Abraham Polonsky: Interviews

Conversations with Filmmakers Series

Gerald Peary, General Editor

Abraham Polonsky
INTERVIEWS

Edited by Andrew Dickos

University Press of Mississippi / Jackson

www.upress.state.ms.us

The University Press of Mississippi is a member
of the Association of American University Presses.

First printing 2013
∞
Library of Congress Cataloging-in-Publication Data

Polonsky, Abraham.
  Abraham Polonsky : interviews / edited by Andrew Dickos.
    p. cm. — (Conversations with filmmakers series)
  Includes bibliographical references and index.
  Includes filmography.
  ISBN 978-1-61703-660-6 (cloth : alk. paper) — ISBN 978-1-61703-661-3 (ebook)
  ISBN 978-1-4968-5796-5 (paperback)
1. Polonsky, Abraham—Interviews. 2. Screenwriters—United States—Interviews.
3. Authors, American—20th century—Interviews. 4. Motion picture producers and
directors—United States—Interviews. I. Dickos, Andrew, 1952– II. Title.
  PS3531.O377Z46 2013
  791.4302'33092—dc23   2012025769

British Library Cataloging-in-Publication Data available

Contents

Introduction

The indelible noir images in Abraham Polonsky's *Force of Evil* (1948), vivid with New York City's propitious allure yet tinged with the melancholy of one's aloneness in the city, resonate in our imagination long after the film ends. The power of these images cannot be divorced from the power, poetic and incantatory, of Polonsky's dialogue. Every technical component—from the eloquent tirades exchanged by Joe and Leo, to the dramatic tonal variations of David Raksin's score, and on to the richly evocative cinematography of the New York City of our noir imagination—achieves a completeness and discreteness that becomes part of a near-perfect fugue of visual and aural poetry that complicates the narrative whole in such manner as to look and sound uniquely strange—and haunting. When I first saw *Force of Evil* as a teenager, on the late show on television, I was hypnotized by John Garfield's performance, especially in his Polonsky-penned voice-over. It was a voice searching to silence the disquietude of a tormented consciousness, and I was aroused to find out all I could of Polonsky's life and career in an attempt to better understand the genesis of this melancholy passion. I read his first interviews, and the essays written by him, published in film journals in this country. There were later interviews in France, after he had been blacklisted by the Hollywood film industry during the 1950s because of his Depression-era membership in the American Communist Party (at the time a fashionable association for contemporary writers). I was impressed by his lack of rancor against those who "named names" in the face of the clear moral stand he took not to do so. He pitied their failure of character, but repeatedly said that he wished them no ill. His response was far more humane than any of their more questionable actions, and his humor had not given way to bitterness. "It wasn't as if they betrayed Jesus Christ," Polonsky said, "they just betrayed themselves."[1]

Among the notable interviews he gave then were William S. Pechter's, the first, conducted in 1962 and then followed up with a second interview six years later, both of which were then published in Pechter's

1971 collection of film criticism, *Twenty-four Times a Second*. I remember reading Pechter's prefatory essay to his interviews with Polonsky and lamenting that there wasn't more to be learned there about this most distinctive film artist.

Polonsky was born in 1910 to Russian-Jewish immigrants, a comfortably-off pharmacist and his wife, and was also reared in the company of his aunt, an independent-minded socialist who returned to the Soviet Union during the halcyon days of revolutionary fervor in the early 1920s to help build the new society (this, before the rude awakening of Stalinism took hold). In the Buhle and Wagner interview, Polonsky talks about the flavor of his upbringing and early years—especially those heady student years at City College of New York during the Depression when CCNY built its reputation as a cauldron of left-wing intellectual ferment. His classmates included the sociologist and poet Paul Goodman and the activist and civil-liberties lawyer Leonard Boudin, and he studied under the famous philosopher Morris Cohen, taking a degree in English before another one in law. In those early, lean, Depression years, Polonsky decided to take up law as a hedge against unemployment and to teach English at his alma mater in the process. The law held no passion for him, and he finally opted for a chance to write for radio star Gertrude Berg and, later, accompanied her to Hollywood in 1937 to help her write a movie for the juvenile screen star Bobby Breen. There, he discovered his affinity for screenwriting, but, with no prospects for more screen work at the time, he returned to New York with Berg and resumed writing radio plays for her, for Orson Welles's *Mercury Theatre* on radio, as well as doing other radio dramatizations up until the War.

In the course of these pursuits, Polonsky developed a leftist political consciousness long embedded in his family's background. He sought to create a modern literary aesthetic to express his humanistic and socialist values in contradistinction to many narrowly Marxist proletarian writers of the 1930s and '40s. He wanted to write with a social conscience of a material world that left some advantaged over the price paid by others left powerless and voiceless, and he wanted to do the work of an artist and not that of an ideological hack. Polonsky applied his aesthetic to a range of writing, including not only screenplays, radio plays, and teleplays, but novels, short stories, and film criticism. He thought of himself always as a writer, regardless of the circumstances he confronted and circumvented in his creative life, most notably the War and, later, the blacklist. All of Polonsky's teleplays written during the black list were collected by John Schultheiss and Mark Schaubert in 1993, and all of Polonsky's film criticism is collected here in this volume.

After a stint in the service during World War II working as an OSS agent in Europe, Polonsky returned to Hollywood in 1945 to work on the screenplay for Mitchell Leisen's *Golden Earrings* (1947) at Paramount. Although the Cold War had started, pre-blacklist Hollywood was an attractive and hospitable place for the American Communist Party. The party recognized the movie industry as having a role in shaping public attitudes and sentiments that complemented the socialist ideals promoted by Rooseveltian democracy. Polonsky was a supporter of organizations that extolled these goals, but he also had no illusions about the appeal of Hollywood to most leftist writers. They, like he, came west for employment. "I came here because I had a job waiting for me," he noted. "When I went to Paramount, I made sure I saw every movie they had in stock."[2] Polonsky's Oscar-nominated screenplay for Robert Rossen's *Body and Soul* (1947) and his masterwork, *Force of Evil*, both written and directed by Polonsky, are so much more than bold expressions of the pervasive corruption a materialist society faces when it loses its mooring. Few filmmakers have created first works of such poetic impact and sure mastery of the medium as he did with these two films.

What distinguishes Polonsky's achievement in these works from that of other screenwriters-turned-directors in Hollywood? Clearly Abraham Polonsky, like John Huston and Preston Sturges, wrote intrepidly, his screenplays unfettered by the self-imposed censorship that so often weakened the films of other studio filmmakers. Polonsky wrote scathing allegories of the capitalist system—the very system that produced his works—and did so on humanist grounds: his characters carry no placards, have no overt political agendas, and are no martyrs. They are the people and faces encountered in modern urban society that suffer in the grip of a corrupted and greedy capitalist culture. Sixty years later, rarely does such a theme have more power than in the post-recession America of 2012.

However, were that all, Polonsky would emerge as a timely throwback to the pre-blacklist studio period but not as a striking creative presence. Polonsky took the elements of word and image in these first two films, especially in *Force of Evil*, and excavated their expressive possibilities in the dramatic technique of doubling where, as discussed earlier, each element of the story commands attention for its own expression of an emotion or theme that is then complemented by another element iterating the same emotion or theme in its own distinctive manner. Joe Morse's voice-over spoken by Garfield expresses his conflicted emotions—indeed, his soul—just as the image of Joe in Garfield's performance places him in conflict with his social obligations, to his corrupt allegiance to Tucker as well as to his loyalty to his brother Leo.

Abraham Polonsky's screen stories have been discussed for their intimate approach to genres and the themes of justice, loyalty to family and community, and the corruption in greed and bigotry that debase them. Critics have insisted on labeling him a leftist writer and director, but that approach alone ignores the supple philosophical awareness of his characters' anguish: these characters transcend the function of a sociopolitical statement and are deeply human examples of spiritual torment. "What're you gonna do? Kill me?" boxer Charley Davis asks in *Body and Soul* when his backers' goons threaten him for not throwing a bout. "Everybody dies." In a similar vein, Wall Street lawyer Joe Morse, in his taxi-ride confessional to Doris Lowry in *Force of Evil*, rationalizes his discomfiture over his older brother Leo's selfless paternal regard by raging:

> It's a perversion. Don't you see what it is? It's not natural. To go to great expense for something you want, that's natural. To reach out to take it, that's human, that's natural. But to get your pleasure from not taking, from cheating yourself deliberately like my brother did today, from not getting, from not taking. Don't you see what a black thing that is for a man to do? How it is to hate yourself?

Polonsky's poetry articulates Joe's rage against his brother's selflessness, against the expression of human decency that obstructs Joe's untroubled rise up the corporate criminal ladder. These protagonists lash out all the more vividly through the performances of John Garfield in the roles, and the New York City tableaux of these characters, just as for the characters in the later Polonsky-scripted *Odds against Tomorrow* (1959) and *Madigan* (1968), place their struggle for self-worth in the city Polonsky knew best, and, indeed, which he savored on screen as few other filmmakers have.

After his auspicious debut as screenwriter and director of *Force of Evil*, Polonsky wrote *I Can Get It for You Wholesale* (1951) for Michael Gordon at Twentieth Century-Fox, starring Dan Dailey and Susan Hayward. A drama about labor relations intrigue in the garment industry, the story was filmed just before the House Un-American Activities Committee

(HUAC) called him to testify about his Communist Party activities and past and present associations. Polonsky knew the employment problems awaiting a blacklisted writer, and yet he refused to name others under oath. His exile from Hollywood did not keep him from writing. In France at the time of his subpoena, he moved his family back to New York and, along with other blacklisted writers such as Walter Bernstein and Arnold Manoff, he worked on live television. He wrote his fourth novel, *A Season of Fear* (1956), loosely based on the McCarthy witch hunts, and he pseudonymously penned the screenplay for *Odds against Tomorrow* for Robert Wise and starring Robert Ryan, Harry Belafonte, Shelley Winters, and Gloria Grahame.

In the mid-1960s, Abraham Polonsky was discovered by the English and French critics with the seriousness he had yet to enjoy in America. In the *Cahiers du cinéma* Delahaye interview and the *Positif* Ciment and Tavernier interview, Polonsky is accorded the deference of an old and honorable left-wing warrior who's arrived on the scene at a particularly auspicious moment: the Paris of 1969, after the antiestablishment political demonstrations of the previous year threatened to destabilize the country. Polonsky recounts these experiences in his own essay of "how the blacklist worked in Hollywood" and in the interviews he gave (Sherman and Rubin, Cook and Canham, and Pasternak and Howton) after his return to the screen under his own name in the late 1960s. He also introduces us to his projects of the moment in these interviews—his screenwriting for *Madigan* and the making of his modern western, *Tell Them Willie Boy Is Here* (1969), the latter a parable of injustices all too familiar to the blacklisted Polonsky.

Tell Them Willie Boy Is Here picks up Polonsky's thematic preoccupation with societal injustice and casts it as the crucible of a young but respected Indian in the last days of the Old West. He later tells a variation of the story in *Romance of a Horsethief* (1971), a parable of thievery and lust, plunder and persecution, among a band of Polish Jews in the czarist Pale of 1904, set around the same time as the events in *Willie Boy*. Polonsky originally encountered *Willie Boy* in 1968 as a potential project for a "120," parlance for a two-hour television movie. The project, rejected for television by producer Philip Waxman, was suggested instead as a feature film. Polonsky saw it as a parable for the social turmoil among the youth of the late 1960s, and he took on *Willie Boy* to mark his complete credited return to the screen as writer-director. He discusses the project in the timely interview conducted with Eric Sherman and Martin Rubin.

Polonsky's final films were met with unfortunate circumstances. *Avalanche Express* (1979), which he wrote, was director Mark Robson's last film. Both Robson and Robert Shaw, one of the film's stars, died of heart attacks during filming. *Monsignor* (1982), Polonsky's last film project, for which he co-wrote the screenplay (with Wendell Mayes), got lukewarm praise and poor box office.

During the last fifteen years of his life, Abraham Polonsky taught film aesthetics and screenwriting at UCLA and availed himself of the opportunities to discuss that period of his life that aborted his promising career. He used his own story as a history lesson of how the blacklist detoured many creative lives and how, as he tells Bernard Eisenschitz in his 1969 *Cahiers* interview, it lives on in various permutations to this day.

In his great first films, as screenwriter and then as screenwriter and director, Abraham Polonsky created a vivid urban world where his characters rail with passionate insistence to be noticed among the many as they struggle to act honorably in a corrupt material world. But their ultimate struggle is to rid themselves of the spiritual anxiety that fuels this passion. Even in his later work as a screenwriter and director, Polonsky's characters remain anxious and restless. Dan Madigan in *Madigan* struggles to stay within the official contours of his job as he tries to make sense of how his law enforcer's badge can permit him to function effectively as a just human being, and Willie Boy wrestles unto death with his dislocation as a Native American in a confusing landscape where even his warrior's shirt, a talisman of invincibility, cannot save him.

Polonsky's screenwriting has always been recognized for the poetic inflections of its urban lament and in the cadences of emotional urgency in the voices of those dispossessed. His writing, however, needs to be appreciated in tandem with the visual correlatives that deepen the meaning of his words. His dispossessed struggle beautifully. Charley Davis in the ring in *Body and Soul* plays out an opera of suffering between the ropes and Polonsky's screenplay inspires James Wong Howe's cinematography to animate the bouts with sharply angled chiaroscuro camerawork. In *Force of Evil*, Polonsky elevates New York City as a visual altar in his paean to all that has made Joe Morse great and fallen. Willie Boy becomes the mystical embodiment of an old, honorable, native people, shot as he is in a hypnotic desert twilight, insisting on his self-respect and refusing to be servile. Joseph McBride's interview with Polonsky, conducted in 1980 and appearing here for the first time, focuses on *Tell Them Willie Boy Is*

Here and parallels this episode of persecution in a changing American Western frontier with the blacklist era of Hollywood almost a half century later that claimed but did not vanquish Abraham Polonsky.

I am grateful to those who consented to have their interviews with Polonsky included in this omnibus: Paul Buhle, Joseph McBride, Patrick McGilligan, William S. Pechter, Martin Rubin, Eric Sherman, and Dave Wagner. Michel Ciment graciously extended his permission to use any of the interviews conducted with Polonsky published in *Positif.* Thanks go to Brenda Fernandes of *Sight and Sound* and Maxine Ducey of the Wisconsin State Historical Society for their assistance in securing interview permissions. I am also grateful to Hannah Low, Anne Panos, Rob Hugh Rosen, and Ilene Singh for their encouragement in the completion of this project as I am to Leila Salisbury of the University Press of Mississippi for giving me the opportunity to do this entry in the Conversations with Filmmakers Series and to Valerie Jones for working on it with such care. Finally, I am indebted to the film scholar and author Ed Sikov for the invaluable counsel and support he offered me when I needed it. His was a testament of true friendship.

AD
New York City
Spring 2012

Notes

1. "Abraham Polonsky: The Most Dangerous Man in America." Interview by Mark Burman. *Projections 8: Film-makers on Film-making*, ed. John Boorman and Walter Donahue (London: Faber and Faber, 1998), 270.

2. "Abraham Polonsky." Interview by Paul Buhle and Dave Wagner. *Tender Comrades: A Backstory of the Hollywood Blacklist*, ed. Patrick McGilligan and Paul Buhle (New York: St. Martin's, 1997), 484.

Chronology

1910   Born Abraham Lincoln Polonsky on December 5 to pharmacist and socialist Henry Polonsky, a Jewish Russian immigrant, and his wife, Rebecca (née Rosoff).

1928   Enters City College of New York (CCNY), where he joins the literary society, Clionia, and helps revive its literary magazine, *Lavender*. His classmates include future writer and sociologist Paul Goodman and future lawyer Leonard Boudin. All studied under the legendary philosopher Morris Cohen.

1935   Graduates from Columbia University Law School while having taught night courses in English literature and composition at City College.

1937   Abandons law to write and to work for radio and film star Gertrude Berg. Accompanies her on his first trip to Hollywood to work on a screenplay she is contracted to write. Becomes involved in the Hollywood writers' community and its predominantly left-wing political activities.

1939   Returns to New York to teach literature at City College while writing radio scripts.

1940   Publishes his first novel, *The Goose Is Cooked*, under the pseudonym Emmett Hogarth and coauthored with Mitchell Wilson, for Simon & Schuster.

1941   The Rapp-Coudert hearings take place at the City College, presaging the House Un-American Activities Committee (HUAC) Congressional hearing ten years later.

1941–42   Abraham and Sylvia (née Marrow) Polonsky wed in 1937, have their first child, Susan, in 1941, and their second, Abraham, Jr., in 1942.

Early 1943   Enlists in the Office of Strategic Services (OSS), precursor to the Central Intelligence Agency, and serves as an operative in England and France during World War II. Publishes his second novel, *The Enemy Sea*, for Little, Brown.

1946   Returns to Hollywood to write a screenplay about the Liberation of Paris for Paramount. The project is not realized, but instead Polonsky co-writes *Golden Earrings*, directed by Mitchell Leisen and released in 1947. Joins the editorial board of *Hollywood Quarterly*, in which he publishes film criticism. Publishes short stories for *American Mercury* and *Collier's*.

1947   Assigned the screenplay of Dan Wickenden's Depression novel, *The Way-Farers*, to star Edward G. Robinson, but the project is not realized. Writes *Body and Soul*, directed by Robert Rossen for the independent production company, Enterprise Studios. The film stars John Garfield and Lilli Palmer and is released by United Artists. Polonsky receives an Academy Award nomination for his screenplay.

1948   Writes and directs *Force of Evil*, based on Ira Wolfert's novel *Tucker's People*, for Enterprise Studios. The film is his second collaboration with John Garfield and is released by MGM.

1951   Writes the screenplay for *I Can Get It for You Wholesale*, directed by Michael Gordon for Twentieth Century-Fox. Publishes his third novel, *The World Above*, for Little, Brown. Called to testify before the House Un-American Activities Committee (HUAC) about Hollywood associates involved in the Communist Party or its front organizations.

1951–55   Writes teleplays in New York City for live television. (See filmography.)

1956   Publishes his fourth novel, *A Season of Fear*.

1959   Writes the screenplay for the film noir, *Odds against Tomorrow*, using a front, John O. Killens, a friend of the film's star, Harry Belafonte, for credit. The credit is rightfully restored to the film by the Writers Guild of America in 1996.

1968   Writes the screenplay for the police noir, *Madigan*, directed by Don Siegel.

1969   Writes and directs *Tell Them Willie Boy Is Here* for Universal, with Robert Redford, Robert Blake, and Katharine Ross.

1971   Directs *Romance of a Horsethief* for Allied Artists with Yul Brynner, Eli Wallach, Serge Gainesbourg, and Jane Birkin.

1980   Publishes his fifth novel, *Zenia's Way*, a tribute to his grandmother, for Lippincott & Crowell.

1982   Coauthors screenplay (with Wendell Mayes) for *Monsignor*, directed by Frank Perry and released by Twentieth Century-Fox.

1996   The Writers Guild of America formally acknowledges Polonsky as the scenarist of *Odds against Tomorrow*, the 1959 film noir classic.

1999   Polonsky dies on October 26.

Filmography and Bibliography

Cinematography: James Wong Howe
Special Effects: "Special Montages" directed by Guenther Fritsch
Editing: Robert Parrish
Sound: Frank Webster
Music Score: Hugo Friedhofer, "Body and Soul," music by Johnny Green
    and lyrics by Edward Newman, Robert Sour, and Frank Eyton
Music Direction: Rudolph Polk
Art Direction: Nathan Juran
Set Direction: Edward G. Boyle
Costumes: Marion Herwood Keyes
Makeup: Gustaf M. Norin
Production Manager: Joseph C. Gilpin
Assistant Director: Robert Aldrich
Cast: John Garfield (Charley Davis), Lilli Palmer (Peg Born), Hazel Brooks
    (Alice), Anne Revere (Anna Davis), William Conrad (Quinn), Joseph
    Pevney (Shorty Polaski), Canada Lee (Ben Chaplin), Lloyd Goff (Rob-
    erts), Art Smith (David Davis), James Burke (Arnold), Virginia Gregg
    (Irma), Peter Virgo (Drummer), Joe Devlin (Prince)
Black and white, 104 minutes

FORCE OF EVIL (1948)
MGM/Enterprise
Director: **Abraham Polonsky**
Producer: Bob Roberts
Screenplay: **Abraham Polonsky** and Ira Wolfert, based on Wolfert's
    novel *Tucker's People*
Cinematography: George Barnes
Editing: Art Seid
Sound: Frank Webster
Music Score: David Raksin
Music Direction: Rudolph Polk
Art Direction: Richard Day
Set Direction: Edward G. Boyle
Wardrobe Direction: Louise Wilson
Makeup: Gus Norin
Hair Styling: Lillian Lashin
Production Manager: Joseph C. Gilpin
Assistant Director: Robert Aldrich
Cast: John Garfield (Joe Morse), Beatrice Pearson (Doris Lowry), Thomas

Gomez (Leo Morse), Howland Chamberlin (Freddy Bauer), Roy Roberts (Ben Tucker), Marie Windsor (Edna Tucker), Paul McVey (Hobe Wheelock), Tim Ryan (Johnson), Sid Tomack ("Two & Two" Taylor), Georgia Backus (Sylvia Morse), Sheldon Leonard (Ficco), Jan Dennis (Mrs. Bauer), Stanley Prager (Wally), Beau Bridges (Frankie Tucker), Perry Ivans (Mr. Middleton), Cliff Clark (Police Lieutenant), Jimmy Dundee (Dineen)
Black and white, 78 minutes

I CAN GET IT FOR YOU WHOLESALE (1951)
Twentieth Century-Fox
Director: Michael Gordon
Producer: Sol C. Siegel
Screenplay: **Abraham Polonsky**, based on an adaptation by Vera Caspary from the novel by Jerome Weidman
Cinematography: Milton Krasner
Special Effects: Fred Sersen
Editing: Robert Simpson
Sound: Roger Heman
Music Score: Sol Kaplan, Alfred Newman (uncredited)
Music Direction: Lionel Newman
Art Direction: John DeCuir, Lyle Wheeler
Set Direction: Thomas Little
Costumes: Charles Le Maire
Makeup: Ben Nye
Assistant Director: Ben Chapman
Cast: Susan Hayward (Harriet Boyd), Dan Dailey (Teddy Sherman), George Sanders (J. F. Noble), Sam Jaffe (Sam Cooper), Randy Stuart (Marge Boyd), Marvin Kaplan (Arnold Fisher), Harry Von Zell (Savage), Barbara Whiting (Ellen Cooper), Vicki Cummings (Hermione Griggs), Ross Elliott (Ray), Richard Lane (Kelley), Mary Philips (Mrs. Boyd)
Black and white, 91 minutes

ODDS AGAINST TOMORROW (1959)
United Artists
Director: Robert Wise
Producer: Robert Wise
Co-Producer: Harry Belafonte (uncredited)

Associate Producer: Phil Stein

Screenplay: **Abraham Polonsky** (fronted by John O. Killens) and Nelson Gidding

[On August 11, 1996, Polonsky took questions after the screening of *Odds against Tomorrow* at Lincoln Center's Walter Reade Theater in New York. He remarked that he wrote the script for the film while working with Tyrone Guthrie on a stage production of *Oedipus Rex* in Canada. He never met with the cast or production people of the movie. The story, based on William McGivern's book, was essentially "rewritten" by Polonsky. "I changed the book and wrote the screenplay from the new book," he said. The occasion of the screening, as part of the theater's John Garfield retrospective, was the formal acknowledgment by the Screen Writers Guild thirty-seven years later of his screenwriting contribution to the film.—AD]

Cinematography: Joseph C. Brun

Editing: Dede Allen

Sound: Edward J. Johnstone, Dick Vorisek, Kenn Collins

Music Score: John Lewis

Production Design: Leo Kerz

Set Direction: Fred Ballmeyer

Costumes: Anna Hill Johnstone

Makeup: Robert Jiras

Production Manager: Forrest E. Johnston

Assistant Director: Charles Maguire

Cast: Harry Belafonte (Johnny Ingram), Robert Ryan (Earle Slater), Shelley Winters (Lorry), Gloria Grahame (Helen), Ed Begley (Dave Burke), Will Kuluva (Bacco), Kim Hamilton (Ruth Ingram), Mae Barnes (Annie), Richard Bright (Coco), Carmen De Lavallade (Kittie), Lew Gallo (Moriarty), Lois Thorne (Edie Ingram), Wayne Rogers (Soldier in the bar), Zohra Lampert (Girl in the bar), Allen Nourse (Melton police chief)

Black and white, 96 minutes

MADIGAN (1968)

Universal

Director: Don Siegel

Producer: Frank P. Rosenberg

Screenplay: **Abraham Polonsky** and Howard Rodman, based on the novel by Richard Dougherty

Cinematography: Russell Metty

Editing: Milton Shifman
Sound: Lyle Cain, Ronald Pierce, Waldon O. Watson
Music Score: Don Costa
Music Supervisor: Joseph Gershenson
Art Direction: Alexander Golitzen, George C. Webb
Set Decoration: John Austin, John McCarthy
Makeup: Bud Westmore
Hair Stylist: Larry Germain
Production Manager: Wes Thompson
Assistant Director: Joseph C. Cavalier
Cast: Richard Widmark (Detective Daniel Madigan), Henry Fonda (Commissioner Anthony Russell), Inger Stevens (Julia Madigan), Harry Guardino (Detective Rocco Bonaro), James Whitmore (Chief Inspector Charles Kane), Susan Clark (Tricia Bentley), Michael Dunn (Midget Castiglione), Steve Ihnat (Barney Benesch), Don Stroud (Hughie), Sheree North (Jonesy), Warren Steven (Captain Ben Williams), Raymond St. Jacques (Dr. Taylor), Bert Freed (Chief of Detectives Hap Lynch), Harry Bellaver (Mickey Dunn), Frank Marth (Lieutenant James Price)
Color, 101 minutes

TELL THEM WILLIE BOY IS HERE (1969)
Universal
Director: **Abraham Polonsky**
Producers: Jennings Lang, Philip A. Waxman
Screenplay: **Abraham Polonsky**, based on the book *Willie Boy: A Desert Manhunt* by Harry Lawton
Cinematography: Conrad Hall
Editing: Melvin Shapiro
Sound: David H. Moriarty, Waldon O. Watson
Music Score: Dave Grusin
Music Supervisor: Stanley Wilson
Art Direction: Henry Bumstead, Alexander Golitzen
Set Decoration: Ruby Levitt, John McCarthy Jr.
Costumes: Edith Head
Makeup: Bud Westmore, Marvin G. Westmore
Hair Stylist: Larry Germain
Unit Production Manager: Hal W. Polaire
Assistant Director: Joseph E. Kenney
Cast: Robert Redford (Deputy Sheriff Christopher "Coop" Cooper), Kath-

arine Ross (Lola), Robert Blake (Willie Boy), Susan Clark (Dr. Elizabeth Arnold), Barry Sullivan (Ray Calvert), John Vernon (George Hacker), Charles Aidman (Judge Benby), Charles McGraw (Sheriff Frank Wilson), Shelly Novack (Johnny Finney), Robert Lipton (Charlie Newcombe), Lloyd Gough (Dexter), Ned Romero (Tom), John Wheeler (Newman), Eric Holland (Digger), Garry Walberg (Dr. Mills)
Color, 98 minutes

ROMANCE OF A HORSETHIEF (1971)
Allied Artists
Director: **Abraham Polonsky**
Producer: Gene Gutowski
Executive Producer: Peter E. Strauss
Screenplay: David Opatoshu, based on the stories by Joseph Opatoshu
Cinematography: Piero Portalupi
Editing: Kevin Connor
Sound: John Ireland, Peter Keen, Michael Sale, Doug Turner
Music Score: Mort Shuman
Music Direction: Robin Clarke, Carl Prager, Eric Tomlinson
Art Direction: Vlastimir Gavrik, Otto Pischinger
Set Designer: Slobodan Mijacevic
Costumes and Wardrobe: Ray Beck
Makeup: Sergio Angeloni
Hair Stylist: Anna Graziosa (Anna Graziosi)
Production Manager: Donko Buljan
Assistant Director: Svetolik Maricic
Cast: Yul Brynner (Captain Stoloff), Eli Wallach (Kifke), Jane Birkin (Naomi), Lainie Kazan (Estusha), David Opatoshu (Schlomo Kradnik), Serge Gainesbourg (Sigmund), Henri Sera [Henri Serre] (Mendel), Linda Veras (Countess Grabowski), Marilu Tolo (Marika), Branko Piesa (Lieutenant Vishinsky), Vladimir Bacic (Gruber), Branko Spoliar (Strugatch), Alenka Rancic (Sura), Oliver Tobias (Zanvil Kradnik)
Color, 89 minutes

AVALANCHE EXPRESS (1979)
Twentieth Century-Fox
Director: Mark Robson, Monte Hellman (uncredited)
Producer: Mark Robson
Associate Producer: Lynn Guthrie
Screenplay: **Abraham Polonsky**, based on the novel by Colin Forbes

Cinematography: Jack Cardiff (uncredited)
Director of Photography: Boat Battle Sequence: Howard Anderson II
Editing: Garth Craven
Sound: Wayne Ardman, Tom Beckert, Fred Brown, Michael Jiron, Charles
    McFadden, Michele Sharp Brown, George Stevenson, Caryl Wickman
Music Conductor: Allyn Ferguson
Music Editor: Ken Johnson
Production Design: Fred Tuch
Set Decoration: Elke Etzoid, Travis Nixon
Makeup: Ago Von Sperl, Rudiger Von Sperl
Assistant Director: Welland Liebske
Cast: Lee Marvin (Wargrave), Robert Shaw (Marenkov), Linda Evans
    (Elsa Lang), Maximilian Schell (Bunin), Joe Namath (Leroy), Horst
    Bucholz (Scholten), Mike Connors (Haller), Claudio Cassinelli (Moli-
    nari), Kristina Nel (Helga Mann), David Hess (Geiger)
Color, 101 minutes

MONSIGNOR (1982)
Twentieth Century-Fox
Director: Frank Perry
Producer: David Niven Jr., Frank Yablans
Executive Producer: Peter E. Strauss
Screenplay: **Abraham Polonsky** and Wendell Mayes, based on the
    novel by Jack-Alain Léger
Cinematography: Billy Williams
Editing: Peter E. Berger
Sound: Roy Charman, William Hartman, David M. Ice, Aldo De Martino
Music Score: John Williams
Art Direction: Stefano Maria Ortolani
Set Designer: Joe Chevalier, Carlo Gervasi
Costumes: Theoni V. Aldredge
Makeup: Franco Corridoni
Hair Stylist: Maria Teresa Corridoni
Production Manager: Kurt Neumann
Assistant Director: Gianni Cozzo
Cast: Christopher Reeve (Father John Flaherty), Geneviève Bujold (Clara),
    Fernando Rey (Cardinal Santoni), Jason Miller (Don Vito Appolini),
    Joseph Cortese (Ludovico Varese), Adolfo Celi (Cardinal Vinci), Rob-
    ert Prosky (Bishop Walkman), Joe Pantoliano (Private Joe Musso)
Color, 121 minutes

Written for Television

During the early 1950s, Abraham Polonsky wrote for television under pseudonyms or fronted by other writers. The two series for which he wrote episodes were *Danger*, from December 1951 to January 1954, and *You Are There*, from February 1953 to March 1955.

DANGER

Episodes written as George Marrow: "The Face of Fear," December 11, 1951; "Prelude to Death," February 5, 1952; "Benefit Performance," March 4, 1952; "Border Incident," April 29, 1952; "Date at Midnight," July 29, 1952; "A Thread of Scarlet," October 7, 1952

Episodes written as Jeremy Daniel: "Carpool," March 24, 1953; "Subpoena," May 26, 1953; "Prodigal Returns," July 14, 1953; "Return to Fear," January 19, 1954

YOU ARE THERE

Episodes written as Jeremy Daniel (unless otherwise noted): "The Landing of the Hindenburg," February 1, 1953; "The Execution of Joan of Arc," March 1, 1953; "The Conquest of Mexico by Cortes," April 5, 1953; "The Crisis of Galileo," April 19, 1953; "The Signing of the Magna Carta," June 7, 1953; "The Flight of Rudolph Hess," June 14, 1953; "The Fate of Nathan Hale," August 30, 1953; "The Secret of Sigmund Freud," October 4, 1953; "The Recognition of Michelangelo," November 15, 1953; "The Crisis at Valley Forge," December 6, 1953; "The Vindication of Savonarola," December 13, 1953; "Mallory's Tragedy on Mt. Everest," January 3, 1954; "The First Command Performance of *Romeo and Juliet*," February 21, 1954; "The Surrender of Burgoyne at Saratoga," March 21, 1954; "The Scopes Trial," May 16, 1954; "The Emergence of Jazz," September 5, 1954; "The Return of Ulysses," September 26, 1954; "The Great Adventure of Marco Polo," October 10, 1954; "The Torment of Beethoven," January 2, 1955 (as Leo Davis); "The First Flight of the Wright Brothers," January 16, 1955 (as Duane Berry); "The Tragedy of John Milton," January 30, 1955; "The Liberation of Paris," February 20, 1955 (as Leo Davis); "The Hatfield-McCoy Feud," March 20, 1955; "The Triumph of Alexander the Great," March 27, 1955

KRAFT SUSPENSE THEATRE

"Last Clear Chance," March 11, 1965

SEAWAY

Polonsky wrote twenty-nine teleplays for the adventure series, which he created and was produced in Canada by ASP Productions for the Canadian Broadcasting Corporation (CBC) from 1965 to 1966.

Radio Play

"The Case of David Smith." *Hollywood Quarterly* 1 (January 1946): 185–98.

Essays

"*The Best Years of Our Lives*: A Review." *Hollywood Quarterly* 2.3 (April 1947): 257–60.
"*Odd Man Out* and *Monsieur Verdoux*." *Hollywood Quarterly* 2.4 (July 1947): 401–7.
"Hemingway and Chaplin." *The Contemporary Reader* 1.1 (March 1953): 23–31.
"Une Expérience Utopique." *Présence du Cinéma* 14 (juin 1962): 5–7.
"How the Blacklist Worked in Hollywood." *Film Culture* nos. 50–51 (Fall–Winter 1970): 41–48.
"Making Movies." *Sight and Sound* 40 (Spring 1971): 101.
"Introduction." In *The Films of John Garfield*, by Howard Gelman, 7–9. Secaucus, N.J.: Citadel, 1975.

Short Stories

"A Little Fire." *Collier's*, August 3, 1946, 18+.
"No Neutral Ground." *America Magazine*, June 1946, 163.
"The Marvelous Boy." *The American Mercury*, November 1946, 550–62.
"A Slight Disturbance." *The Contemporary Reader* 1 (August 1953): 54–64.

Novels

The Goose Is Cooked. With Mitchell Wilson. New York: Simon & Schuster, 1940.
The Enemy Sea. Boston: Little, Brown and Company, 1943.
The World Above. Boston: Little, Brown and Company, 1951.
A Season of Fear. New York: Cameron Associates, 1956.
Zenia's Way. New York: Lippincott & Crowell, 1980.

Abraham Polonsky: Interviews

The Best Years of Our Lives: A Review

Abraham Polonsky / 1947

From *Hollywood Quarterly* 2.3 (April 1947): 257–60.

N'est-ce pas parce que nous cultivons la brume?—Mallarmé

About this time each year, the Academy Awards remind us of the fictional odds and ends produced in the Hollywood studios. I suppose everyone will agree that *The Best Years of Our Lives* stands above its competitors as life itself dominates our fictions.

We are offered a view of three veterans from different social classes adjusting themselves to modern times in Boone City, America. It is a pattern of reality as Wyler and Sherwood see it, the life that touches their imagination with truth, with warmth, with communication. The social environment of former Captain Fred Derry is treated reluctantly and without a true perspective, but if Wyler and Sherwood knew better, like their most sympathetic protagonist, the banker Al Stephenson, they realize that some version of the Boone City bank is in control of the film industry. Author and director bowed and passed. Nevertheless, the area of human character which the *Best Years* makes available to its audience is a landmark in the fog of escapism, meretricious violence, and the gimmick plot attitude of the usual movie. It becomes very clear that an artist who happens to bring even a tag of daily experience into the studio is making an immense contribution to the screen. The *Best Years* indicates for every director and writer that the struggle for content, for social reality, no matter how limited the point of view, is a necessary atmosphere for growth in the American film.

As the plot goes, three veterans meet by accident and return to their city in the same plane. Each goes home and is welcomed: one to the rich emotional sympathy of an upper-class family; one to an earnest but narrow white-collar house; and one to a poor man's broken home and a slut

3

of a wife. Al Stephenson is a hit-the-beach sergeant, and, oddly enough, a banker. Homer Parrish is an enlisted man from the Navy, now equipped with hands in the form of two hooks. Fred Derry, the poor boy, is the Air Force captain, formerly a soda jerk. Director and writer were intensely interested in these three men, but the same understanding was not brought to bear on their special problems. Homer, the petty bourgeois, has a girl whom he loves and who loves him. She wants to marry him, but Homer is self-conscious about his hooks, resentful of pity. Wilma, in a slow and lovely scene, faces up to the broken flesh; Homer is rescued from himself; and we are left happily aware of their happiness, recalling a previous scene in which the government pension puts an economic base under their marriage. Fred Derry comes from "across the tracks" (we even hear the trains); his father is a drunk, his stepmother anomalous, his wife less so. Fred is forced back behind the soda fountain, loses his job with a punch, his wife to another man, an ex-G.I., and decides to leave town. His wife is going to divorce him because he can't make money, and finally he is magically offered a position as a laborer, which he accepts. Al Stephenson, the banker, has a "wonderful" wife and two of the "finest" children in the world. He gets a bigger job in his "old" bank, this time as a vice-president in charge of G.I. loans. Unable to grant such loans without collateral, Al gets drunk (evidently the forms of courage in the economic system need different stimuli than in combat) and makes a speech in which he beautifully points out that the soldier asked no collateral for his final sacrifices in the war. Al doesn't lose his job, and the final scene, although unresolved, is not unhappy.

These three unrelated plots are bound together with some wire left over from a million movies: the poor boy, having found himself, gets the daughter of the well-to-do veteran. Homer stays with us because his uncle owns a bar, in which some of the scenes are played.

It is obvious enough that we are here faced with the general stereotypes of the film industry and popular fiction. The original novel by MacKinlay Kantor is even more run-of-the-mill, and the Wyler-Sherwood changes move the story progressively toward realism. In Kantor's story, Al leaves the bank to become a small-time farmer and Fred narrowly escapes becoming a bank robber. The film's drive toward truth is evident in every sequence. There is immense patience for detail and emotional texture, especially in the homecoming scenes of Al and Homer, where the inventive commentary on human behavior is enormous. A passion for insight smashes the stereotypes, around the edges. The lesson for directors and writers is evident: writing for the movies is writing under censorship. The censorship forces stereotypes of motive and environment on the creators, and the problem is to press enough concrete experience into the mold to make imagination live.

Unfortunately, in the *Best Years*, as in most social-problem fiction, the artist falls into the trap of trying to find local solutions in existence for the social conflicts, instead of solving them in feeling. This is, of course, the industry's demand for happy endings. Now the truth of the matter is that veterans have been sold out *en masse* by society. The picture exposes the fraud of America's promises to the soldiers, the promises of businessmen and cheap publicists. We all remember the refrigerators that became planes and flew off to the lonely beaches and mud; we all remember the girls who waited at home and the jobs that would be there. The new world was articulate in the newspaper editorials. The soldiers would take care of the fighting, and the powers-that-be would take care of the peace and prosperity. In the *Best Years*, fakery is laid bare, but the plot forces easy solutions on its creators. Fascism is solved with a punch; a bad marriage by the easy disappearance of a wife; the profound emotional adjustment of a handless veteran by a fine girl; the itchy conscience of a banker by too many drinks. The future is not to be predicted out of such formulas.

Despite the fact that the Hollywood fog which hangs over modern life as portrayed in film is cleared from time to time, the basic stereotype holds constantly. Where the economics of life make naked the terror of a return to a bad old world, the southern California mist moves in and obscures the truth. This is why the crux of the story lies at the point where the veteran's problem is the most mental, least rude and real. Al, the banker, has a bad conscience about the abandoned ordinary veteran. What happens to these "buddies" bothers him, and this intellectual approach is both sound and useful. But a story which has a Fred Derry who must meet the brutal indifference of society, solve it, or be destroyed, seems suddenly oddly accented when the story point of view is that of the man least involved, Al Stephenson.

I suspect that Wyler and Sherwood are not really emotionally conscious of the Derrys, the majority of veterans. People of the kind the author and director best understand, with whom their sympathies lie, are good people like the Stephensons. So it follows that the only family in the story with size, roundness, dignity, beauty, sympathy, and passion, is the family of the good banker. For Derry the environment of action has been specialized to mere plot, built for violent contrast, and localized in the inability of the poor boy who made a little easy dough flying a bomber to adjust himself to his former economic status. The concentration of human virtue in the least affected of the social strata lends a certain lopsidedness to the understanding of veterans' adjustment.

Two scenes most sharply indicate the attitude.

One is Al's daughter accusing her parents of being smug with happiness, of not understanding Fred's desperate plight of joblessness, a broken marriage, of general reorientation. The daughter tells her parents that they have escaped the basic conflicts of the times in a decent standard of living, a good job, and a honeymoon in the South of France. Smug self-pity replies that mama and papa have had their emotional ups and downs, that sometimes mama didn't like papa and vice versa. The girl is defeated and cries. This is blindness.

The other scene is a wonderful metaphor. Captain Fred Derry, the junked bombardier, walks in the graveyard of the air fleet, seen first from his point of view. The camera lifts until at last he is small and abandoned in what seems an endless pattern of power nailed down to uselessness, objects chosen for oblivion. A whole society has poured forth its strength to create these marvelous machines, and a whole society has combined power to train this former soda clerk to the machine. Now, both (the film tells us) are not needed. Finally, Derry climbs aboard a motorless bomber, sits in its nose, in the dust, in the sun, staring through the dirty plastic into the sky. The camera, returning to the outside, catches up in music the noise of the gunning motors, then advances head-on toward the bomber, and from a low angle imaginatively lifts the plane into the clouds. Inside again, the music roaring like motors, Derry relives the terror, the individual destiny of combat—then the junkman appears, the bombardier is chased from his plane.

A life and a society are supposed to be summed up in this, one of the ultimate scenes of the film. Here for a moment the plot became almost identified with reality. Here the plastic values of the different arts merged as in some fabulous area; and then, as always, the Hollywood fog moved in, obscuring what we have just seen and almost realized. Derry gets a job from the junkman, takes off his jacket, and we are all enormously relieved to know that the intense experience of the last few minutes has meant just nothing at all.

The movies just seem to find it impossible to deal with people who work for their living in factories and on farms. This submerged majority of the public is left inarticulate by the artists, covered with a fog which occasionally breaks to reveal a Capra pixie. Greatness was possible for the *Best Years*, but this meant examining Fred Derry where society hurts hardest. It was not done.

Technically, the picture is free from the nervous cutting for mechanical pace so holy in Hollywood, and close-ups do not pop in to fill dramatic vacuums. There is no excess of moving shots having the aesthetic value of vertigo. The style of shooting is round, built about the people in relation to one another, held in the shot to let the story come through.

Within its imposed limits and compromises the film is an enormous success, something like the war itself, which has invigorated many a European country and stirred vast colonial peoples, while here at home we have returned to cynicism from our betters, sharpened social conflicts, and a mood of vulgar despair among the artists.

The Best Years of Our Lives, RKO, 1946. Director, William Wyler. Screenplay, Robert E. Sherwood. Based on the novel *Glory for Me*, by MacKinlay Kantor. Photography, Gregg Toland. Music score, Hugo Friedhofer. A Samuel Goldwyn production.

Odd Man Out and *Monsieur Verdoux*

Abraham Polonsky / 1947

From *Hollywood Quarterly* 2.4 (July 1947): 401–7.

Whenever I think of modern times, I see a continuing crisis. Above the airplanes that circle the globe, scientists tell us, is an atomic cloud, radio-active, created at Bikini, and now a kind of planet to our own. Upon the earth itself every headline proclaims new disasters, and if every dream dreamed this night were continuously flashed on a screen we would see how general secret problems had become. In such an age a great moral danger is that the individual may lose hope and with it the will to struggle.

How, then, can the artist function in this crisis to feed consciousness with iron and fragrance? It is a deep question, rooted in the ambiguities of the recent war and its qualified victory. How can reality, reconstructed in art, issue into experience as a further mastery of the daily world? The objectless anxiety on so many faces will not be cured by metaphysical solutions. You can take fear into the street and beat it like a stupid, stubborn dog; but when you have exhausted your temper on it and returned into the house, it will be sitting on your best rug, drooling saliva on the floor, panting to be cured again. The artist cannot pleasure his audience except with some fragment of reality, no matter how superficial or hidden. What do we mean when we say that a work of art is written from the point of view of reality?

Two recent films, *Odd Man Out* and *Monsieur Verdoux*, offer interesting material in this regard.

The two films have the same abstract theme: a man, or men, challenging the authority and going habits of a modern society. In *Odd Man Out* the leader of a nameless revolutionary group in Ireland holds up a mill to get money for his organization. In the course of the robbery a mill representative is killed, and the rest of the plot is taken up with the efforts of the police to capture the wounded killer. In the end he is shot down by authority.

In *Monsieur Verdoux*, a discharged bank teller tries to support his family by marrying and murdering a number of women for their money. Pursued by the police, he successfully escapes every trap until a new depression wipes out his resources, his family, and his will to resist. He is then captured, tried, and executed.

Odd Man Out uses the style of melodrama and tragedy; *Monsieur Verdoux*, that of satire and low comedy.

From the opening shot of *Odd Man Out*, we are immersed in the sentient atmosphere of a real city and a real dramatic tension, for haunted men are planning a crime which very soon will involve death. The screen is crowded with *actual* objects; people are opaque personalities; the light moves from real daylight through grayness to rain, and then the soft, spreading silentness of snow. The whole atmosphere of fog and decay which so characterizes the milieu of the nineteenth-century realistic novel or the street films of pre-Hitler Germany floods the eye. Bars, joints, a boardinghouse; the endless rows of stoops and windows; factories pushing their nighttime death upon the avenues; the fracturing glare of traffic; a busload of people: all launch their scraping presentness upon the senses, even to the threatening eyes of the police-car headlights glaring into our own. Such clothes, too, lived in, inhabited, holding the body shapes!

There are flashes of reality that plunge deeper than the foregoing: the men plotting the crime; the lovers in the air-raid shelter as the Leader waits in the dark corner for them to leave; the scenes with the children crying for their pennies, and the little girl who points and will not talk until she scurries off on her single skate. We are, we feel, delivered into some darker kind of living reality.

There are collateral truths of a social nature: the doctor will heal the dying Leader so that he may be executed; the priest will confess him; the sympathetic will bandage him before flinging him into the night; the bar owner will brace him with a drink; the others will buy him or sell him. For the Leader, as he moves and is moved from place to place, thrusts his condition into parallel ways about him.

But as the story moves on, our anxiety for the safety of the Leader begins to pass into the question, Why is this man important? What does his struggle mean for him so that it can mean something for us? What, in short, is the conflict in the picture? What is the object of the terror, the suspense, the suffering, the meanness, and, for 'the girl,' the love that goes with the Leader into death intoned by machine guns from the police and covered gently with the falling snow?

The organization the Leader represents is nameless, its people pursued by the police. The city is Irish, the time the recent wartime or its aftermath. We do not know for what the organization is fighting. We do not know why the police must suppress it. From the reactions of people, we see that they fear the police as well as the organization. The men in the organization struggle to find the wounded Leader, and we do not know why. Themselves, they are timid, garrulous, unheroic, like the ratty gangsters of our own films of the twenties. One man alone shows determination and skill; but the question is, For what, for whom, to what end?

The feeling seems to be that a question larger than a historical one is being posed, a question of some ominous general truth being filtered through simulated realistic symbols. It is humanity itself that is on trial. If we grant, without evidence, that it is for the people, for truth, that the Leader offers himself; then he offers himself against no historically conditioned repressive state, but just against authority itself. In short, it is man's inner soul in conflict with abstract authority.

It is here, early in the film, when Denis, the aide to the Leader, makes a violent effort to save him, and fails, that the whole trend of the presentation falters. There is a gap, and now we are offered a series of discursive incidents in which people discuss their inner relations to the helpless dying man and his use to them. A cabby, a birdman, a priest, a mad painter, a doctor, even the girl in love, are all suddenly flung into a deep inner struggle to determine what their non-historical, unconditioned responsibility is to authority. The steady, quiet, fatherly police official and the eternal law of civic order which he represents, must be satisfied, so each of the characters will now have his use of the helpless baggage of a man before authority claims its creature.

This sudden shift in the midst of the film from narrative to moralizing is a traditional philosophical method called raising the question from the accidental to the eternal. The film then proceeds at this high level to put the struggle aside and considers a series of general notions *out of relation* to the first presentation of the subject matter.

With the change of perspective the nature of the scenes changes and one wild vignette follows another, culminating in a hysterical and rather cliché morality play in an artist's garret. Nothing remains but to kill this wretched, dying creature, and he and his girl are slain.

The closer we examine *Odd Man Out*, its confusion of motive, its drift from facing out toward what conditions morality to the inner world which denies it, the more adequately we estimate our own reactions, the clearer it becomes that the film, although invested with all the trappings of realism, is nothing more than an enormous fantasy, a fantasy of the unconscious, a confession, a private dream. *Odd Man Out* is actually a stereotype of realism in the literary form of melodrama. Its *content*, as differentiated from its mechanical form, is essentially antirealistic, a consideration of a metaphysical and not a social struggle.

In treating social events it is necessary to know their precise historical conditions in order to evaluate the operation of moral choices. In a metaphysical inquiry we are mainly interested in defining the abstract terms for logical manipulation. Nowadays, a whole literary school has arisen, antirealistic in nature, which is devoted to deciding whether organization-as-such is evil (not whether this organization is evil or not), and whether man's inner agony is a condition of physical existence (not whether this social existence or that creates terror and anxiety in his spirit). Such questions are not considered useful from the point of view of reality.

Monsieur Verdoux is more like a clever dream than a copy of reality. The notion of turning Bluebeard into a sentimental husband compelled to run a small murder mill on the side to support a loving family and give them *all the things* society expects families to have, is outrageously unrealistic. Verdoux is a wretched criminal, busy as a bee in his work, happy among his flowers, counting his ill-gotten money, terribly earnest about the stock market, making love to miserly women, killing them; Verdoux is a bigamist, an adulterer, a murderer, a buffoon.

Cinematographically, the film is awkward, the physical backgrounds improvised and unlived in, and the story meanders confusedly from sequence to sequence.

From the first stiff and awkward scene in which the members of a French family snarl at one another and worry about a missing sister, her money, and the new husband, through the bread-and-butter scene in the detective bureau in which the search for Verdoux is presented for plot reasons, we know there will be no realism of character, décor, or treatment. And then we are borne on a magic carpet into the presence of

Verdoux cutting his roses, nimble-footed in his garden, while an incinerator smokes behind him. This is the fabulous Charlie in another visitation on the earth, the profound artist of a generation of millions, the imp of perversity whose defiance of reality has released for a stray moment the social wish to be free. Neither the clumsy editing nor the stiff head-on acting of the other characters takes away from the marvelous flow of gesture with which Chaplin has contributed to our understanding of human vitality.

It is a strange, lost world that we inhabit in *Monsieur Verdoux*, a world filled with examples of the forlorn mentality of the little bourgeois. He is so devoted to his vice, which is gambling on the stock market, so precise in his business, which is murder.

There are many styles of storytelling, and the symphonic form is not necessarily the best; but the bits and pieces of plot do not pattern themselves in Verdoux. The scenes with his crippled wife and child are incredibly sentimental, the scenes with his victims almost insane with satire. But artists have more resources than those which inadequate premises force upon their works; from the very depths of Chaplin's understanding of needs, from his sensitive awareness of our times, reality begins to infiltrate the film as passion does a just cause.

Who is Verdoux? Suddenly we want him not to be captured, because he is clearly caught in the dreadful hazard of the day, the insecurity of the individual in a world where social forces move like landslides without pity or charity or justice. This little bank clerk, faithful to one bank for fifteen years, has been thrown on his own resources by a depression. He provides for his family in a way not commonly accepted as socially useful. He applies himself with an employee's devotion, a businessman's acumen, a workman's skill, and a philosopher's gaiety to the task chosen. And only when another depression wipes out his family does he lose his heart. It is economic depression, avarice, the indifference of society which are his enemies. He holds them off for a while in scenes of desperate comic gravity, in scenes of hysterical burlesque, and even falls victim for a moment to his own death-dealing intentions. At the end, all hope gone, he leads a merry chase just for the fun of it, then gives himself up.

In court his defense is traditional. Necessity forced him to run a small business. He objects to being called a mass murderer since his record is petty compared with that of the munition kings and the lords of our life, the warriors, the statesmen, the great owners of death. He refuses the consolation of religion, although he regrets that he has missed some of the sweetness of life. And like countless honest rebels he goes to the guillotine. He has acted with all his will, tried to master existence. The defeat is his personal tragedy; the struggle, his gay contribution to his fellow men.

The real conflicts that men must face in our world are permitted to operate in *Monsieur Verdoux*, although the artist lets them in through every device but a door. Somehow we are not satisfied by the film since it does not seem to have found an appropriate form for the conception. But it is a free film, made with an artist's freedom from censorship, freely invented, and always brought into relation to a living social condition. He does not take refuge in some eternal disaster which a false condition of existence presupposes. Life is not an endless wheel; it is an endless set of chances.

Now, we must not and cannot hope to be otherwise than most appreciative of all art, no matter from what point of view it is created, for works of art are apt uses of a section of history which is withdrawn from abstraction (and therefore imaginative death) for the uses of human consciousness. If in literature, film, and painting today there are perverse and terribly sad forms of human frustration and self-deception, we who are also subject to both, even when we are not suffering them, should be particularly sympathetic. Just because these distortions brood with melancholy clarity over the problems of certain artists, and just because we, too, have been nourished on their neuroses and, in part, think aesthetically in terms of them, we must not abandon their particular contributions. (For example, the contribution of Kafka, who taught himself to write very calmly, as if objectively, about *the* terrible dilemma of human existence when all he knew was his own crisis, an incapacity to discharge his feelings into society as an act of will.)

Like all works of art, or attempts at them, *Odd Man Out* and *Monsieur Verdoux* are not complete illustrations of the point of view I am trying to develop. The two tendencies in modern thought which they in part represent are general orientations. A specific art work is concrete, enormously complex, influenced by current opinions of nature and history, generated deeply by the artist's specific personality and experience, partly autonomous, richly attached at numberless places to the changing processes of life, inheriting the fruitful as well as the sterile attitudes of the past, and plunging into the future as a hope. The two films under consideration are superior accomplishments and will not ever be mere examples of any one thing.

They do remind us, however, of a schism affecting much modern aesthetic musing; it is not accidental that *Odd Man Out* moves away from reality and *Monsieur Verdoux* toward it. Today, the aesthetic avant-garde is mystic, illiberal, and extremely sensitive to the psychology of self-consciousness.

Faced with the violent social upheavals of the last hundred years, the turmoil of everyday choices, the horrible wars and plagues which we have endured, and the worse wars promised by our political and military leaders, many delicate minds have ransacked intellectual history for malleable modes of thought that will comfort them. In scholasticism they have found a nomenclature of exceptional rigor which gives them strength; in romantic idealism, a breath of energy which gives them courage; in existentialism and a distorted Freudism, a psychic primacy over outer reality which allays their fears; in symbolism and the works of Kafka, a literary vocabulary which, like music, permits wishes to daydream their anxieties away. These artists have finally "undiscovered" the real world and substituted an *Innerlichkeit*. They have turned away from history to vast internal structures of subconscious consciousness. Occupied by psychological symptoms of the real world, they do not look beyond into causes, but estimate, analyze, and dramatize their apparently autonomous inner materials. As a result, the realists have discovered many an important truth about themselves (and us) and created some ravishing works of sensitive discrimination; but they have abandoned their audience to the turmoil. The search for inner truth suddenly externalizes itself as a radical verbalism which accepts the status quo no matter where. The discovery of man's inner agony yields up to the artists controllable neuroses while we are delivered over to objective agonies and uncontrollable death. The decision that the *universe as such* is socially dangerous leads to the luxury of not having to struggle in the market place and obscures the truth that social systems change and agony is not man's condition on earth.

These are the long, dark steps leading down from the life of reason, of the passion, of accomplishment, the retreat from rational efforts to irrational abdication of the will. Such personalities are created for the concentration camps of authority, for the torture cells and agonized pleasure of self-abasement.

It is somehow in this general antirealistic context that the content of *Odd Man Out* appears. You cannot pretend to examine life without opening a floodgate of truths, for the real world is generous in revealing its systems, its laws, eager to provide opportunities for human success. But when these truths conflict with presuppositions rotted in interest, then you must obey the truth or refuse to look. In *Odd Man Out* the story-tellers refused to look. To the senseless world they say there will always be authority, needed, aided, loved; and there will always be rebels, both weak and heroic; and people are torn with fears of self and not-self; and man is a storm-tossed creature adrift on the dark seas of eternal conflict and misery; but if we have some inner dignity, and charity toward others and ourselves, while we cannot change life, we can learn to endure it. If we cannot change human nature and the conditions of its existence, let us at least be kind to each other. Let us *indeed* be kind! We can get used to not being used to life, as many a suffering neurotic can vouch for. This is, of course, plain antirealistic perversity with which the psychiatrist is more familiar than I, and no décor of objectivity, not real street lights, street signs, tenements, mills, not any real object or place, makes this position aesthetically realistic. These works are not created from the point of view of mastering reality. You cannot master reality unless you recognize its content, and this, despite its bravura clownishness, *Monsieur Verdoux* does. *Realism is based on content.* Realistic works are those created from a certain point of view with respect to this content. The accidents of a literary verbal heritage or stylistic modes are not central to the method of realism.

In general, the orientation of works written from the point of view of realism is: (1) that objective reality is the condition of man's consciousness, and, therefore, his morality, not the other way round; (2) that the life of humanity cannot be made available for understanding unless it is limited to a specific society and to conflicts in which men are struggling, desiring creatures; and (3) that man's development is directly related to this ability progressively to master reality, for that is the condition of his social life.

I am reminded here of an old conversation between Hegel and Goethe as reported by Eckermann in 1827:

"The discourse then turned upon the nature of dialectics. 'They are, in fact,' said Hegel, 'nothing more than the regulated, methodically cultivated spirit of contradiction which is innate in all men, and which shows itself great as a talent in the distinction between the true and the false.'

"'Let us only hope,' interposed Goethe, 'that these intellectual arts and dexterities are not frequently misused, and employed to make the false true and the true false.'

"'That certainly happens,' said Hegel; 'but only with people who are mentally diseased.'

"'I therefore congratulate myself,' said Goethe, 'upon the study of nature, which preserves me from such a disease. For here we have to deal with the infinitely and eternally true, which throws off as incapable everyone who does not proceed purely and honestly with the treatment and observation of his subject. I am also certain that many a dialectic disease would find a wholesome remedy in the study of nature.'"

Odd Man Out. Universal-International (Rank), 1947. Producer and director, Carol Reed. Novel, F. L. Green. Screenplay, Robert Scherriff and F. L. Green. *Monsieur Verdoux.* United Artists, 1947. Production, direction, and screenplay, Charles Chaplin.

Hemingway and Chaplin

Abraham Polonsky / 1953

From *The Contemporary Reader* 1.1 (March 1953): 23–31.

In the lifetime of an artist after he has created a body of work, an instant arrives when the pressure to speak with his own voice, as if privately, becomes irresistible. All works of art whether they are called objective or subjective and no matter who pays for them, the artist, the patron, the publisher, or the state, express the artist's point of view. This is one of the fascinating things about art as with the manufacture of munitions; even when you say I'm saying this because they make me or I'm manufacturing this because I have to, to eat, to survive, to get away with it, in the end there is something in you, some interest which is the same as the one you pretend to detest. So everything an artist does reflects his point of view or part of it and yet all these works are different from the one in which, with a passion for autobiography, he confesses to his irresponsibilities, his quirks, his fancies, his egotism, his irony about himself, and his commitment to historical destiny. The intimate work keeps repeating "in spite of my weakness" and "because of my strength" and between the confession and the boast, truth becomes personal and we no longer are bearing the abstract social opinions which everyone can share or condemn without ever living; we begin to hear those on which the artist has founded his life, changeable often, but nevertheless real.

The artist's need to speak out is always his whether he decides the occasion or a subpoena does it for him. Chaplin's *Limelight* and Hemingway's *Old Man and the Sea* are psychological self-portraits and it is hard to tell when we are dealing with art and when with simple testimony.

All cunning storytellers prefer to speak through invented characters even when the character is mostly their own. The artist feels more freedom that way. It is a way to get around the constant demand to be one thing at a particular moment, as if everything were being put to a vote and the decision were going to be final (as in Zeno's old jokes). Fiction makes it unnecessary to eliminate real contradictions which the artist finds in life, in the heart of his conscience, and perhaps just in his ignorance. He can always claim it was Calvero or Santiago who said it, who felt it, who did it, and it is up to us to point out when it is Chaplin or Hemingway speaking directly for themselves as they have lived and wish to be remembered. I know also that the artist likes to be found out, the reader likes to find him out, and this is the way they influence each other in private.

Limelight and The Old Man and the Sea are just about the same story, the tale of an old man once supreme in his field whom time has weakened and circumstance faced with a test of strength and philosophy. Both heroes affirm and do not alter their vision of life. Chaplin is involved with a girl and Hemingway is involved with a fish.

Limelight deals fundamentally with the conflict between Chaplin and his American public. This public includes almost everyone who can hear and see: the mass audience which resists the transformation of the magical tramp into a realistic satirist and lyric poet; the avant-garde, nowadays the rear-guard, who are embarrassed by his simple ideas of human perfectibility; the special organizations of Catholics and veterans who picket his politics; and the governmental bureaucracy always one jump ahead of the grand jury but still with the power to keep a Chaplin in involuntary exile.

The scene of the film is the London theatrical world early in the century and the hero of the tale is the aging clown, Calvero. Until he appears it is hard to tell whether this is going to be Chaplin in the world of fantasy or in the real world. His beginnings are always deceptive and the test is never the laughter but the nature of physical pain. Even in M. Verdoux where Chaplin experimented with the transition between two worlds, the old roué fell out of the window without worrying too much about gravitation and human engineering. In fantasy everything is a symbol even when it is as real and human as your child's rag doll. The moment, however, Calvero comes down the street and goes up the steps, so gay and light and human on his feet, we know this is a man who will act the clown, who might become a symbol, as did Lear, but is not himself symbolic of anything, who will mean what his actions and thoughts mean according to the laws of the socially real world and this includes the American Congress, supply and demand, and the fact that the human heart pumps eight thousand quarts a day (and this is why Calvero will die). Our clown is a dancer, a comedian, a humanist, a lover of life and, as he says, of women ("I've had five wives already. One more or less makes no difference." The audience chuckles. They are familiar with history). This is then our real world and we know as we laugh that here pain is real pain and love is real love and to die is to die as we die on earth, forever.

Chaplin uses rather special material as he moves into the world of artistic realism, ballet dancers, actors, impresarios, and clowns, characters touched with make-believe in an atmosphere of charming boarding houses and bars, the backstage, the stage itself, a bench at dawn on the Thames Embankment. There is an air of *La Vie de Bohème* about the whole thing, but bourgeois artists have always found that cast and milieu interesting. It is a way to protest against the detestable economy of the boulevards, and in Greenwich Village and the Montmartre you can say things that the police won't mind since no one is even remotely respectable, but times have changed, and there is no protection against political persecution by calling yourself an artist. Of course, you can still show a bare behind to a twelve-year-old on Broadway and get away with it, but don't try to say anything about reality or teach evolution and political science, *even if you make clowns say it.* Our world is now a total Broadway filled with shooting galleries, cafeterias, and tourists, violence and pornography up in lights, common sense and truthfulness written by hand on alley walls.

The actual plot of the film is simple and haunts us with memories. It is one that Grimm might have begun with his "once upon a time." The aging clown, a failure and a drunkard, rescues the beautiful young ballet dancer and turns her mind toward life. He tries to re-establish his own career and fails. She goes on toward success. She loves him, but he will not take her pity or her help and leaves her. In the end she arranges a benefit to help him financially but he converts his last appearance into a triumph for his talent and dies happily while his gift for life lives on in her. It is a story out of the old chapbooks. Naturally Satan is played offscene, in command at Ellis Island so to speak, and the magic elixir is not in a phial but is man's consciousness. Artists use folk tales as folk tales use props, whatever is handy, and each generation has to satisfy its own sense of verisimilitude.

Throughout the film there is a relaxed fooling, sly when Calvero is sober, fantastic when he is drunk, which takes the place of the slapstick in the old comedies. Set scenes contain all the preparation and explanation of the characters, and are told in exchange of gnomic wisdom ("life is a local affair") or run out into sheer prosiness as in Terry's tale of love for the poor music student. (In real life the student happens to be Chaplin's son. Two patrons talked about this as we left the theatre. "What can this possibly mean?" one asked. The other replied, with a backward glance to an imaginary couch, "It's a Freudian joke." At any rate it is a joke because Chaplin has three other children in the film.) In addition to the drama there are separate vaudeville turns, the ballets, and one piece of old-fashioned slapstick with which Chaplin and Buster Keaton so exhaust the real audience that it drowns in its own laughter.

A kind of creative irresolution mars the interweaving of these elements as if Chaplin could not or would not determine the boundaries of functional distortion. For example, the social background of Terry is stereotyped beyond acceptability. Even Calvero says it sounds like a novelette and I suppose he means Michael Arlen. Then, the clown's fall from popularity is neither explained by his dreams nor his actual performances at the Middlesex Variety Hall or at the benefit, while in the second of the dream sequences Calvero does a turn with Terry which belongs to the world of modern poetry and is connected as a poetic aside might be with the culminating dramatic scene where the dying clown is borne aloft like Siegfried but on a broken bass drum. Finally Chaplin uses *plot* coincidence as most of us use punctuation—wherever it fits.

All these weaknesses give an unfinished tone to the film and because we love the man and his performance a certain careless charm. They do not become irrelevant but they become unimportant as actor and idea link up in superb patterns of filmic images that progress in meaning and soar in arias. Within these lyrical outbursts Chaplin creates the new things that have to be made and uses the old things that have to be used and says those private thoughts that have to be uttered.

Limelight runs along as a love story between a young woman and an old man. What unites them is need, character, philosophy, and sex, not paternalism and gratitude. There are no *psychological* coincidences in the relation between the clown and the ballet dancer whom he has rescued for life. As a result, love is founded on the exchange between age and youth develops with musical logic, through growth, through understanding, and not in conventional psychology, literary and scientific, by the process of misunderstanding, malevolence, and emotional insanity. (We know this well, the usual drama of love in books and plays, on the screen, the radio, television: I didn't know what you meant. What? You mean I thought you felt that I thought? O! if I had only *known* . . . and so on through the gambits of miserable self-pity and pornography.) Here in

Limelight the love flowers, and what is so immense for our social world of sexual boredom and violence, it flowers without sexual play, sexual fight, and sexual jealousy. We can even imagine at a certain point the clown and the ballet dancer became complete lovers, if only for awhile, and had the film been made in another country, I suppose we would have had some indication of it to emphasize the shift in dependence between them.

After Calvero's audience abandons him at the Middlesex Variety Hall (and the scene which is real is shot as if it too were a dream like the earlier ones, faceless seats and no face there but his own) the film springs from his defeat to Terry's liberation to her exalted cry repeating and repeating that she can walk, that she is walking, *I'm walking, I'm walking.* In this scene there is a close-up which states in a single image the opposite pole of the weary but fulfilled face we see at the end of the benefit. Here it is Calvero removing his make-up with cold cream in the provincial dressing room. Out of the heavy impasto stare suddenly the pain-ridden eyes. The make-up, the whorls of chalky white, the lighting all make everything dead *except the eyes*, and as they look into their inner defeat, they too suddenly die, and all is dead, everlastingly dead beneath the light of the dead moon. It is from this death that Terry springs alive, and it is from this death that Calvero finally triumphs and then dies as men should, happy to have lived.

Between the *moral death* of the scene at Middlesex and Calvero's *human* death extends his need, and this is why he turns down Terry's offer of marriage. Calvero wants his audience again. "In the few years I have left, I must have truth. That's all I want of life . . . truth. And if possible, a little dignity."

Of course this is to ask everything of life and the question is what does Chaplin mean by truth, what truth is it that he wants?

He wants to make a statement about all of his life now that he has lived so much of it and crowned it with those great comedies which finally achieve in his later career some of the massiveness and cumulative weight of a school: *City Lights, Modern Times, The Dictator, M. Verdoux,* and now *Limelight.*

The truth he wants to assert is that life stifles as its form becomes fixed in the past, that human life is not content to perish this way and it will struggle to disintegrate those dead social forms which maim it. Now Chaplin does not erect a system in the film. He acts out, he creates plastically the full content of his passion for life and belief by asserting it in every image and by the flow of action, by illuminating the vision that life is change and the struggle is not between the moral absolutes of good and evil but between progress and reaction. In this whole film there is not one character or one scene that can stand by itself and be labeled: moral evil, bad man. We master reality by liberating human energy, human potential, human creativeness. This is the lyrical note of the film and as an actor he dares the limits of sentiment in his compassion, his affirmation, his refusal to accept Napalm as the universal solvent for life which "is a desire and not a meaning." The meanings are in the social order.

Within this frame of reference is Chaplin's truth, and the proof of his truth and his right to utter it, is his relation to his audience.

Chaplin wants his audience and he needs them but so does the audience, blinded and bewildered by lies and censorship, need Chaplin's truth.

Chaplin speaks directly of the problem in a number of ways. In the scene with his theatrical agent, Redfern, Calvero is filled with rebelliousness, consummate pride, stubbornness, and finally a pathetic humility when he hears: "Your name is poison to them. They don't want you any more."

The scene between artist and agent has gone on for some years now in America as the blacklist has grown, the artist dumbfounded by a career abruptly terminated, the agent feeling the same about his ten per cent. The sadness is mutual and the mutual resentment comic.

The fact is that Chaplin's name is not poison to his audience. He is poison to the special spiritual and material interests that live comfortably within dead forms and refuse to change, hate change, and fight change. All animal and human history cannot convince these dead that this time will not be different from all other times, and so again we have political persecution and again we have censorship.

There is some evidence within the film that Chaplin feels his own growth as an artist has also helped rob him of his audience.

He is talking with Terry in their little magic mountain:

> Calvero: Y'know, as a man gets on in years he wants to live deeply . . . a feeling of sad dignity comes upon him . . . and that's fatal for a comic. It affected my work. I lost contact with my audience.

And then very bitterly:

> Calvero: I'd like to forget the public.

Terry: Never . . . you love them too much.

Calvero: I'm not so sure . . . maybe I love them, but I don't admire them.

Terry: I think you do.

Calvero: As individuals yes, there's greatness in every one. But as a crowd I distrust them. They're like a monster without a head that never knows which way it's going to turn. It can be prodded in any direction. . . .

It is the public's reaction to *M. Verdoux* about which he is talking. But the failure of any particular work of art, and I don't think the film is a failure, is not central to Chaplin's problem. As artists move in their work trying in one way or another to master reality, as they grow *because they are working* and *because* life is changing (so sound comes and dooms the little tramp and a whole mode of comment is gone as if part of the brain were destroyed and its powers had to be reorganized elsewhere), as this everlasting change occurs, artists lose a familiar, easy relation with their audience, or any audience, only to regain it more deeply in their time or history. In *Limelight* with a sad cheerfulness Calvero leaves the pub and sums up his first career: "There's something about working the streets that I like. It's the tramp in me, I suppose." Chaplin's tramp is gone, but a memory-touched reminder of him now appears with nostalgic pantomime on television in the person of Ben Blue.

In Europe, Chaplin met with a wave of love and admiration from his world audience. Naturally, the crowds in countries where it was necessary used the occasion for some kind of political protest since like Chaplin they did not wish to live, in life or in literature, in a graveyard. As Sartre said, the *brochette des intellectuels pâles et doux comme des demoiselles qui récitent des compliments appris sur la culture et la liberté*, were met by silence, empty streets, and a great many improper signs. The man who affirmed life was met by those who want to live, and met with that enthusiasm which he prophesied in the film, the benefit for Calvero which is really for our benefit.

Calvero finds his truth; it was what he knew and believed all the time, and fulfilled, he dies. His spirit, his love of life and gusto for it, his love of beauty and form, of truth pass to Terry. This is what we are made to feel, we know it, we triumph in it, and as they take Calvero away, his shoes turned out, she is alone on the stage in an immense hollow of shadow where the light of his consciousness and ours illuminates her as she whirls, turning, turning, posing in arabesques as every work of art does so that we can possess it, going on and on as life must, endlessly flinging up forms in which our desires become social triumphs through the endless change of things.

Like Chaplin, and for the same reason, Hemingway picks a romantic area in which to display his story, *The Old Man and the Sea*. He wants his statement to be personal and he wants the freedom to explore symbols without foundering on the practical issues of the day. He does not quite get what he wants and perhaps in a way he did not want to escape altogether.

What is the story of *The Old Man and the Sea*, of Santiago, the champion? It is a tale, even more old-fashioned and touched with received tradition than *Limelight*, of an old and poverty-stricken fisherman who goes out to sea alone to catch one of the big fish for market. His expedition has already been shadowed with heavy meaning. He is going alone because the boy who loves and reveres him has been forbidden to go with an old man who has lost his *luck*. We know that *not* to be lucky is to be cursed by the gods and nature, to be cast out, to be an outlaw, naturally the old man catches the biggest fish ever. He loses the flesh to the sharks after a desperate struggle and in the end the boy rejoins him:

> "The hell with luck," the boy said. "I'll bring luck with me."
> "What will your family say?"
> "I do not care. I caught two yesterday. But we will fish together now for I still have much to learn."

And now the world knows as the village knows that this old man is one of the chosen of the world and his luck is our fate and our fortune, his gift to us whether we cherish him or not.

In spiritual self-portrait Hemingway tells us what he wants us to believe of him and reaffirms his place as a man and an artist in our world. He says it most clearly after the old man kills the first shark that comes for his great fish.

> "I killed the shark that hit my fish. . . . A man can be destroyed but not defeated. . . . Perhaps it was a sin to kill the fish. I suppose it was even though I did it to keep me alive and feed many people. But then everything is a sin.
> . . . You did not kill the fish only to keep alive and to sell for food.
> . . . You killed him for pride and because you are a fisherman. You loved him

when he was alive and you loved him after. If you love him, it is not a sin to kill him. Or is it more? . . . Besides everything else in some way. . . . Fishing kills me exactly as it keeps me alive. The boy keeps me alive. . . .

"And what beat you, he thought. . . . Nothing. . . . I went out too far."

Hemingway has never anywhere said more of what he is and believes and all of it is true enough. By now I think we can believe him that he believes it. The point of view that he is re-affirming here he has asserted from the very beginning through all the marvels and mishaps of his work, from the early time when his style was a manner, a method of getting at the truth, to the time when his style became a mannerism and obscured the truth. We are involved with the fundamental Hemingway situation in love, in sport, in war.

He sees existence as a terrible struggle with the external world and in every fight with a bull, an army, a fish, a talent, a woman, the man is inevitably fighting the crisis in himself, for man lives in a perpetual crisis of courage and persistence in which all actions by their very nature are defeats and the only victories are triumphs of man's proud and sinful inner spirit. This attitude toward existence is habitual with those who believe in subjective monsters and angels, the familiars of religion and psychoanalysis. It is a magical notion based on the assumption that nothing in the external world can transform us because we are actually not part of that world. It is a famous disease in morality and philosophy, and we can appropriate Thomas Mann's comment on Wagner for Hemingway, "His disease, after all, consists in being a variation of the bourgeois variety of health."

In the Hemingway disease, which he believes is his position in the world as an artist and a human being, the true man always goes beyond all the other stupid and cowardly ones who hang back, makes his hopeless attempt, flirts with the absolute and death, and often dies because he ventured beyond. Life, Hemingway is accustomed to say, is shorter than death. Therefore, let us think of death and defeat which are longer than life. Let us be serious.

What can we do with this Hemingway story which is so much like all his other stories? This great fish which it is our fate and destiny to catch and destroy, this Leviathan which is the state and society, this irrevocable trend of time and history, this hope, this work which the sharks destroy, which the critics abuse and misunderstand, this great fish of a man and a work, what can we do with all this? Is it true enough?

Yes, it is true enough.

Having rejected a position which lets life in to mold and be molded, a position such as Chaplin asserts, Hemingway is forced to survive with a gesture. Mystic honor supplies a way to live, and the honor is honorable enough; it is the mysticism that dishonors it.

In all his stories there is always this gesture of absolute courage in the face of absolute defeat, and generally there is death too, for only dying can prove the seriousness of the action. This notion of behavior is one of the few general ideas that Hemingway has. To emphasize the radical hopelessness of man's fate, the built-in sinfulness of the world, he often cripples his hero with some form of impotence so that the gesture is utterly doomed and therefore all the more illuminating.

Now the gesture of courage in the face of overwhelming odds (and sometimes defeat) is habitual with the poor and oppressed. It is the common morality of their lives and a way to prove hatred of the oppressor. However, the poor and oppressed do not make this gesture for metaphysical comfort but to add to the certainty of the common victory. It is a way to prove confidence in the future which begins now with this *gesture*. Among the oppressed real heroism is measured by liberation and victory, not by the mystical value of courage assigned to the individual man. The oppressed, who are many, know that as events begin to move in unison and millions therefore move together, individual courage is translated into the force of the situation which carries forward all actions, and it no longer matters who is brave and who is not. In the general fighting everyone fights. The thing is to win. A hero, then, can be an individual with individual courage but he becomes genuinely a hero as he assigns his actions to the common victory and not to any metaphysical IQ in courage.

What Hemingway explains about himself and his work in *The Old Man and the Sea*, he once tried to say through a more socially distinguished character in *Across the River and into the Trees*. Into this novel of Venice, Hemingway flung all the elements of his earlier successes, a battle-weary colonel wounded almost to the death by heart disease, a city ancient with romance in the center and good hunting on the outskirts, a comradeship of *types*, and to cap it all a young girl, aristocratic, who could make the earth move from the second balcony. This colonel is straight *Death in the Afternoon* Hemingway in terms of self-consciousness and memory content. Hemingway, who outgeneraled most of the other war correspondents in France, lets his wishes daydream him out of his artist's conscience and consciousness in this memoir in the form of parody. And the Colonel, like most of the Hemingway heroes, gets to be very funny as the great torero of love, his conviction being that love between the sexes is more like marksmanship than passion, the virtues being good aim, a steady hand, and a true instinct for the bull's eye.

Having failed with a Colonel, Hemingway tried again with Santiago, and for the first time in many years we begin to hear again that wonderfully clear note with which, in one form or another, he founded the main literary movement of our time and then by direct descent a good fifty percent of the film, novels, radio shows, and television dramas of the next two generations.

Hemingway tries to assimilate the fisherman into the Hemingway hero. What happens is that the Hemingway hero is overwhelmed by the powerful image of Santiago, the representative of the poor and oppressed. This Cuban colonial must now in addition to the weight of the American sugar empire bear the sophisticated burden of the Hemingway philosophy. He does and he can. His true life absorbs the alien artist and gives a wider meaning to the fable. In the end it writes a new finish to a favorite Hemingway story.

Santiago's consciousness and memory give Hemingway a great deal of trouble. The writer throws in some of his own philosophy, some strange and curious dialogue about baseball which just will not get to be like bullfighting, and finally an incident from Santiago's youth to prove that the old man like the author was a champion. Hemingway's terrible ignorance of social reality which has crippled him from his earliest days makes him stumble in public where even a Missouri tourist has learned to stumble in private: Hemingway can't spell Negro. In the *Green Hills of Africa* you will find that he can spell all the dirty words which the white man uses against the Negro people. Such ignorance of the moral world is innocence at twenty and wickedness at fifty, and this is why the inner world that he assigns to Santiago makes a murmur such as we hear from a machine, that is noise, and not music. But the objective story of *The Old Man and the Sea* contradicts almost all of the weaknesses of the author's philosophy. Hemingway, like most dominating artists, has a wonderful eye for significant subjects and a sense of their timeliness. He knows who the heroes of our time are and out of what world they will come. Santiago belongs to the colonial peoples. So does the future. And here in the sea off the shores of Havana there is a victory and this time not only of the spirit but in fact. The old man returns safely and the boy returns to the old man. There is something to pass on.

The story is a psychological self-portrait and Hemingway, it seems, would like to survive and hand down his wisdom and accomplishment.

Who can blame him? Like all mystics and idealists he lets reality in through the kitchen after nobly flinging it out through the parlor. All to the good, as a certain politician once said.

Hemingway has force and we worship force in America even when it is used against us; he has control and we lavish fortune on our professionals who work at what should be our play; and yet he began his career within a narrow circle of aesthetes and his first book was privately printed, three hundred copies, I think. Today he is a popular novelist whose name has value even in the beer advertisements. Chaplin began as a popular entertainer of the poorest and most numerous part of our population and rose to be the darling of the little film journals. These two men are representative American artists in the most historic sense of the word, and yet they are still trying to estimate and educate themselves. This is why I particularly like their testimony at the moment. We live in a time when Sartre goes to the peace conference and Upton Sinclair and John Steinbeck join the chair-borne atom bombers

In one way or another I think we will be hearing from most of our writers and artists in the near future and some of the testimony will be peculiar and most of it will be just as we expected, and a lot of it will be shameful. Every now and then we will get *The Old Man and the Sea* and *Limelight*.

We have to realize that we too live in historical times and a lot of it is going to be filled with surprises.

A Utopian Experience

Abraham Polonsky / 1962

From *Présence du Cinéma* 14 (juin 1962): 5–7. Translated by Andrew Dickos.

I am often asked if it is possible to conceive a scenario as a particular literary form. Having tried this experiment, I hope my story might interest all those who, like me, have had the most disappointing results in this pursuit. It is mainly in the obstacles of three hazardous conditions: the producer, the director, and the script itself. (I suppose the writer, director, and producer are people whose competence cannot be questioned and who will not question the characters and scenes fixed in the story.)

What does the producer expect from the screenplay? To make possible an assessment of the cost of production. This means that in addition to dialogue, the script should produce a text that specifies the additional shooting time predicted for each page. Good writers have learned to divide their text this way. This requirement is clearly arbitrary and unrelated to the real needs of this work. (Naturally, there is the creative producer, recognized as a truly responsible force behind the making of the film and who *utilizes* a director, screenwriter, and actors; the creative director who dictates the needs of the scenario to the screenwriter, and finally the creative actor, who animates the scenario and sets the pace for the producer, director, and screenwriter.)

What does the director expect from the scenario? The dialogue and dramatic organization which will allow the action to be clear, the best sequence of scenes to follow, and an understanding of each motivation. This collaboration with the writer varies from simply working together to the alternating of orders and compliments, and thereby creating links to a real friendship. Those who are excluded from the sacred mysteries of the screenplay conferences are fascinated by what they learn of this annihilation ritual in which a writer's idea is praised, then his work analyzed, and finally destroyed completely, for these ideas are to be reborn through the director.

An American screenplay generally follows this particular style of setting up shots, designed so that directors, producers, and actors who are not accustomed to texts without pictures can read the screenplay without fatigue. They are used like headings of chapters and paragraphs. Such shots are not entirely to be discounted as inappropriate. A traditional scenario is composed of scenic and dramatic progression in a manner that convinces the director, actor, or producer they are the true creators of the film. Variations may occur, but it remains the general rule, true even if the writer is also the director or producer, since then the script will work as a contribution to the production. The shape the screenplay takes actually becomes a simplified system of notations used by film editors to set up those beginnings and ends in ideal order.

In this environment, nobody would admit to a properly prepared scenario that did not have this exact form—which necessarily frustrates the scriptwriter. The only concept of freedom of expression that may be the screenwriter's is literally to stage through the screenplay the film he imagines. By a comprehensive analysis, he can try to specify each scene and report it with all the images, speed, size, leadership, diversity, and power of impact of what is to be shown. But it is ultimately impossible, not only because no verbal description can fully account for the action of a scene or sequence, but because no scenario can be structured precisely enough to determine the total content of each scene; it would make the scenario thicker than all the volumes collected of the Encyclopedia Britannica, and equally insufficient.

What the director hopes to find in a scenario is a storytelling strategy that can and should work. Meditating and improvising on the set, along with the actors, he draws his inspiration from a screenplay whose dialogue, from the first draft, shapes what will become the film. The result of this work is a set of images extremely complicated and changeable, surprising and disturbing to both the director and the screenwriter. The tension the screenwriter faces to counteract the traditional scenario and his desire to create something truly ambitious is based on the fact that an essential part of the script remains unwritten. This part is as intended in the mind of the director and takes form when the film is actually shot.

The modern film is a set of images and a set of dialogues. Under the best circumstances, and working with a modest director, sensible and acquiescent, the maximum a writer can have is that most actions suggested, and dialogue written, should not be altered. But what is clearly the creation of the film—this set of images with movement and an aesthetic structure—the true center of it, must remain unwritten.

Controlling no more than half of the film, the screenwriter can, through this work, claim a literary ambition. Screenwriters know that a scenario is not a play. The text of a play, even if it lacks the actor's and director's talents, still connects them to the dialogue at hand, which, by implication, contains all the necessary references for future plotting. Actors and directors in the theater are only interpreters, which is what a filmmaker is not. And no writer, producer, actor, or businessman can assume the role of mere interpreter without destroying the film. The dialogue of a play is expressed in real time on stage. *The dialogue of a film is expressed in psychological time that creates the images which occur in real time.* Inexperienced writers may confuse these two styles of dialogue because both use common literary origins and may sometimes, to a limited extent, be interchangeable.

The writer's desire to share personal creative control forces him to become the director of his screenplay or to introduce those technical improprieties that a capable director then ignores. In theory, a serious writer who is not capable of directing his own work should stop writing for film.

I suggest however that there may be a solution to this problem, a solution that is unrelated to the technique or an exhaustive analysis of the shots, but one that could be sought in a defined structure with intensity and elegance; by metaphor, synthesis, and size; and with richness. I'm speaking about poetry, and the literary form of scenario I have in mind is the poem.

I use the words poem and poetry to define a type of scenario, which, instead of the specific angles of shooting, would clarify the intentions of the writer by concrete images (similar to that of metaphors) and, instead of set directions for action, directly express this action in its intensity; which, instead of summary information on the characters would express their exact behavior; which, instead of a dialogue that brings meaning to the scene when the image is missing would establish the meaning of this scene. These devices of the novel and modern poetry might renew the technique of screenwriting, appealing in the process to their precursors in the old religious and national epics.

We should eliminate this voluntary assemblage of narrative, of psychological analysis, of dialogue and the received wisdom of critics which form the traditional novel. This series of concrete images in the script would not seek to replace the images of the film, but would provide for the director as well as the actors a more human literary and technical richness.

Can scenarios be designed to serve the goals and styles of the director and actors? Certainly, since they contain all the dialogue and establish the strategy of the film. But instead of being a summary of directions to follow, the strategy would be in a series of images detailing the reality of the action to follow and its evolution, providing the director a much wider berth to realize his vision. Of course, the director should read and the writers should be poets. It is possible to create a cinematic literature to match the work of the director and, possibly, to exceed it. We would thus free ourselves from the paralysis of naturalism which has completely distorted the description of our modern condition on the screen.

Not long ago I tried to write such a scenario, but in the smiles of the conference that followed, I was asked to give up my resentment as a recently blacklisted writer and undertake a more traditional approach to the project at hand. This I did.

Conversations with Abraham Polonsky

William S. Pechter / 1962 & 1968

From *Film Quarterly* 15, no. 3 (Spring 1962): 48+; and from *Twenty-four Times a Second: Films and Film-makers* by William S. Pechter (New York: Harper & Row, 1971), 147–61. Copyright © 1971 by William S. Pechter. Reprinted by permission of the author.

In 1948, a writer, whose experience, with the exception of two previous screenplays and two unmemorable novels, had been primarily in radio, made an adaptation of another writer's undistinguished, journalistic novel to the screen, and directed a film of it. The event would not seem to be a particularly auspicious one nor much of a novelty for Hollywood, where every other day finds one hack adapting the work of another hack into a piece of adapted hack work. Nor would it have been much more promising to know that the film made use of several elements that were sufficiently familiar—the good-bad guy involved in the rackets who finally goes straight, the ingénue who tries to reform him, etc. Yet, apparently, to have known all this was not to know enough. How else to account for the fact that out of it all was created an original, moving, and even beautiful work, whose only tangency with clichés was at the point at which it transformed and transcended them? I think it is accounted for by that phenomenon which never ceases somehow to be inexplicable and unpredictable: by the presence of an artist.

But the event was, perhaps, not quite so unpredictable as I may, somewhat Hollywoodishly, have made it sound. The artist's name was Abraham Polonsky, and his film was *Force of Evil*; previously, he had written the original scenario for the film *Body and Soul*. *Body and Soul* did not lack acclaim; although independently produced, it won an Academy Award, and was financially successful. *Force of Evil* went largely without acclaim or appreciation; noticed chiefly by the British film periodicals, it was allowed to die an inconspicuous death, a gangster film with only muted violence, a love story without romantic apotheosis, a Hollywood film without a happy ending. Both *Sight and Sound* and *Sequence* cited it among the best films of the year, and it still occasionally crops up in catalogues of neglected works. Lindsay Anderson, in his analysis of the last sequence of *On the Waterfront* which appeared in *Sight and Sound*, invoked *Force of Evil* as foil to that film's inflation and dishonesty. The habitual British reader may have caught the aptness of the comparison; for the American one, it must have been merely a little baffling.

In theme and meaning, *Body and Soul* and *Force of Evil* form an extraordinary unity. In each, the protagonist, played in both films by John Garfield with his most characteristic combination of tough cynicism and a dreamy sense of the city's promise of exaltation, allows himself knowingly to become involved in some kind of corruption only, finally, to experience an intense self-revulsion, and to attempt to wrest himself free. In both films, the protagonist is not moved to this final breach without first having caused some irrevocable violence to those most close to him, and both films end not with any cheap and easy redemption, but deep in anguish and ambiguity. "What can you do? Kill me? Everybody dies," are the final words of *Body and Soul*, as the fighter says to the gambler whose fight he has refused to throw, and, heroic as the words may be, they do not undercut the essential bleakness of the film's concluding prospect, or transform it into any conventional concession to an audience's expectations. What the audience was given, however, was the physical excitement of the prizefight scenes, dynamically photographed by James Wong Howe on roller skates, and the comfortable familiarity of the basic plot: ambitious young man from slums climbs ruthlessly to success. Probably, it is these elements in *Body and Soul* that account for its commercial success and Academy Award, but the film's true distinction is rather to be found in its lyrically rich language, its evocative sense of an urban poetry, and the sensitively observed drawing of characters and their relationships which flesh out the success story's skeleton and give it life.

Force of Evil is not so accessible a film, one without *Body and Soul*'s more immediate compensations for its serious demands. Joe Morse, the protagonist of *Body and Soul*, is not so simply and understandably the product of social determinations as is the fighter in *Body and Soul*. We first see him as a successful lawyer, propelled not by lack of advantages but by the drive to acquire more. Nor is he unaware of the nature of his corruption, or without moral insight. One is never certain to what extent the protagonist of *Body and Soul* is capable of self-knowledge, but Joe Morse acknowledges responsibility for his acts, and without pleading weakness. In his own words, he is "strong enough to get a part of the corruption, but not strong enough to resist it." But this is not so much weakness as a perversion of strength, a defect not in quantity but in kind. The progress of *Force of Evil* is that of the painful burgeoning of a moral indignation. This is not miraculously attained through romantic love, but achieved only after the death of Joe's older brother, whom he had tried both to advance and protect within the racket into which he tempted him. There is a romantic love story in the film, but the relationship which lies at its heart is that of the two brothers, a relationship exacerbated mutually by guilts and thwarted love, and ending agonizingly in the death of one brother and the other's acceptance of his responsibility for this. In its unfolding, the film moves with great charm and vivacity, but also with an underlying tragic momentum toward its painful conclusion, and the painfulness remains largely unmitigated. There is no final, solipsistic kiss; "I decided to help" are Joe's last words as the film concludes on his decision to confess after he has found his dead brother's discarded body. It is a moment entirely free from the pieties which customarily attend Hollywood-style reformations, nor has it any of that sense of straining to engage some good, gray abstraction like Society, which hangs so heavily over the last sequence of *On the Waterfront*. *Force of Evil* ends in moral awakening, but it reaches not so much outward toward society as inward toward communion: toward a shared responsibility; toward a sense of the oneness of human involvement without any diminution of that involvement's complex difficulty and ineluctable pain.

Were this all, one might still have simply a film of the delicacy, compassion, and, I believe, somewhat vitiating softness of, say, *They Live by Night*. Even *Sight and Sound* tended to relegate *Force of Evil* to the status of a sensitive but "minor" work; I think this is other than the case. The film was said to be too essentially literary, and there can be no doubt that it is a work which relies indispensably on its language; we have still to free ourselves entirely from the constrictive dogma that language is not properly an element of film. Simply to observe that the language of *Force of Evil* is beautiful is probably not to the point. The impression of that language is of really hearing for the first time in films the extraordinary sound of New York City speech, with its distinctive repetitions and elisions, cadences and inflections, inarticulateness and cryptopoetry; much as Odets had brought it to the stage. As in Odets, the effect is naturalistic, and, as in Odets, it is achieved by an extreme degree of stylization. But the radical accomplishment of *Force of Evil*, perhaps more obvious now in light of such conspicuous rhetorical experimentation as that of *Hiroshima, Mon Amour*, is in the way the word works with the image. Nothing is redundant, or unnecessary. Joe Morse finds his brother's battered body where he has been told he will, flung upon some rocks, and says in narration what has already become known both through dialogue and image: "He was dead"; yet the effect of this is never superfluous. The narration is the image refracted through an individual consciousness, and thus, however subtly, reimagined. Throughout the film, the protagonist is constantly commenting upon the action, telling us not only what he and the others are thinking but describing events even as we see them; creating through the free flow of language, a context of perception and volition which constantly urges on us the sense of his moral responsibility. But, beyond this, the aesthetic effect of all the film's oblique repetition, with its language overlapping image and language overlapping language, is to impart an almost musical resonance to the agon of the brothers which is at its core.

The more one sees *Force of Evil*, the more one becomes aware of the intricate synthesis of formal means by which it is unfolded. The language becomes a kind of insistent presence, and the images move both congruently and dissonantly with an extraordinary autonomy and freedom. A brief conversation is composed from a remote angle above a gracefully curving stairway; the moment exists both in and independent of the action; and, independently, in its abstraction of light and space, it is startlingly beautiful. Such astonishment is to be found in profusion throughout the film, from so relatively simple an instance to others as complexly moving as the image of Joe Morse running senselessly down a deserted Wall Street at night, knowing that he will never again be rerunning to his "fine office up in the clouds." The film's critics are right. *Force of Evil is* a literary film, but only insofar as the film *is* a literary medium, and perhaps no other work until Godard's has pressed forward with such exploratory imagination to test the boundaries of the literary capacity of films. But beyond its exploratory thrust, the achievement of *Force of Evil* remains in what it is in itself: an original, moving, and even beautiful work. Its beauty directly engages the paradox of art: that it can be both deeply painful and provide pleasure; the pleasure, ultimately, of having one's vision extended. Perhaps nowhere in *Force of Evil* does this fusion of the harrowing and the beautiful command more power than in the film's concluding passage. In the breaking light of early morning, Joe Morse descends a seeming infinity of stairs to discover his brother's body where it has been discarded "like an old rag" upon the rocks at the base of a bridge. It is a descent to "the bottom of the world," to a kind of hell; the symbolic death that must be suffered before regeneration. "Because if a man can live so long, and have his whole life come out like rubbish, then something was horribly wrong . . . and I decided to help."

The "interview" with Abraham Polonsky related below was conducted entirely through correspondence. I have taken the liberty of some slight rearrangement so that there might be a clear relation of answer to question, but the words remain unchanged. Therefore, while the exchanges may occasionally approximate the give and take of conversation, they may be accepted as having the value of written reflection, such as that may be. —William Pechter

Q: Would you begin by giving me some idea of your background before you began working on films? Somewhere I picked up the information that you originally wrote for radio, and, if my memory doesn't play tricks, I recall reading a radio script of yours in the old *Quarterly of Film, Radio, and Television*. I also seem to remember hearing that you taught for a while at the University of Southern California and even the City College of New York, although I am not sure of the chronology (i.e., before or after film-making), and virtually certain that I must have dreamed the latter. Would you also refer to your published fiction and film criticism?
A: I led the usual restless street life: gang (East Side); (CCNY, A.B.); Law (Columbia); volunteer in politics (Democrat, Anarchist, Radical, Confused). I taught at City College from 1932 to the war; never taught at the University of Southern California. I am familiar with the learned professions (teaching and law), the vagrant ones (sea, farm, factory), and the eternal ones (marriage, fatherhood, art, science). The most extraordinary shock in my life was not the war which I survived, but the films which I did not. I always wrote, produced little motion in my life, and never stopped talking.

My first novel (*The Discoverers*) was accepted, announced, advertised by Modern Age Books and then withdrawn as unreadable. I retired to silence in art, action in politics, and gibberish in radio (Columbia Workshop, Orson Welles, Goldbergs, and I forget). Two potboilers (Simon and Schuster; Little, Brown). The war (O.S.S.). My blueberry pie was Paramount.

Excluding the movies for the moment, I managed a semiserious return to the novel with *The World Above*, and, after being blacklisted, *The Season of Fear*. These attempts were laced with some short stories, criticism, and genteel scholarly editing (*Hollywood Quarterly*, *Contemporary Reader*).

The guerilla life I pretended to practice in the war I played with some amusement and frequent disgust in the jungle of TV as a blacklisted writer. Likewise in films. Those minor victories and major defeats admit no obituaries at the moment.

Q: How did you begin your work in films?

A: By accident. I signed with Paramount before going overseas. However appalled I was by the industry and its product, the medium overwhelmed me with a language I had been trying to speak all my life.

Q: Since I am under the impression that it is not extensive, would you mention all of your screen credits, official and unofficial, if the latter case is such?

A: Credits. *Golden Earrings*: direction, Mitchell Leisen. Assigned to an incredible romantic melodramatic stew, I painstakingly studied gypsy life under the Nazis (they were incinerated) and very cleverly worked the whole thing around to something else. The film, starring Marlene Dietrich, appeared as an incredible romantic melodramatic stew. I never could sit through it. I know there isn't a single word or scene of mine in it, but I was instructed to rejoice in the credit which I shared with two old hands, Helen Deutsch and Frank Butler.

Body and Soul: original screenplay; direction, Robert Rossen.

Force of Evil: screenplay with Ira Wolfert from his novel, *Tucker's People*; my direction.

I Can Get It for You Wholesale: screenplay based on Weidman's own treatment which simply kept the title of the novel. A comedy of sorts, directed by Mike Gordon with Dan Dailey, Susan Hayward. It was a stopgap for me to return to Europe to write another book and set up *Mario and the Magician*. Before I left, Thomas Mann told me he felt his exile was beginning all over again since fascism was inevitable in America. The novel I completed years later. No one wanted to finance the film.

I returned to Hollywood and made a deal with Sol Siegel at Twentieth to write and direct a picture, but the blacklist intervened.

Q: Was your scenario for *Body and Soul* a wholly original work, or was it derived from some other source?

A: It's an original screenplay. A folk tale from the Empire city.

Q: Was Rossen to direct the movie from the time of the script's inception, or did he only come to do it through the contingencies of film production?
A: Rossen was hired after the script was done.

Q: Did your work on *Body and Soul* end with the scenario?
A: No.

Q: Were you present on the set during shooting?
A: Continuously.

Q: Of course, it is easy to look knowing in retrospect, but to judge from Rossen's other work, *Body and Soul* would seem to have closer affinities with *Force of Evil* than with the other films of his, even in the elusive matter of visual style. Or am I just second guessing?
A: There was a struggle during the shooting to prevent Rossen from rewriting the script and changing the ending. In fact he shot an alternate finish in which the fighter is killed and ends up with his head in a garbage can. I think a comparison of *Body and Soul* with *The Hustler* might indicate not only the uses Rossen made of the former but where his temperament and style inevitably lead him.

Q: Are you satisfied with the realization of *Body and Soul* as a film?
A: I liked *Body and Soul*. It was a surprise to see something I had written become film. I have an animal faith that survives moral weakness and defeat. To urge this against Rossen's metaphysical identity and everyday cynicism and the journalism of sense and sex indicated the realities of film-making. Our resources on the set were immense: Garfield, James Wong Howe, Robert Aldrich, Lyon and Parrish, Don Weis, Pevney. A slew of directors emerged from the film. Rossen's talent is force applied everywhere without let-up. My only concern was to save it from parody, except where deliberately I had kidded *Golden Boy* and that dear old violin. However, I'm not so sure any more that the obvious isn't one of the strengths of film language. If so it violates a bias of my nature.

Q: What attracted you about *Tucker's People* as an original source?
A: Experiment. Garfield and Roberts suggested that I direct. I had already been brooding over this notion. Being a novice didn't prevent me

from sharing all the illusions and frustrations of more seasoned writers. I was under fire long before I knew I had volunteered.

I knew *Tucker's People*. It had an allegory, true then and even more bitterly apt today; a milieu and characters familiar as my own habits; a hint of the language of the unconscious I could use as dialogue. In realization, necessities of the medium evaporated the allegory, leaving great uncharted reefs of symbolism to wreck the audience; the people emerged except where I agreed to wrong casting; and the language almost obeyed my intention to play an equal role with the actor and visual image and not run along as illustration, information, and mere verbal gesture (wisecracks, conventional middle-class slang, elevated notions drawn from the armory of Longfellow and Hemingway).

Q: In the course of adaptation, you altered the novel rather radically, excising some characters and events, combining and condensing others. What particular problems did you feel were fundamental to your decisions in making the adaptation? I don't mean so much with regard to *Tucker's People* in particular as with the question of adapting to the screen in general.

A: I no longer remember anything except the days Wolfert and I spent endlessly talking along the beaches. Under the windy sun we didn't reason so much as proclaim discoveries. In effect, we eliminated the discursive power of the book and substituted for it so to speak centers of suggestion. We reimagined the novel as if it were an aborigine again. Then it became obvious that some characters would play larger roles and others disappear. Adapting a book to film is fundamentally a moral crisis. Assuming the intention is serious, the book is not chosen to be translated for non-readers but because still embedded in the conception is a whole unrealized life whose language is a motion of images. Where a book in unfulfilled a frightful problem arises. The film, if successful, is a critique of the author's failures. I am a coward here and prefer my own stories.

Q: Do you have any particular conception of the nature of the medium? One of the original reviewers of *Force of Evil* (Robert Hatch in *The Nation*, as I recall) suspected the presence of blank verse, and was truly horrified; but even admirers of the film have characterized it as "literary." Does this have any meaning to you? Do you have any ideas about the relation of word to image in the film; yours, and, perhaps, the film in general?

A: I've heard them talk in talking pictures. Might talkies be like the opera? The main thing is the music but O the joy when the singers act and the songs are poetry. Let's pretend, I assumed for *Tucker's People* (*Force of Evil*) that the three elements, visual image, actor, word, are equals. (After all, the human personality is the medium of the total human expressiveness. After all, language has been a medium for an art of two.) I didn't project anything important, just an experiment in which each of my resources was freed of the dominance of the other two. I was too inexperienced to invent novel visual images or evoke great performances. And certainly there was nothing in my literary record to suggest a New Voice. All I tried to do was use the succession of visual images, the appearances of human personality in the actors, and the rhythm of words in unison or counterpoint. I varied the speed, intensity, congruence, and conflict for design, emotion, and goal, sometimes separating the three elements, sometimes using two or three together. As for the language, I merely freed it of the burden of literary psychology and the role of crutch to the visual image. Blank verse? No. But the babble of the unconscious, yes, as much as I could, granted the premise that I was committed to a representational film. It was a method I would have tried again and again. After all, we had that big Hollywood machine which the success of *Body and Soul* had delivered into our hands and we didn't mind seeing what we could do with all that horsepower. But the blacklist took the machine away from us. While we had possession, like those bicycle fanatics at Kitty Hawk, we couldn't wait to waken in the morning, knowing that each day would surprise us. We had the right feelings. Only our plane never flew.

Q: Would you say you have been influenced by any other film-makers?
A: Vigo.

Q: Mention has been made in a way I think might be valid of Odets as a literary influence. What is your opinion of this?
A: We both derive from Jewish jokes and street quarrels. I live dangled between the formal and argot without solution. I've tried to avoid American Standard Movie dialogue which is a genuine Hollywood convention. But I can write it and have for a living.

Q: What film-makers do you particularly admire?
A: I like going to the movies.

Q: What Hollywood films have you thought commendable since the late forties?

A: I seem to remember liking some but I can't remember which.

Q: Is there an identity of theme and meaning between *Body and Soul* and *Force of Evil*?
A: Yes, but in *Force of Evil* every character and situation is compromised by reality while *Body and Soul* is a folk tale.

Q: Eric Bentley has made the point that in both Elia Kazan's *On the Waterfront* and Arthur Miller's *A View from the Bridge* there is, scarcely beneath the surface, an apologetics for each of their respective positions on political informing, a certain acting out of private crises; informing being the crucial act in both works, good in the former and evil in the latter. *Force of Evil* ends with the hero about to confess to the police, and "help" them. I do not mean to suggest that the final act is ever simply this, but do you feel that there is any political parable underlying the conclusion to your film?
A: Not a parable, a fact. The hero is about to confess to the police because that was the way we could get a seal. There was an allegory underlying the film. It got lost somewhere and had nothing to do with confession or avoidance. Bentley is certainly right in his estimate of those works although the distinction between good informing and bad escapes me. One escapes not only to escape punishment and regain acceptance but to share once again in the authority of the state. It is a hard life outside the pale.

Q: Do you believe or know that you were blacklisted?
A: I know it and I believe it.

Q: How did you discover this?
A: I was told by the studio, my agent, the newspapers, Congress, and my landlord.

Q: How is one blacklisted; I mean, what is the typical nature of the process?
A: One is named in a hearing by an informer, or one is summoned to the hearing in person. The consequences are the same.

Q: Do you know of particular individuals who were behind the blacklist, or was its authority always kept anonymous?
A: The cold war was behind the blacklist and everyone participated,

from those on the political right through those who had no politics. It was like collaboration under the Nazis. And it was like the resistance. The spectrum took in everything human including the inhuman.

Q: Did you ever appear before the House Un-American Activities Committee?
A: Yes.

Q: Was there any opportunity for compromise in order to "clear" yourself?
A: Then and now and frequently in between.

Q: John Cogley, in his *Report on Blacklisting*, observes that there was virtually no political content in the films of the blacklisted, and when it did exist it was usually in the form of so generalized a commitment to democratic ideals and justifiable revolution as could be subscribed to by any member of the audience but the most avid Hitlerite. Do you agree? Would you ascribe this to a lack of intent, or lack of accomplishment? Or lack of talent?
A: Hollywood radicals were mainly moral humanists and their films when they reflected anything at all allowed a concern for the suppressed elements in human life. Political programming of any sort, left, middle, right, couldn't ever appear because producers wanted to make money. When political programming did appear as in the so-called anti-communist pictures they were made in deference to the climate and not from the usual expectation of profits. Cogley's argument that blacklisting radicals is silly because they're too stupid or talentless to use the film for direct Marxist propaganda is jejune. He is talking about journalism, not story telling.

Q: Do you have any thoughts on the career of Edward Dmytryk, who went from the Hollywood Ten to "exoneration," and eventually was to film such a tribute to conformity as *The Caine Mutiny*?
A: He probably thought it was capitalist realism.

Q: It has been suggested that John Garfield's political difficulties and debarment from Hollywood work were a considerable influence in accelerating his early death. Do you have any opinion on this?
A: Yes. He defended his streetboy's honor and they killed him for it.

Q: In the publisher's blurb for *The Season of Fear*, it was implied that you left film-making voluntarily in order "to go abroad and devote [yourself] to serious fiction." Aside from the thinly veiled, characteristic cultural snobbery, is there any truth in this?
A: No.

Q: Inasmuch as you have any such self-image, do you regard yourself primarily as a novelist or film-maker? Or both?
A: Neither. If I were younger you might say I had promise.

Q: Were you aware of the sympathetic reception accorded *Force of Evil* in *Sight and Sound* and *Sequence*?
A: Yes.

Q: Was their appreciation of any personal importance to you?
A: Pure oxygen.

Q: Was *Body and Soul* a financial success?
A: Very much so.

Q: Was *Force of Evil* commercially successful?
A: No.

Q: Did you have any criticisms of the latter film's distribution?
A: It got lost in the general dissolution of Enterprise studios. Had we stayed in business we could have rescued it and made some money.

Q: How did you come to use Beatrice Pearson?
A: She was brought to my attention by Martin Jurow, now a considerable producer himself. He worked for our company at that time.

Q: Where had you seen her previously?
A: Nowhere.

Q: What became of her?
A: She was in a few films and disappeared. They didn't know how to use her.

Q: In what work are you engaged at present?
A: Grub Street.

Q: Have you had any opportunity to make films since *Force of Evil*?
A: No.

Q: Have you imagined any new subjects you would have particularly liked to work into a film?
A: Indeed I have.

Q: Do you see any possibility for your prospective return to work in the film?
A: No.

Q: What are your plans for the future?
A: None.

The interviewing of an artist is chancy; the pitfalls are familiar. On one hand, there is the kind of gulling Lindsay Anderson suffered at the hands of John Ford in his well-known *Sequence* interview; on the other, those dreary chronologies of how The Studio mutilated this film, and how They butchered that. Both alternatives may be valuable in their way (and the Anderson piece, I believe, does reveal, even inadvertently, a good deal of Ford's nature as an artist), but I was interested in achieving neither. Existing somewhere in that uncharted area between the put-on and the death toll, I tend immodestly to think that my "encounter" with Abraham Polonsky was something of a success. In anticipating critical intelligence of the artist, one proceeds at one's own risk. In Polonsky, I found this sort of intelligence, and the ability to articulate it.

Not all of the questions were answered as thoroughly as they might have been, but I conceived my role not as inquisitor; I was not out to "get all the facts"; rather, to open up certain areas for discussion, to that extent which Polonsky was interested in going into them. Politically, for example, it may be observed that, although the specters of the blacklist and the House Un-American Activities Committee are pointedly raised, no question is put as to Polonsky's actual political affiliations. I don't think of this as an evasion. My own attitude toward the pursuit of this line of questioning (from an anti-Communist position, it may not be irrelevant to add) is simply: So what? The fact remains that Abraham Polonsky, having earned the right to work in Hollywood on the terms which Hollywood unfailingly understands, those of having proven the ability to show a profit, was denied the exercise of that less-than-glorious right. The fact is that since 1949 a film-maker whom I regard as one of the richest talents to have appeared in Hollywood in the past fifteen years (and, I believe, the richest literary talent to have appeared in the American film) has not been able to work in films. One need not respond emotionally to that fact. One need not respond emotionally to any fact. (1962)

• • •

Abraham Polonsky wrote *Body and Soul* in 1947, directed *Force of Evil* in 1948, and was politically blacklisted in America until 1968.

In 1962, I contacted Polonsky, and soon after published an "interview" with him done solely through correspondence. I met Polonsky a short while later, and have seen him on those several occasions when we have been in the same place at the same time in the years since; a time during which our relationship progressed, I think it fair to say, from that of critic and film-maker to one between friends. And it was, I think, in the latter relationship that Polonsky telephoned to tell me the news that he was going to direct a film again and to invite me to visit him once shooting had begun, although it was more in reversion to the former that I brought along a tape recorder which ran intermittently throughout much of a long day that I spent with him soon after.

I visited the set of *Willie Boy* [subsequently retitled *Tell Them Willie Boy Is Here*—AD] several weeks after filming had begun; I had hoped to observe filming at one of the desert locations, but was frustrated in this by some last minute changes in the shooting schedule. I arrived at the studio some twenty minutes after the beginning of the working day at 9 a.m., and reached the set to find it had been cleared of the crew, which, as I learned subsequently, some disagreement was taking place between the director and Conrad Hall, his director of photography. Later, Polonsky spoke of it; he was going through a stage with Hall that was not uncommon, he thought, to the working relationships between directors and their directors of photography: he was trying to get Hall to loosen up. "I need more freedom for the actors because they're complaining bitterly. He's holding them to too many marks." But Polonsky wasn't complaining. "He's interesting, temperamental, and a gambler with light. The actors are both obedient and creative. What more can you ask?"

It had been some time since I'd been on a working set, and, generally harmonious as this one was, the feel of it—the numbers of people performing small tasks or just hanging about, and the numbers of temperaments requiring solicitous orchestration—reminded me how unappealing I had always, by my own temperament, found that side of film-making. Yet Polonsky seemed not only good at it but genuinely to enjoy it, and I asked if he did.

"I enjoy it, yes. It's almost as good as writing because it is a form of writing. I like it and I feel it as we do it. It's excellent; I feel this whole thing, and I feel it all coming together and coming apart all the time, and that's part of the pleasure and part of the operation and part of the contest you have with yourself, if you have any contest at all. That's the wrong word; it's . . . it's the living sense of the set. The set is a live thing—a more complex writing experience."

I asked if, in seeing someone else's films, he could see from what was on film where, if there's some failure, it may be that kind of failure—a failure in working with people.

"I don't think I could . . . I mean, I wouldn't know."

Though I had read a copy of the script, the scenes being taken that day weren't in it, and one thing in particular, the start of tracking movement, was giving the camera crew some difficulty. I asked if it might be possible to achieve the desired effect with a particular cut, a jump cut, though I'd failed to visualize it as that.

"Jump cut? . . . Why not, if you intend it. It's all right; there's nothing wrong with it if you mean it . . . You feel that at once in a picture where that isn't the style. If it's not a general style, then it's a particular emphasis. But, if it's an emphasis, what do you mean? Well, I don't mean that sort of emphasis here."

Someone suggested what a jump cut there *might* mean.

"That's true. But that would be an explanation after the event, not an intention now. That's what you can do, rationalize a meaning. When you shoot, that's a prediction; not an explanation . . . after something happens."

The shot was finally made as Polonsky wanted it, and, while the next one was being lit, the director secluded himself with his actors in rehearsal. Afterward, Polonsky spoke of this and amplified on the issue over which he had confronted his director of photography.

"The reason for the rehearsal was to find out where they would go naturally in the scene. I don't want to tell them to go there and go there and go there—just to help out with the lighting. Not today, anyway. It turned out they were going to go exactly to the places I had asked them to originally. That happens very often. Excluding documentaries where you take the camera and expose yourself to the scene, whichever way it works . . . in this kind of a film, what you do is construct a *cage* of light around these actors—and they are not really free in this cage because, if they are really free, neither the sound nor the light works in it. One of the ways to eliminate the sound problem is to loop it. But you can't eliminate the light problem. You can't eliminate the cage of light, and this is true outdoors too. Depending where the sun is in the sky, and how your scene is going, you can't see the expression on a face even if you're two feet away. So what you do with the kind of film we're used to seeing—clearly full of expression in every detail—is construct this geometrical thing . . . and live with it.

"If you ask the cameraman to loosen up, and if he just falls back and lights it generally, you're not going to see anything. I'm shuffling around from heads to bodies in the same shot and moving them. There are very grave difficulties for the actor and all the technical crew . . .

"Now the problem is that professional actors, in this cage, give you *their* performance, which enables them to survive the cage. And if you want anything else, they're fighting with the cage. So there's a dynamic set up between how much you're going to go for and how much the technical crew can give you without hobbling the actor."

Later, at lunch, some comments on a few of the stars whose giant photos decorate the walls of the studio commissary led back to the subject of actors.

"Well, some have a performance that they own. Let's say they have nothing but this one performance. It's often more than enough for a film, where personality is rampant and effective."

Someone remarked that most actors don't even have one performance.

"Not really . . . Most of them have many. But most of them come to rely on one performance for other reasons. When it's a successful one, for instance."

Thinking of *Madigan*, I said, "Now Henry Fonda's been doing that bit—"

"That's right!"

"But Henry Fonda can do a lot of other things."

"Oh, yes! . . .

"When I cast these characters for the posse, I was very careful not to pick Western actors simply on the grounds that they wouldn't have a stock set of performances as a posse to give. Otherwise, you have to fight that battle too. I'm not sure what I'll get from them, but I won't have that."

The conversation turned to the direction of actors.

"Very often what you do is substitute energy for expressiveness. You drive the actors and get a lot of energy going on the set, and it feels like life, but it's not necessarily life; it's mechanical life. The way we live."

"Of course," I said, "if you're not as concerned with your actors as you are, you can get expressiveness in other ways, and use the actors more as props."

"But then you can't use my actors; you'd have to cast others."

"Well, you can't use you as a director on that film either," I said.

We discussed the morning's takes, and I mentioned my interest in seeing how some things looked in the rushes.

"Dailies can fool you. They're full of momentary energy. You have no way of knowing till they're cut together in the whole film if anything is going there . . . Accidental energy cancels out, and things just lie there."

With us through the day was Robert Gilman, one of the most talented and technically proficient young Americans now making short films outside the industry. He asked Polonsky: "How do you work with your editor? His idea of rhythm is going to be different from your idea of rhythm."

"Well, when we first met, I picked the stakes I thought were best and gave him a general idea of how I wanted to go and he went and edited and assembled. And he showed it to me, and the rhythm was different from what I wanted. So I went back with him to the Movieola, and edited it piece by piece, and he saw what I wanted.

"Now, as we go along, I select the takes I prefer and give him a general idea of how I want it go. Then he edits the film. Where the rhythm is different from what I want, we work together until it has my feeling, where that's possible. Then my rhythm runs."

"He's quite willing to do what you want?"

"Yes. He's good. There are editors who won't do that; you can't work with them. He's only done two films, I think, before this one. The last one was *Finian's Rainbow*; he worked with Coppola, who works the same way I do; he edits his own films."

One difference between them, I remarked judging from the one film of Coppola's I'd seen, was that Coppola didn't seem to care about his actors.[1]

"No. He's interested in technology," Polonsky said.

The afternoon's shooting moved slowly, a few brief takes surrounded by long intervals for lighting. During one of these, I commented to Polonsky that it seemed a peculiar predicament for an artist to have such periods of tedium inescapably interwoven with periods of working creation.

"That's why experienced directors learn to live their lives between shots—writing letters, calling on the phone, making dates with girl friends, investing in the stock market . . ."

Later, during one particularly long pause for lighting, we left the set, where, the actors having been rehearsed, the director was as dispensable as I was. In a small trailer, the director's equivalent of a dressing room, we were able to talk without interruption.

"Now to maintain full expression throughout the course of the film, and freedom, is the problem."

"By full expression you mean the expressiveness of the actor?"

"And my own. But the liberation of the actor in the scene, the liberation of the content of the script, and the excellence of the technical apparatus to make it visible . . . and audible; to make this all come together in sound and talk and light and clear expression. What you tend to do is *settle* . . . for technical excellence. What you do is find yourself settling for a passing grade. It tells the story, it's pretty good, there are no big mistakes; thank God, let's go on. Disaster."

"Settle for technical excellence?"

"And performance; competent, excellent performance. That's not the same thing as a real performance by anyone, including the camera. By the end of the day, you're willing to settle too. This is where you have to stop. Your greatest problem is not to settle for what's good enough; to try to go a little further. You have pressing on you schedule, cost, all those things which are forcing you to settle.

"I suppose the advanced stage is when you don't know that you're settling."

"Well, then, as in all things, you've succeeded in your profession. You are now successful."

A bit later, while we were still alone. Polonsky said, "I'm kind of amused by all this."

"What do you mean, it amuses you? You love it."

"I love it, but this is, in a way, too late."

"Too late to be struck by the glamour of it you mean?"

"Well, it's not glamour. . . . Marcel Proust said—or was it Marcel Proust who said someplace that—don't wish too intensely for anything because you'll get it . . . but too late . . . Or something like that . . . some witty remark of that nature . . .

"I don't know, it isn't really too late, but there's a lot of—something of that in what I feel . . . like I don't really care any more, but I do. Twenty years is too long. . . . In a strange kind of way I'm doing this and I'm saying, well, I'll do it, but I don't really think it's worthwhile bothering with all this stuff any more. Now that may just be—"

"What do you mean by all this stuff? Films?"

"No . . . perhaps just weariness as you work . . . I mean so many people are such a drag . . . I'm surrounded by hundreds of people . . . I ought to retire to my mountain and meditate, that's what I mean. . . ."

"Maybe you should be making films in a different setup?"

"Maybe I shouldn't make anything is what I mean. . . . I don't know what I'm saying really. . . . I mean—what I don't know what I'm talking about. . . . I'm talking about something. . . . I don't know what it is . . . I mean something."

"I've often had that feeling."

" . . . There's something wrong with what I'm doing. On the set, everything's fine. I'm having all the freedom anyone gets. . . . The management doesn't even look at the rushes. . . ."

"Is it anything to do with the feeling that you could make a good film or a bad film and it wouldn't make any difference to most of the people you're working with—I mean that they wouldn't *see* the difference?"

"No. No, it has nothing to do with that. They'll see the difference; of course they will. They may not like the same things I like, but, in general, they know the difference. All they want is for it to be a good film. If it turned out not to make money, they wouldn't be horrified because they know that happens very often . . . so there's no problem with that. . . . I'm talking about something else, I think . . . but I don't know what it is. . . . I don't know how it even came out. I didn't intend to say it. . . ."

Before returning to the set, we talked a little about the blacklist, which Frank Rosenberg had broken for Polonsky with a co-author's credit for the screenplay of *Madigan*, a project to which Polonsky had come late, following the departure of the first writer, Howard Rodman (who has pseudonymous co-author's credit for the film as "Henri Simoun"). Earlier, I had referred to *Madigan* (a film I had enjoyed despite or, probably, as much because of its forties-melodrama clichés, as well as for its occasional passages of genuine feeling and the performance of Richard Widmark) as "hack work," meaning only that I assumed it had been a job undertaken while waiting for or as a means to the more meaningful work of direction, and Polonsky had been somewhat defensive, thinking I was simply accusing the work of mediocrity. (He agreed with me, of course, that there was a good deal of mediocre work in the film, but hoped I'd realized that his share of it wasn't done with a free hand.) He had thought there would have to be a succession of *Madigan*-level assignments before he'd have a chance to direct again. But then he was given the chance to do *Willie Boy* as a film for television, and, as the project took shape, the studio was persuaded to produce it as a theatrical feature; Polonsky, all the while, buying directorial independence by relinquishing his own financial prerogatives in the film as a business venture. Yesterday, and for twenty years, he was anathema; today he is, with an unusual degree of freedom, directing a film budgeted at three million dollars, and planning three other projects to follow. In America, there is always a happy ending, and all wishes come true. Sometimes, too late.

"And there are still people blacklisted?" I asked him.

"It's about over now. . . . Till there's a new one. . . . It's part of the way the world goes . . . ."

I asked about a few people in particular; John Berry, and Bob Roberts who had produced *Body and Soul* and *Force of Evil.* "They're making films again?"

"Yes . . . Everybody is . . . unless they're dead. Some died . . . some of them left. . . . Everything comes to an end, including you and me. And that's a relief."

After a day's shooting was finished, we went to see the previous day's rushes. In the audience, Katharine Ross and Robert Blake, who hadn't been involved in the present day's shooting, joined Susan Clark and Robert Redford, who had. I saw on film some of the scenes I had read in the script, but there was little I could tell about the finished work other than to get some sense of its visual style and see how those actors whom I hadn't seen working looked in their roles.

Willie Boy is the story, based on an actual incident, of an Indian hunted for killing the father of the girl with whom he has fled; the action takes place in 1909, at a time when President Taft is on a speech-making tour through Southern California, and the single Indian is so incredibly resourceful in eluding his massing pursuers (at one stage, including eleven posses) that rumors reach the press of an Indian uprising and an attempt to assassinate the President. Robert Blake, whom I hadn't seen in films before, plays Willie Boy, the hunted Indian.

Afterward, Polonsky took me to his office; he had something to show me. There, spread over two walls, were photographs of the actual Willie Boy and others involved in the events: Willie Boy in what seemed to be a studio portrait; individual pictures of the participating sheriffs; the full posse, posed for the press, stiff and erect as a graduating class or early baseball team; and, finally, the full posse again, its members proudly smiling, like fishermen with their big catch, as they stood over the corpse of their solitary quarry; all interspersed with pictures of the Banning and Twentynine Palms desert landscapes where the action had taken place. Somehow, it had never occurred to me that the entire episode would be so fully documented. I turned again to the studio portrait, but could not fathom the pathos in that blankly impassive, young yet ancient face; though I had known there was an actual Willie Boy, it was not until the instant of seeing his photograph that he ceased for me to be fictional. Seeing Robert Blake's to me unfamiliar face on the screen while viewing the rushes, I had been impressed by the unactorish verisimilitude he bore as an Indian, but now I felt humbled in this presumption by the eloquent presence of what James Agee used to venerate as "the real thing."

Polonsky, too, seemed slightly awed before the photographs' mute authority. I think Polonsky knew that I had reserved feelings about the script; one of the first things I had asked him that day was whether his commitment to this film was of a kind with that he had given *Force of Evil*, and he seemed surprised and irritated that I had any doubts that it was. Other than that, the day's conversation had tended away from any discussion of the film as a whole to concentrate instead on the meaning of this or that particular shot, a natural course of direction when all one's activity on the set is centered upon the particular shot that is being made. One comes to take it for granted that an actor's performance in a film is pieced together bit by bit from shots made out of dramatic sequence, the sequence of takes in most films being dictated by economic rather than dramatic necessity; but one is less inclined to consider that the director must then perforce work this way too. I had thought that much of the unevenness in even the best of films, especially those made in America, owed to the participation of too many hands, but now it occurred to me that virtually everything in the conventional processes of commercial movie-making operated as a threat to the work's artistic unity. Unless a film-maker's work was episodic of its nature, as, for instance, Godard's, what a feat it must be to keep before you an imaginative vision of the work as a whole through all the fragmentizing stages of its creation. And, given the further enervation in having to bend great numbers of other people around to your vision while yourself striving to sustain it, the sheer labor of making a film suddenly seemed to me almost heroic.

And now, for the first time that day, and in the presence of those photographs, Polonsky began to talk about his vision of the film; of how he imagined it and of its meaning. I had no illusion that the script I had read was any adequate imaginative equivalent to the film that might be made of it, but Polonsky spoke now of possibilities in the material which I simply hadn't seen in the reading; and possibilities not simply for visualization but of realizing the meaning of the action and relationships. It would be untrue to say that what he said utterly dispelled my reservations about the script; whether the film would fulfill those possibilities he saw in it, I couldn't know; but, for the first time, I was brought to see that those possibilities were there. And I recalled what Robert Redford had said to me earlier that day when I had asked him if Polonsky was an easy director to work for. "Yes," he said. "He has passion."

It was almost nine, and dark outside. I didn't run the tape while we spoke thus, or for the short time remaining that we spent together. Exactly what Polonsky said then would mean little without one's having read the script, and, in a sense, it wasn't important; either it will be in the film or it won't. Either it will have its life as art or join the ghosts in that crowded limbo of unrealized intentions. It will be important or it won't. ". . . Like I don't really care any more, but I do."
(1968)

Notes

1. Obviously, at the time of this conversation, Coppola hadn't yet made *The Rain People* [which was released in August 1969—AD], on the basis of which I gladly retract my earlier comment on his direction of actors, justifiable as it may once have been.

Interview with Abraham Polonsky

Eric Sherman and Martin Rubin / 1968

From *The Director's Event: Interviews with Five American Film-makers*, ed. Eric Sherman and Martin Rubin (New York: Atheneum, 1970), 9–37. The interview was conducted in November 1968. Reprinted by permission of the authors.

Polonsky: The trouble with interviews is that everything sounds so damned intended and pompous. It's like someone writing a review of his film after he's made it. A great deal of just plain *living* goes into making a film—that's the pleasure of it—and the interviews never reflect that. They reflect Seriousness and Significance and all that. That's like saying a love affair is all about the time you had these kids. But that's not what it's about, is it? Those are just some of the things that happened. And these interviews always sound like that to me. So, I forgive you. If you forgive me!

I came to make *Force of Evil* because Bob Roberts [the producer] and John Garfield asked me to direct a film. At that time I hadn't the slightest notion that it was possible for me to direct. I'd only written two films: one at Paramount called *Golden Earrings*, which was completely rewritten by Frank Butler, and *Body and Soul*, which was a success of sorts. I had been on the set all the way through *Body and Soul*, and Roberts and Garfield thought it would be an interesting idea if I directed. It was a time of interesting ideas, just after World War II, with plenty of trouble beginning in the United States in political matters. We were all more or less involved with certain radical attitudes and a great sense of loss—who had really won that war?

I knew the novel *Tucker's People* by Ira Wolfert and was fascinated by it. The book had a clear parallel to Fascism. I mean, that's an ordinary metaphor you find in all economic writing and in poetry of left-wing journalism: gangsterism is like capitalism, or the other way round. I don't know if that's true, but anyhow it's a metaphor when you're desperate.

The great thing about success in Hollywood is that everything you say is considered potentially profitable. So, even though this was a particularly arty subject—arty for a studio film—I proposed it and they accepted it.

I arranged for Ira Wolfert to write the first draft of the screenplay. What he wrote was good, but it was clearly Ira Wolfert writing a screenplay from *his* novel. It's very difficult for a novelist to escape his work, and that would go for me, too, I think, if I were to adapt any of my own novels. Eventually I wrote the screenplay, based on his treatment, the book and our conversations. People who read the screenplay were a little upset by it at first—the language put them off. I know how to write in my own way, but not necessarily in the convention of energetic moving picture dialogue. *Force of Evil* wasn't anything like that and it was a little upsetting to them. But, as I told you, success carries you past all such habitual hesitations. So we made it.

Question: Why did you use classical décor in the film, particularly in Tucker's house and in Garfield's office?
Polonsky: Why not? The audience immediately accommodates to that as being recognizable, significant, weighty—suggesting power and authority. Therefore, when you come to portray this story, which is actually a destructive analysis of the system, the décor gives you the tension that's necessary to disrupt the given situation.

Question: Were you attempting an even broader contrast between the décor and what was going on inside of it?
Polonsky: That was the technique of the whole film: unfinished polar relationships. I used the rhythmic line of the dialogue sometimes with the images, and sometimes against the images. In that Tucker scene when they are walking down the stairway, the voices are right on mike but the people are a mile away. I did that all the time. It was the style of the film.

Question: Another example might be the café scene with Gomez and the Bauer character [Tucker's bookkeeper]. When Gomez is kidnapped, it's very different from the usual gangster violence. The dramatic and visual tone of the scene was quite muted, and the music was like a religious dirge. In other words, there was a very noticeable air of detachment, of alienation from the images.
Polonsky: You said it! [Laughs.]

Question: Could you go more specifically into why you were trying for this note of disruption?

Polonsky: To create a sense of general anxiety. When you do a thing like that, what you do is utilize the *familiar* as a way of calling attention to the fact that it's not so familiar after all.

Question: Why did you give so much emphasis to that first shot of Garfield and Tucker going down the stairs? In other words, why did you use a long take?

Polonsky: They're on their way to hell, you see. But in the beginning, it looks like they're coming down a grand staircase. It's only later that you find out where they're really going.

Question: So, you intended a definite parallel between that and the final scenes?

Polonsky: "Down, down, down." Right. Also, there's a knocking on the door downstairs, as in *Macbeth*, isn't there? Death is coming! [Knocks twice on desk.]

Question: Another way in which *Force of Evil* differs from the average gangster film is that you never show the Law Crusade. We never see the law enforcement people, particularly that Special Prosecutor, Hall, who is always talked about.

Polonsky: I originally had a scene with the Law, but I eliminated it. After all, who cares about *them*? I mean, with all their talk about law and order, they're not really saying anything. I'm for law enforcement—but not against *me*.

Question: This made the Law much more ambiguous. By making it so remote, you seem to tie it up with the remote fate that these people are dealing with.

Polonsky: The Law is just another representative of the general evil in which we all exist. I mean, it's nice that someone comes and helps you when you're being robbed or beaten up. I like that. But that's not a metaphysical argument. I'd rather have it that *you* helped *me* and didn't have a badge. You just helped me because you saw me suffering, not because you were the Law.

Question: Why did you attach so much importance to telephones throughout the whole film?

Polonsky: Well, first of all, they're useful . . . but they're more than useful. The telephone is a dangerous object. It represents dangerous kinds of things. I don't like instant communication. I like it to take a long time before I understand you and you understand me. In the film, it forms the structure of the characters' relationships. Everybody is tied up with this phone. Garfield makes his call to order the raid, right? And he makes this call a number of times in the film. It's his way of communicating with one world and receiving messages from another. I had a big telephone made so that it would loom very large in the foreground of those close-ups. I guess the telephone was an easy symbol for the connections between all the different worlds in the film. These worlds communicate with each other through telephones instead of feelings. We're getting our messages in *signals*, not *feelings*. Sometimes these messages are correct, and sometimes, even when you hear them, they're incorrect. And to have your telephone tapped, we know now, is the way we communicate with our government and law enforcement agencies. It's our last means of direct representation except for an occasional riot.

Question: In the novel, much more time is given to the character of Tucker. Why is he a shadowy figure in the film?
Polonsky: It was necessary for what I was trying to do. The more shadowy Tucker is, the more omnipresent the feeling of what he represents.

Question: There seemed to be a direct parallel between Tucker and the Law on the other end of the telephone.
Polonsky: Exactly. You see, the people live in a lane, and on both sides of this lane are vast, empty places. On one side, it says LAW, and on the other, it says CRIME. But, in fact, you can't tell one from the other. Except for the messages you get on this phone, it's hard to know. All I can tell is what happens in this lane, and the rest are murmurs from space outside. It's just history talking to us—murmurs from history.

Question: How much freedom of choice is there in this lane?
Polonsky: Any *single* person can stop anytime, I feel. I don't know if a *thousand* can, but I know any single one can. I believe that. Sometimes, if you stop, you make all the others stop. If you stop believing *that*, you've become the establishment, the organization, the syndicate.

Question: Can this one person ever stop outside of corruption?
Polonsky: Why not? I don't think the nature of life is to be corrupt.

Nor do I think the nature of life is to be good. I mean, the nature of man is to *be there*, as any other animal is there. That's why we invent our moralities. That's the way we handle the world. The fundamental relationship between people is *moral*. That's our social invention—in place of instinct.

Question: I wasn't too clear about the man that Bauer meets in front of the bus with a password. Was he a gangster or a lawman?

Polonsky: I don't remember. In the film, I have two kinds of people around: cops and gangsters. I don't remember which side this particular person was on, because I made that up as I went along. It wouldn't matter to me whether he was one or the other. I can't remember now what I had in mind with that character. I'd have to see the film again, which I refuse to do because I can only see how bad it is. That film, you know, is fundamentally a failure.

Question: The end of the film, where Garfield "returns to society" saying, "I decided to help," is again different from the ending of a normal gangster film. But it also seemed different from the way the story was leading. Do you think this was some real kind of rebirth, or was it the logical development of his character throughout the film?

Polonsky: It was a mixture of cop-out . . . and significance. It was a gangster film, and in those days, censorship was much stronger. So, in a way, his last sentence had to say, "I'm going to see that something is done to get rid of all this corruption." People say that to themselves all the time, and I wouldn't consider that, as you must know, a significant remark then or now. That's not the way things happen. How much history do we have to have happen to know that?

So, it was partly a cop-out. It was saying to the censor, "Look. It's O.K. Don't worry about it. He had a change of heart." But that was *completely* on the surface. I didn't mean it at all. What I really meant were all those words at the end and all those images: "Down, down, down."

At the end of the picture, in Garfield's case, it's like being left back in school. I remember in Thomas Mann's *The Magic Mountain*, when he talks about Hans Castorp's youth. Hans is in school, and he gets left back—and what a *relief* it was to get left back! Because *then* you don't have to get ahead anymore. A kind of liberation and freedom comes from failure. What I tried to do there was to get the feeling that, having reached the absolute moral bottom of commitment, there's nothing left to do but commit yourself. There's no longer a problem of identity when you have no identity left at all. So, in your very next step, you must become something.

In general, that's what the ending was: vague. But then changes in personality are always vague. You only know long afterwards whether they had any significance.

Question: It seemed to me that you framed the cycle of Garfield's corruption. In other words, at the end of the film, a light is flashing outside the exit of the nightclub when he leaves, and near the beginning of the film, a lot of emphasis is given to the light flashing outside the window of Tucker's office. I interpreted that one as sort of an entrance light, as the other was an exit light. Does Garfield's corruption start right there, which I don't think is true, or, does anything start when he's in Tucker's office at that time?

Polonsky: What happens in Tucker's office is not the beginning of his corruption, but that it is called to Garfield's attention. That's the thing. I don't think you begin to get corrupted at any particular moment. You're *already* corrupted when you first begin to notice it.

Life's a kind of corruption, as you live it. Life's a kind of dying, as you live it. You receive messages, as from these telephones, or you receive messages from other people, and slowly you're aware that you're immersed in something. But you don't believe it, because you think you can handle it. And *true* corruption starts at that moment. Because if you realized that you *couldn't* handle it, your corruption would begin to be over. It would be on its way out, wouldn't it? It's that sense of power or control over yourself, that you don't really have, which leads to your tragedy.

Question: Thomas Gomez, who played Garfield's brother, felt that he maintained some kind of integrity because he was only involved in small-time corruption, nickel and dime gambling. But Garfield points out to him, truthfully, that they are in some way equal.

Polonsky: Sure. Gomez was even worse; he felt he had an ethical basis. It's even true in American society today. Small businessmen feel ethically superior to trusts, and our laws reflect it. The base of the bourgeois ethic by which we all live in our society is the small businessman. He sits in his shop; he's honest; he deals well; everybody takes advantage of him—and out of him come all the disasters. That's why Tommy Gomez feels he's an honest man; he reflects the whole society.

Question: What about Bauer, the bookkeeper who informs the police? The film gives particular emphasis to his doom. For example, when the numbers bank is raided, there's a shot of him on the floor which is the exact same shot used when he's killed in the restaurant. Why should we feel that Bauer's more doomed than the other characters, particularly Thomas Gomez?

Polonsky: Gomez thinks he's in charge of his life. Bauer knows he's not. Then, Bauer is an accountant. He has the account book of our society. They balance out, don't they? In the end, one side is equal to the other. God knows what happens in between—which is all this terrible life people lead.

Bauer is the accountant of the whole picture. Therefore, he feels, "I'm only keeping the books! I'm doing something perfectly proper and reasonable. I do nothing but add numbers. What am I guilty of?" And all the while he feels terrible because he knows he's involved in the whole thing.

A man who feels he's doing something reasonable and who's suddenly caught short is the *perfect* betrayer. You know, if you don't have very strong moral principles, it's hard for you to betray other people. You really have to be committed to do that. That's Bauer.

Question: How does he differ from Thomas Gomez, who also feels that he's not responsible?

Polonsky: Well, Thomas Gomez is in a way like Bauer. But Gomez is the employer. He's carved out this little niche which is fundamentally illegal. And he runs this operation as if it were a human society. He takes care of Doris [Beatrice Pearson]. He takes care of his people. He doesn't want them to get into big trouble. He doesn't want his brother to bring him into the big syndicate and involve him in the *big* corruptions of society. He has this little island of human loyalty, human relations, and benevolence, and that's the way he justifies what he does. It makes him feel like a man, and they want to take away his manhood by making him part of the machine.

So he's different from Bauer, because he's in control. Bauer knows he's in control of nothing, and therefore he never fights. How can he fight? He runs like a rat. That's what he is: a rat, keeping the books.

Question: What is Garfield trying to get out of Gomez?

Polonsky: He wants his brother to be his brother—and to forgive everything.

Question: Then why does he victimize him?

Polonsky: Because he's trying to *save* him. If he just let Gomez go down, Gomez would have no problem. But he's his brother, so he's going to save him—and he kills him. Gomez keeps saying, "Stop trying to save me! You'll kill me! Because you're no good!" This is the classical mythological relationship between these kinds of brothers—all brothers.

Question: But does Garfield ever try to destroy Gomez, rather than save him?

Polonsky: They're both trying to destroy each other. The older brother, Gomez, had to live a bad life and a hard life, and he says to Garfield, "I made all these sacrifices for *you*. *You* are the favored one, and *you* have the blessing there." It turns out that this blessing is a disaster. The younger brother finds out that you can't do anything with this blessing in the world, except turn it into power. If you turn it into power, you turn it into corruption.

In that sense, you can interpret everything that one person does for another as a way of destroying him. Everything is double-edged in our relations. The way all stories take on their dynamism is that everything has its double nature. You do a thing for this side, and it's the other side that becomes apparent. As you shift from one side to another, one becomes more dominant over the other. Love becomes death and hate—all love, depending on how you make your choices.

In the end, Gomez is doing everything in his power to make sure that his brother destroys him, because *then* his brother is guilty. Garfield says it all the time, doesn't he? "Why are you trying to do this to me? I'm trying to save you! Do you want to make me feel guilty?" And Gomez says, "You *are* guilty!"

Question: Even with the classical décor the visual tone of the film seemed stark, almost barren.

Polonsky: The cameraman was George Barnes, who, as you know, was probably one of the best cameramen we ever had in this town. He had deep-focus long before other people used it, before Welles and Toland hit it. Now, for years Barnes had been photographing mostly older actresses, making them stay young and beautiful—you know how that's done.

We did a few days' testing and looked at the rushes, and they were beautiful and vague. That is to say, it was the standard romantic photography that he'd been doing, which was absolutely against everything I intended to do in this picture. Jimmy Howe, who photographed *Body and Soul*, doesn't shoot that way at all. He's very clear and precise and naturally anti-romantic. I was used to that, since I'd seen Howe every day on the set of *Body and Soul*.

I tried to tell George what I was looking for, but I couldn't quite describe that to a cameraman, because I didn't know what to say. I went out and got a book of reproductions of Hopper's paintings—Third Avenue, cafeterias, all that back-lighting, and those empty streets. Even when people are there, you don't see them; somehow the environments dominate the people. I went to Barnes and I said, "This is kind of what I want." "Oh, that!" He knew right away what "that" was, and we had it all the way through the film. He never varied from it once he knew the tone I wanted.

Question: The New York exteriors that you used in the film were strange. What were you trying to do with them?

Polonsky: Just what you said. I was trying to make strange exteriors. Just as Tucker's apartment and the offices are full of the nature and power of our society, so are the exteriors full of their beauty and the symbols of their significance: the bank-fronts, the church, the Palisades, the great bridge. Of course, you die at the foot of the bridge, but that happens all the time—we fall off our monuments. We spend our lives falling off our monuments.

Question: The opening shot of the film shows a huge crowd. As the film progresses, it becomes less populated, and the final exteriors are deserted.

Polonsky: Well, by the end, Garfield's flying. He's flying down his dreams or illusions or whatever you want to call them. He's flying to that bridge, and the world gets emptier and emptier. Finally, the only things that are left are his dead brother and this girl—and she's as much a victim as his brother.

One of the scenes that I particularly like takes place after Gomez's numbers bank is raided. Garfield's sitting outside the courtroom, and all these people come out. They have just been let out on bail; everything's arranged. And these people coming out are a freak show, a real one, except for this darling girl. I mean, these people are really beaten. Even if they had had all the success in the world, it's already been stolen from them.

I felt that that scene was shot just the way it should be: the texture of it, the look of it—it's so bedraggled and empty. And then, when Garfield meets the girl, I use a romantic image, through the translucent glass doors of the courthouse. Completely romantic—the complete opposite of the milieu. As if to say that you can still hold on to something beautiful and delicious despite everything. Of course you can! That's the cheat. Garfield still thinks so, because he's not finished yet, is he? Going down those steps, I kind of liked that scene. I thought it was successful.

Question: Why do you consider the film a failure?
Polonsky: Well, it was my first film, and I think there's a difference between what I really intended to do and what came off. I didn't know *how*. And then, despite good reviews, it wasn't a successful picture at the box office. Of course it was a difficult picture, and, of course, it was experimental in a way, deliberately experimental. But, nevertheless, I thought that the general weight of it would be obvious, that people would feel it. But it wasn't felt except by very sophisticated audiences.

Question: Did you try to correct these "failures" in *Willie Boy*?
Polonsky: *Willie Boy* is totally different. There's no relation between the two films, except as I'm related to both of them. The technique is different. Everything in the world of the film is charged with my meanings, everything is present, you see, so I know I don't have to work so hard to make them available. It'll happen anyway. So it's much simpler . . . *apparently* much simpler. If you wrote a sonata when you were twelve, and then you wrote one when you were fifty, they'd be different, wouldn't they?

Question: Could you tell us about your experience with the blacklist? What were you doing between *Force of Evil* and *Willie Boy*?
Polonsky: After I finished *Force of Evil*, I went to Europe to write a novel. The blacklist, of course, had begun to operate by then, although it hadn't yet taken on that momentum and destructive energy in the industry. Blacklisting is part of the political behavior of all societies: you put your friends in and keep your enemies out. But it takes on its own momentum, too. It becomes a *thing* with its own life, which has nothing to do with its original intentions.

I'd written this novel, and then I came back here to work at Twentieth Century-Fox. I knew that it would have been safer to stay in Europe—but not really, because not everybody is suited for exile. I think you have to have a temperament for it. Also, the only kinds of exiles that I admire are those who are doing everything in their power to overthrow the government at home, so they can get *back*. Otherwise, you might as well emigrate and get it over with, finish it off and become another person—if they let you.

Now, it wasn't that bad—yet. But it was happening. Instead of staying in Europe, I came back here. I was subpoenaed to appear before the committee. I appeared, and was blacklisted.

I made a living all those years mainly by writing for television under pseudonyms. I did a very good show, too, called *You Are There*. At the height of the whole blacklist, a couple of other blacklisted writers and I were doing shows about free speech and personal liberty. You know: Galileo, Milton, Socrates, and so on. But we weren't doing it for that reason; we were just making a living.

Then, by and by, the Hollywood producers started appearing in cloaks and black hats, in obscure corners of remote cities—and giving us jobs fixing up scripts. Very shortly we were making just as much money, if not more, than before, but we were doing infinitely worse work. That was the way the blacklist period was.

I sometimes wonder why I didn't go right down and start working in the underground film movement which was in existence then. I don't know why. It never occurred to me at the time. One of the reasons was: I didn't want to do any pictures at all . . . I think.

So I turned myself into a writer, in a way. I'd only directed once, right? I didn't consider myself a director. I considered that I *had* directed. But I'd always been a writer of sorts. I became interested in some little, lefty, avant-garde magazine in New York, and I wrote articles for it. The blacklist world slowly ground to a halt with the McCarthy-Army hearings. It did not disappear after the defeat of McCarthy, but it no longer terrorized those people who gave employment. Now they appeared openly. In fact, some of them, like Otto Preminger, just ignored it. He hired Dalton Trumbo and paid no attention to it. Of course, it was soon discovered that if you paid no attention to it, nothing happened. And finally, some three or four years ago, that happened to me.

Frank Rosenberg, who is a producer at Universal, asked me to write a television pilot. Since I had plenty of money at that time, as a blacklisted writer, there was no particular reason for me to do a television show. I was making a good living fixing up rotten movies. So I said, "I'll do it if you put my name on it." In that way, I thought I was getting rid of the possibility of ever having to do it. My name was submitted to whatever the network was. A generally discouraging kind of report came back, which in a sense said, "Get somebody else. Let's not start this up again."

When that happened Jennings Lang, one of the vice-presidents of Universal, called and told the network to go to hell. And they said, "O.K., we'll go to hell." So there I was, able to do that pilot under my own name.

Then Rosenberg prepared the film *Madigan*. The screenplay was being written by Howard Rodman. Rodman and Rosenberg, for their own reasons, didn't get on very well—this happens. So Rosenberg asked me to work on the screenplay. But this was under my own name, you see. After checking with Rodman to make sure that he wouldn't be working on it, I came out here and did some rewriting.

Soon after that, Jennings Lang proposed that I write and direct what we call a "one-twenty," which is a two-hour film for television. Before this, Philip Waxman, who was to be the producer of this television film, had come to me with a book called *Willie Boy*. I proposed that we make it into a "one-twenty." This is not a very good deal for a producer of a "one-twenty" since you get very little money compared with what you get for a feature film. But Lang—he was at the heart of the whole operation as you can see—thought that we could make a feature film out of it. Waxman took his chances. I wrote the script, and they liked it. And I cast it with their help, and they liked it. And I made it, and they liked it. That's the way it happened. Don't ask me if I like it!

Question: What was it about *Willie Boy* that particularly interested you?
Polonsky: When I read the book originally, I didn't see anything interesting enough in it for me to make a film. I had no particular interest in the Old West or in the New West, or the Old East or the New East, or anything like that. Then, when I was writing *Madigan*, one day I suddenly saw the story, the Willie Boy incident, in a different way. It had nothing to do with the Old West or the New West. It had to do with most of the young people I knew today, living in a transitional period and being driven by circumstances and values they couldn't control. And at that point, I thought it would be an interesting story to do, because then I could play around with this romantic investment we have in the past, along with a lack of comprehension for the realities of the present, and show these two things pushing one way and another. When I saw that, I called up Waxman and said I'd do it.

This picture is intended for you people not yet committed to the disasters of history. If I had one specific intention in my mind, it was to tell my feelings about this to your generation. Not to mine. If mine doesn't know that, to hell with 'em. They should know it by now—and you should know it by now, too. I have a particular feeling about this general problem. Not just because they're Indians, but because this is a general human situation. It's fundamental to human history—this terrible thing that we do. Civilization is the process of despoiling, of *spoliation* of people, which in the past we considered a victory, but we now suspect is a moral defeat for all.

My feeling about this film, in making it, was to address it to your generation and say, "This is what I think about this. This is the way I feel about this. This is the way I see it. This is what this experience is—and you should know it."

By the way how did you like Bobby Blake, who played Willie Boy? Did you accept him?

Question: Completely. I wasn't too sure if Katharine Ross fit into the part of Lola at the beginning, but I think she got better as she got a little more violent.

Polonsky: That was the hardest thing in the film. You must accept Blake as an Indian in 1909. I think any first-rate actor can handle most roles, but to look like it, too, is the hardest thing to accomplish. And I think he made it; he actually seems to look like that person, and he certainly is that person as an actor. Toughest part in the picture.

Ross had the same problem. I mean, how does one become an Indian girl? I tried to overcome that difficulty by making her an Indian girl who wanted to be a white girl. So, wherever she's not really Indian, you say, "Well, that's because she's trying to make it with the whites." Then you finally accept her anomalous position, and she plays into the part. It works out kind of nicely, I think. Of course, you know, in history, no one knows who Lola is, as a person. She's a name from history, that's all.

Question: The grayness of the rocks in the film reminded me of brimstone.
Polonsky: Great rocks, weren't they?

Question: I felt that the film was starting at the end of *Force of Evil*, going down, down, but going far beyond that.
Polonsky: *Force of Evil* dealt more with what they used to call *angst*. This film ignores that. It starts long after we're used to *angst*. It's too serious to worry about generalized metaphysical anxiety. And that's what I meant when I said that I don't want to look at that other picture again. The point of view seems so limited to me.

Question: The chase was handled unusually. You seemed to eschew all melodramatic value—suspense, people catching up to other people, decreasing distance between the pursued and the pursuer, and so on.

Polonsky: Well, I treated it as a formal structure. I took the whole chase and changed it from someone chasing someone to just a formal structure, like writing a fugue, see, so that you wouldn't get mixed up in the pursuit but pay attention to the meaning.

I had it written out originally as a real chase, with events and so on, which you do to make it interesting. Then it occurred to me, just before I started to shoot those scenes, that I didn't really care very much about that. What did that have to do with my story? With what I meant? What I did was reorganize all that into this formal structure. I treated the ambush in that way, too.

Question: I had no sense of time throughout the film. This seems unusual for a chase film, where time is usually so important. It was as if time stopped.

Polonsky: Well, why do you think that happened?

Question: At one point Lola says, "They're white. They'll chase you forever." And Willie says, "How long is that?"

Polonsky: ". . . less than you think." It has no duration, has it? Which is why I finally formalized the chase, because if I had used that chase in a dramatic way, I would have brought chronological chase time in and destroyed the picture, I thought.

Question: When Willie leaves the Twenty-Nine Palms oasis, several locations are repeated. This gave a great sense of futility to the whole chase; it seemed as if he were retracing his steps. Was this intended?

Polonsky: Well, everything is kind of intended. But sometimes intended things have magnificent results in a direction opposite of what you hope for. Then you're happy to see it and take advantage of it. [Laughs.] Hooray for accident! Father of us all!

Question: Outside of the four main characters—Blake, Ross, Robert Redford [the sheriff], and Susan Clark [the government agent on the reservation]—everybody else seemed almost irrelevant.

Polonsky: Right. But of course everybody's characterized, you see. No one is just a neutral thing, or else the motion picture would be unseeable. But, at the same time, I want these other characters to be the environment, just like the stones, the sky, the water, and everything else—with these four living creatures in it. When many persons are your environment, are within your life, the prime question is one of focus.

Question: One character who stood out among the posse was Calvert [Barry Sullivan].

Polonsky: He wishes he could live a little again, because everything seems so boring now. Our main use of the Western, in our mythology of pleasure, is to deny its reality and substitute what we like to imagine our history was for what really happened. Everybody does that with history; it makes the present more tenable. So Barry Sullivan plays out this untenable mythological Western, you see. For example, he says to Redford, "Your father was lucky. He died when it was still good to live."

He also says, "I was telling them about the year your daddy and me followed a party of Comanche two hundred miles into Mexico. We brought back six scalps that time." And sitting around that fire with the posse are three Indians! Indian police, who are out chasing this other Indian. The posse members never pay any attention to whether these Indians react to this. All the conversation about Indians, even at the end, is done in the presence of Indians, who are not supposed to have any reality. They're not supposed to think like Indians—they just exist. And we do that all the time, of course, with people whom we think are inferior to ourselves.

But I put in a slow alteration in mood. These Indians finally start to identify with Willie, and then they start to get pretty hostile, and finally Redford says, "Bury him," and they burn him!

Question: The turning point seems to occur when Lola's body is brought up, and the other Indians say that they think she killed herself in order to save Willie, not that she was murdered by Willie. That seems to be where these Indians started to swing over.

Polonsky: That's right. And that sort of thing actually happened in history. In real life, unlike in the movie, Willie had committed suicide early in the story. They had twelve posses out looking around for a man who no longer existed.

I used that general feeling of identification, developed between Willie and the other Indians, which arose from the fact that the posse couldn't capture him. Therefore, and Indian was making some kind of stand, in that sense, at a time when Indians made no stands at all. 1890, I think, was Wounded Knee, the last of the Indian massacres. About two hundred Indians, who were wearing those ghost shirts, were wiped out. The Sioux believed if they wore the ghost shirts, white bullets couldn't go through. When Willie runs at the end, you know he's not trying to escape, if you're really tuned in, because he's wearing a ghost shirt. He put his father's ghost shirt on.

Also, Lola killed herself because they would have surely caught Willie if she had stayed with him. Alone he had a chance. Well, instead of making a stand at Twenty-Nine Palms, he really *escaped*. They couldn't catch him; therefore, Lola hadn't died in vain. After that, he was ready to do what he wanted. In other words, she didn't kill herself for nothing: he did escape. But after that, he had no reason to be free anymore.

Question: The Susan Clark character, the woman agent on the reservation, was benevolent toward the Indians yet had very little real understanding of the situation.

Polonsky: Yes, I think she did a marvelous job of creating the establishment—humanized, but at the same time, infinitely dangerous and infinitely involved. I wanted to show that, despite all of Clark's sympathies for the Indians and her desire to help them, her concern is only with sanitation, education, health. She doesn't have a spiritual concern. She's helping them, and Willie says, "Yeah, she's a helper!" What he means is, "Who wants that kind of help? We don't need any help. We just have to *be*. Our problem is to *become* someone." But Lola doesn't know that until the very end.

We don't really admit the Indians' existence, because their existence means that we don't really belong here. They have no being, except anthropologically.

Question: In this light, the only character who "becomes" is Willie Boy. He becomes through his death.

Polonsky: That's right. This is a story of an anti-hero, to use popular phrases, who is Redford, and of a real hero, who is Willie. A real hero is someone who fulfills his destiny. And an anti-hero is one who struggles to find his identity in a destiny that he refuses to fulfill. What he's really fighting against is the power structure, the organization, the set-up. Willie is struggling with that, too, but he has a real destiny to fulfill. He's a hero. All he has to do is become himself, and he does. What else can a poor Indian do?

Question: In the filming of Willie, it doesn't look like he's making choices along the way. It looks like every step he takes is predestined. On the other hand, every step that Redford takes looks like he's making choices—the way he carries himself, rides his horse, follows Willie's trail. Willie has laid the trail; Willie is the one who *had to* step there.

Polonsky: Exactly. And that's what's good about Redford's performance. That's why I called him Coop in the film: Gary Cooper, the great Western sheriff. And he plays this role with a great deal of uneasiness. I think he does it very well.

Question: When Willie and Lola were making love in the orchard, you cut to a long shot of the people closing in on them. That was one of the darkest love scenes I'd ever seen.

Polonsky: It's what happened in the Garden of Eden—after they ate of the tree. It's shot like a Garden of Eden scene. They're completely nude, and yet their nudity is irrelevant. They're not nude; they're in their skins. That's their costume for that scene.

Question: You intercut a lot between the two love affairs: Willie and Lola, and Coop and the Susan Clark character.

Polonsky: I treat both love affairs as a single affair, being acted out by different people at different times. All during the story, that's what it is.

Question: The whole thing is who acts out what part. For example, there's an obvious sense of Willie and Lola consummating the affair for the other two people.

Polonsky: That's right. That's where the significance comes in. That's the way I make the social significance work without having anything to do with it.

Question: All through the film, the town is awaiting a visit from President Taft. The local officials prepare for his arrival by constructing a chair large enough to hold him and by deploying an extravagant number of small American flags all over the place. Again, this seemed to do away with any surface political or social intonations to the story. You see all these flags, and that settles that!

Polonsky: [Laughs.] That's it! You see these flags and this immense chair for Taft to fill, and what more can you ask of a President? It's so specific, that suddenly it's irrelevant.

Question: About the end, the burning of Willie's body. The posse comes for souvenirs . . .

Polonsky: Something to show for all of it! They have to have something to show for all this work they've done—this chase, the money, all this nonsense they've invented.

Question: What does Susan Clark's inscrutable expression to Redford at the end mean?

Polonsky: Well, ask yourself this question: What do you say to a man who finds himself a prisoner of a situation which he feels he must play out? He feels he must fulfill a role in this situation in order to become a man. And the moment he does so, he realizes that that's precisely the one way he *can't*. In that last scene, he now knows this, and he's washing the blood off his hands. What do you say to him? Nothing. How do you look at him? What do you do? You stay away from him! What does she do? She stays away from him. And that's the end of the film, as far as she's concerned. By the way, while we were filming it, it was Redford who urged this approach.

Question: So this man thought he had a job to do, and he thought he would define himself by doing it . . .

Polonsky: Not necessarily to *kill* Willie. Coop didn't go out to kill him, just to capture him. He was *prepared* to kill him. I suppose to be prepared is somehow already to have killed.

Question: But he did kill Willie, and in doing so he destroyed himself. But, by the nature of his self-definition, it had to be done. When we were discussing *Force of Evil*, I asked you how much freedom of choice these characters have. Did Coop have a choice *not* to commit this act?

Polonsky: Well, he offered Willie and therefore himself the choice to go peacefully, but after Coop had killed him and discovered that Willie's rifle wasn't loaded he knew that there had been no choice after all.

And it's that irony, which is in all events, that defeats all the illusions we have about the choices that we make up for ourselves. *Long* before that event, we have committed ourselves to courses of action which are folly and disaster. And all along the line, we invent choices which we think are real but are just cover-ups.

I think that's the nature of the fake morality that we live by. We invent right and wrong, so that we seem to be making very good choices all the time—and that's a trap! Long before that, we've committed the disaster. And all these choices that we seem to be making are not choices at all.

That's why, long after terrible historical events pass, people say, "But I didn't know!" "I didn't know what was going on in those camps." "I didn't know that was what the war meant." "I didn't know that he was going to die." "I didn't know she was going to be so unhappy." Those are great *I-didn't-know's*. You've heard them all over. Popular fiction, whether in television, films, novels, or plays, is made of these false *I-didn't-know's*. That's what you call sentimental writing. That's the pornography of feeling. And that's the way we cop out, to use a favorite phrase of your generation.

Question: At the end, these people who are breaking up the fire look extremely desperate and futile. They're not really breaking up anything.
Polonsky: No, they're not. They've got nothing to bring back. These Indians burn Willie's body because you could burn the bodies of chiefs in those days. I originally had a line in the script about that, but I took it out—too noble. Now he's burned beyond salvage, and there's nothing to bring back except cinders. So the posse rides in and starts pulling the fire apart—a boot, a shoe, an ear, *anything* to bring back. And they're dancing around this fire, trying to find something. Then Sheriff Wilson goes up to Coop and says, "God damn it, Coop, what've we got to show for it? What will I tell 'em?" And Coop says, "Tell 'em we're all out of souvenirs."

And that's what I want to tell everybody. Never mind all those souvenirs that they keep pushing down on us, all the sacrifices *they* made in the past. I don't care about them. The past is not now. It's just a souvenir, and we shouldn't be bound by souvenirs. If we are, we're not going to live here long. Well, you know that. We're not living here long anyway. They've extended our life expectancy but decreased our chances of living long.

Question: Is there any affirmation in this dark ending?
Polonsky: Well, we know *they're* in the dark; *we* don't have to be. Willie isn't in the dark. Coop isn't in the dark anymore either, is he?

Question: Although Coop may not be in the dark, will his next step be of his own choosing?
Polonsky: Far from it. That's why there should be no movement be-

tween Redford and Susan Clark at the end that gives you any sense of warmth or affection. It would obscure the ending. It would make you feel, "Oh, well anyhow, Love goes on!" We didn't have anything like that. By then, she knows this man, doesn't she? She comes at Coop's moment of disillusionment, which is Willie's triumph, since he's become himself. And she doesn't do anything. She doesn't weep a single tear, she doesn't show any kindness toward Coop. She just passes him by.

You only kiss returning soldiers in real wars. In these kinds of wars, which, in a certain way, are much more important than real wars, you don't do that. There's no comfort and no company. You're alone, and you want to be alone, and Coop is alone at the end of the story. He walks away from history.

In effect, he says at the end, "It's no use explaining how all these things come about, because all you do is explain. The terrible thing is that they happen." Historical explanations and moral explanations, and explanations of tenderness and love, and *all* such explanations, are irrelevancies beside the fact, as you look at the fact. Now, you look at this fact and face it. I say that to you and anyone. Know this fact and face it.

Interview with Abraham Polonsky

Michel Delahaye / 1969

From *Cahiers du cinéma*, no. 215 (septembre 1969): 30–39. Translated by Andrew Dickos.

Polonsky wrote in 1966: "The blacklist has never been abandoned. It has extinguished itself little by little. Those who haven't perished in the course of these witch-hunts are still around, for the most part doing new projects. Me too." Polonsky co-wrote the screenplay for Don Siegel's *Madigan* (1968) under trying conditions and, in 1968, wrote and directed *Tell Them Willie Boy Is Here*, which we will see here this fall [in 1969].

The Hollywood witch-hunt period has recently aroused a rather suspect interest over one aimed at learning about its oppressive mechanisms—collective or not, pathological or not—of certain groups. One prefers to indulge in a purely anecdotal research of it, whether about the exemplary conduct during the period or about naming names, strongly resembling in the opposite the witch-hunts themselves and attempting to restore the limitless complacency of the past from fear of recognizing the present. Many will be more interested to know that Polonsky worked clandestinely on a (justly) celebrated antiracist police noir [the 1959 *Odds against Tomorrow*] to understand that the blacklist has far from limited his activities to the "silent decade" of tyrannies under J. Parnell Thomas and Senator Joseph McCarthy. One sees that Polonsky does not share their views, and that the climate, if not the word, of such views still exists today. The problem of the blacklist is many-sided: political, moral, practical, creative. These considerations have generally been confused and, apart from some strictly historical works, painful to recount. In Polonsky's case, for example, it is of interest to explore his relationship with Enterprise Pictures, as well as his stay in Europe (Polonsky: "I always considered myself as being a 'passenger,' before I discovered Europe. There, I understood that, for better or worse, I wasn't an American like

the others.")¹ To speak of, or to, Abraham Polonsky, one needs to avoid confusing him with his contemporaries, a difficult task to undertake given their intersecting work and careers. "Everyone makes his choices, everyone follows his nature, and we've managed rather badly. I believe *Force of Evil* reflects all this," Polonsky observes. Recollections are hasty to take the temperature of actual conditions and forget that the connections, the relationships, are not established or necessarily only within a group (blacklisted) or genre (the police noir). To paraphrase Tynianov about Khlebnikov, only when these matters cease to be spoken of over the years will they begin to crystallize. . . .
—Bernard Eisenschitz

Cahiers: Can you tell us about the movie you just finished, the first one you've had the possibility to do since *Force of Evil* in 1948?
Abraham Polonsky: The title is *Tell Them Willie Boy Is Here* and its starting point an incident that took place in 1909 in California, in a desert region near the towns of Twenty-nine Palms and Banning, between the San Bernardino and Bullion Mountains, at the moment when the Old West was changing into the modern U.S. And, seeing as we too are living in a transitional period at this moment, I thought that that could be interesting. It had to do with the problem of the oppressed races, of political problems, and their numerous connections with the situation presented. I'm summarizing the history for you to understand it well.

In California, in 1909, lived an Indian named Willie Boy, and whose Indian name was Running Fox. He was an Indian unlike the others in that he didn't live on the reservation with them, he played on a baseball team in Victorville, in California. In fact, he distanced himself from the Indians as well as the whites. He was the kind of guy who drew a line around himself and said, "Stay outside the line, I can live; cross my line, I cannot live." At that moment, he was in love with a young woman, an Indian, whose father threatened to kill him if he continued to see her.

Finally, Willie kills the father. Some white men and three Indian policemen begin to pursue him. They chased him five hundred miles into the desert and never caught him. At that moment too, and in the interest of history, thirty miles away from there President Taft was making a trip across the United States trying to get members of Congress elected, just eight years after the assassination of President McKinley by an anarchist in Buffalo. When the President arrived in Riverside, there was noise suddenly being made of an Indian uprising in the region, led by Willie Boy, who himself planned to kill Taft! All of a sudden there was much agitation in the country. And this is the context of the event, which interested me and drew me to the story of *Willie Boy*. Willie Boy, who only looks to defend himself and to protect the simple way of life he prefers, suddenly becomes the object of all the hidden guilts of the white community, which at heart knew that it had stolen territory from the Indians.

The pursuit, therefore, becomes a gesture of destroying the illusion of resistance, which, in fact, isn't even real, but which today, among the oppressed in the United States and around the world, is a reality. I preserved the time and place transformed a bit by the people and details of the event. There are some unquestionable analogies with today, particularly in our relations with blacks.

I wrote this story in a very simple and direct style, which I usually do not do, and I filmed it that way. In other words, I eliminated contrived effects as much as possible.

Cahiers: What commonalities, what kinds of relationships, did you see or search for between *Force of Evil* and *Willie Boy*?

Polonsky: In fact, I believe that *Willie Boy* has more in common with *Body and Soul* than with *Force of Evil*. *Force of Evil* is a realistic film, truly realistic, whose screenwriting is perhaps modern, but *Body and Soul* was a fairy tale, an urban myth of life on the streets of New York, just as *Willie Boy* is a myth, a parable. However, despite these connections, the structure and composition are much more complex: I used musical structures—the fugue structure, for instance. I have two or three themes; I go from one to the other, and I work in all capacities—with the photography, for example—to create the *mise en scène*.

Cahiers: That was already felt in the composition of *Force of Evil*. Do you think that we will discover it again in your next film?

Polonsky: I don't really know, but it's certain that the musical references are those which preoccupy me the most when I make a film or when I write it. I worked on this project two or three years, and it deals with life in the U.S., in Mississippi, between blacks and whites, a month before the Civil War. The story, like everything I write, involves what might be seen as metaphors or hidden meanings, related no doubt to what I am and what I cannot escape. Again, I'll try to uncover the reasons that brought us to this place.

Harry Belafonte worked with me on this film, but I'm producing and directing it myself. I would liken the film more to a war than a work of art. If I were a painter, I would say that maybe I'm entering a new period in my style. In any case, in *Willie Boy*, as in the following project, I abandon what you commonly call "psychology." In *Willie Boy*, there are no motivations given, no time wasted over that. There are the historical elements that are in themselves their own explanation. The film's structure works so that the meaning of the behavior stems from the environment.

Cahiers: Will your third film be made for the same company, Universal?
Polonsky: Yes. They left me relatively alone for *Willie Boy*. Of course it was a studio product, for the film was controlled by them financially, but once the agreement was made over the budget and distribution, they left me entirely free to make the film. I could, for instance, choose my own technicians, which they say is rare, but perfectly natural to me.

Cahiers: It's strange enough because Universal has a rather bad reputation . . .
Polonsky: I know. . . . But, you know, this is like the woman who was married twice, whose first husband says, "I could never trust her," and the second says, "All I can say is that she was always faithful. . . ."

Cahiers: We love *Force of Evil* a great deal. How do you find it today, twenty years later, and just after finishing your second film?
Polonsky: I love it slightly less than you do. I do not consider it a total success. I absolutely could not do what I wanted; I didn't know very well how. I tried to separate and empower the various components—the commentary, the dialogue, and the images, for example—to separate them and only make them work together when it seemed necessary. I have the impression that the story, the narrative, is linear, and initially it was not supposed to be that way. When I saw the film again, I realized all that I missed, and that embarrassed me. But on the other hand, people are trying to persuade me that this is fine.

Cahiers: What did the pubic think at the time?
Polonsky: The public was very lukewarm toward the film, whereas the critics all were positive. Since its release, the film has found its audience, but never on a grand scale. It's shown all the time on television, and I often encounter it there. I think what happened is that some narrative techniques I tried have since become more accepted. Anxiety, anguish, and guilt aren't very popular things to show, but, today, any housewife

has her anxieties, her misplaced anguish, unspecific, floating, that she believes are a part of modern life.

Cahiers: What interested Universal in *Willie Boy*?

Polonsky: The studio believes that the film works because the story is very intense, very dramatic, full of potent moments, because it's bound to the very feelings and concerns people have today on the question of oppressed peoples. The story concerns the freedom to be, so common today. There's some physical action, so everyone's happy with that. On the other hand, there's action involving a short guy and others pursuing him. For these reasons, the producers hoped that the film would be popular, as I did too. Besides, this aspect of the story really exists in actuality. I don't want you to think that it's a trap masking another aspect of the story. The story is well told. I improvised quite a bit during the shooting. I wrote the screenplay, and I could have gone with that—it was what everyone originally agreed to. But the actors were very good, the context interesting, and the film took shape and a different balance was struck than I expected. And I found it exciting, fascinating. . . .

Cahiers: You use color this time. . . .

Polonsky: I spoke at length with my DP before starting the film, and we decided to use exterior colors in such a way to eliminate the "snapshot" appearance of the desert, which makes it appear less menacing than it really is. This place is fierce, magnificent. We used a new film stock rapidly and overexposed it. The sky is not so blue but snow white; there are no vibrant colors, just pale ones. As for the interiors, the colors are soft, familiar, like the costumes, the tunics.

In most of the roles, I made the Indians come off as they were actually treated, and we revived their customs, traditions, and games. Every family, for example, has its own songs. I also recorded their music, apart from its use in the movie, for my own purposes. The Indians in question are the Cahuillas from the Morongo Reservation; they are grouped around the same language. They are passionate, very sophisticated today, and very conscious of their history and what happened to them. The elders, for example, believe that Willie Boy is not dead, that he fled to Mexico, and that the whites lied. But younger Indians, modern in all senses of the word, socially concerned by what happens, demand their rights. They have their own museum, and they do their own anthropological research. They want to know why they should be white Americans; they prefer to be red. Of course, I don't treat all that in my film, at least directly, explicitly, but I'm using it in the background. I present these facts as they occurred from those I interviewed for the demands of the story, without too much distortion.

Cahiers: Some anthropologists think that Indians have more and more influence—underground—on Americans. . . .

Polonsky: In America, all oppressed people for so many years—Hispanics, blacks, American Indians—today constitute a force to be reckoned with. With regard to the Indians, I've been noticing since I was in Canada with them that they are still strangers in their own country. This is the big problem in the world; it's acute in America but also elsewhere. There are oppressed people in all parts of the world, no? In other words, this is a conflict and constant paradox: those who were all taken now say "Let us return," and they say above all "Let us live" and "All of your inventions belong to us because we are part of the human race." Today is the beginning. This combination of economics and race is the most important problem of our time. What Hitler saw, and disastrously attempted to solve, remains for the world to do what it takes to accomplish. I cite Hitler, as I hope you can imagine, only because the problem existed on a global scale: the entire world was involved in the fight, and the entire world is still involved in the fight since oppressed peoples want their liberation. We have to address this problem, and I, of course, will do it within the limited scope of my power. I hope that *Willie Boy* reveals what I feel, since my feelings are a mystery to everyone but me. . . .

Cahiers: Would you be interested in a film directly concerned with the politics of today's youth in America, for example?

Polonsky: I would do a film on the subject, and I've already thought about it, but it would be very difficult. Maybe I could do it after my third film, which is ready, as I told you. That this has happened in every city in the world is extraordinary; it's as if the awareness was a malady spread from city to city among its young. It's like 1948. Suddenly in all of the centers of civilization in Europe, among certain segments of the bourgeoisie itself, a strange kind of revolutionary consciousness has clearly taken hold. In socialist countries, and in capitalist ones, wherever you go, you encounter this fantastic phenomenon. It was extraordinary to read in the newspapers the accounts of the events in France: one day a few hundred students argue with hundreds of policemen, and the next day all of France explodes. Soon there'll be a lot of movies about it in the country. . . . Although these films have already been made—the French films of the last ten years were the testimony anticipating what's happening with the young today. In *Bande à part*, for example, and in several other films, you already felt something, a malaise. And here too one felt it. Several years ago, it was the race problem; my next movie project, for instance, [the never made] *Mississippi*, was something I conceived six years ago, and nobody wanted it or wanted to listen to us, [actor and producer, Harry] Belafonte and me. Sometimes you can just sense if things are going to happen.

Cahiers: Have other films like *Bande à part* in France seemed to predict such attitudes?

Polonsky: Yes, even movies called "erotic." When you see a film as a story, when you see ten of them as stories, this is testimony to an historical period. Seeing French films of this period, you cannot help appreciate such an historical map for the cinema, technical and other. Ignoring the other stuff that came out, we knew that as a body they represented an historical whole, and that's why these movies are so exciting. If you look at American films today, even commercial ones, you know something's happening, but you don't know what. And even when you think you know, afterward, you realize that what's happened was different from what you expected—worse.

Cahiers: What do you think about one part of the American cinema represented, for example, by films such as *In the Heat of the Night* or *Bonnie and Clyde*, which, ideologically, seem to depend upon the same film-making institution they claim to denounce?

Polonsky: The real question is not posed by each of these films taken separately. Of course, here as elsewhere, when someone makes a movie, he tries to be modern and sometimes—and this is the danger—to look modern. You take current events, which, shown stylistically, combine to give you a "modern" movie. I don't know how else it would be done if you're talking about movies. Anyway, this is what you seem to imply. I know to what end the taste for the modern can be artificial and irritating; but try to look beyond it, elsewhere, to what's sought in these films and, regardless of their singular value, is symptomatic of change. In these films—which you may or may not like—you can detect symptoms, reactions to a lifestyle, to economic constraints, to all kinds of repressions. Seen up close, these films may not be of great interest; perhaps by dint of wanting to be modern, they're just outdated artifacts, but taken together, as a whole, it's altogether another thing.

Cahiers: What American films have you seen recently? Have you seen John Cassavetes's *Faces*?

Polonsky: I have not seen films in the past five months, but I saw *Faces*. Cassavetes is one of my friends. He has a lot of talent, and he's interested in the things that interest me and often feels the same difficulties in achieving them, and that's unfortunate. He's also a good actor. He and the people around him also represent something important for America today, and not only for the American cinema.

You never know how things will turn out. At the beginning of all important literary movements, there are little magazines that no one takes seriously or that they demolish with insults. But you can't ask young people to summarize their lives in print before they've even lived them. If I were young, and I wanted to be engaged, I'd do the same thing, I think.

You know, everything happens in a very complicated and unexpected way. There are youth the world over now who feel a general malaise and are provided a difficult life to face. Indeed, by all appearances we dominate the universe, but we can't live in it. It's a huge paradox. To begin with, we couldn't control the universe, and when we tried to do it, we found it unwieldy. We had to learn a great number of things and ways of life, and we discovered our social life. Now, we apparently have the means of doing what we want, but we can't live in the world because it's full of destructive elements. Of course, people in general live in far better conditions than in the harsher, horrible, conditions of the past. The sons of these people—workers, established citizens—seem to be in positions of absolute power but, in fact, really have none because things happen that no one wants. Consequently, they react in a very complicated manner: they think the world must change first before they change it. However, we know historically and philosophically this is a big mistake and the best way not to identify the real problems of the world, because one cannot change without changing everything around him, starting with the economy. Such people are "experimenting." . . . It's much easier to change your clothes than to change the world outside, believe me. I don't think we transform the world by making ourselves better or worse—but we change the world for better or worse.

To believe the reverse is to demonstrate a very old-fashioned psychology, impulses, instincts. . . . Psychology invented a model that we apply to everything, but we are much more interesting than the models. The world outside is not like physics or chemistry. It's more than that, right? Psychology is outdated; moral issues are outdated; the old liberal politics are outdated—they're all in the past.

Take the case of the hippies, for example. The parallel culture that they're creating is a reflection of the society from which they escaped. Their metaphysics is old, their philosophy outmoded. I understand very well the reasons they do that: the idea of creating a liberated counterculture is without a doubt a good idea, and an especially utopian one. And at any moment, they can rejoin our society.

I believe that changes arrive only when one is forced to change. Poverty, which is imposed upon people by their conditions, is a real force, whereas the poverty that you choose in a group that's like a corporation is just an experience in one's life. I don't disapprove of that; I say that if a lot of young people create a subculture in which they refuse the values of today's society, this is neither a solution to their problems nor those of society. That may be a psychological preparation for change, but it is not a real one.

Cahiers: And a start for change, a ferment?
Polonsky: Perhaps, but these kids are not aware of themselves; they can't know or foresee what will happen. This is why someone should deal with this issue. Everything begins with the rejection of established society; even the old-fashioned artists of the nineteenth century started with that. All frustrated artists of our time rejected society in one way or another; it served as a model. Then they become part of this society because it changes and absorbs them, rejecting nothing and accepting all. You have to play with it, be wary of it, and also know how to fight from within it.

Cahiers: You yourself have been rejected by this society. This is the reason why you haven't made this film in twenty years. Can you tell us about this moment?
Polonsky: Everyone knows the reasons, I've explained them often. Would you like me to again?

Cahiers: Yes.
Polonsky: Good. During the worst period of the Cold War—the McCarthy period—McCarthy wanted the United States to maintain a blacklist.

Of course, it didn't touch only film people, but people in all areas, attacking Communists and neo-Communists. And, in fact, in Hollywood this list lasted twenty years until social conditions changed it into something else. So those who survived have been validated, found usable again—if they had enough strength to want it. In fact, many have died, disappeared, were killed off by the blacklist because, you know, when you become a stranger in your own country it's very difficult to survive. Either you go and wait impatiently to return, or you leave and become a citizen of another country. Or you go and die. As for those who remain, they can return to work if they still have the strength and desire.

But, also, there are blacklists today. Other blacklists. Other more insidious blacklists. The blacklist isn't a dated phenomenon; it's constantly creating new victims for one reason or another. For example, if you are for peace in Vietnam, or if you're a student who's arrested and gets a record, you can't find a job. In this sense, in all countries, there's always a blacklist. It's a means of control in this or any country—by those who run a country, those in charge, those who feel comfortable defending themselves and their positions by refusing others work, or even by those denying others the liberty to disagree with them.

Cahiers: Who are the people who could never return to work after the blacklist?

Polonsky: You never know the reasons why someone isn't working any more: sickness, old age (after all, the list is twenty years old and you're twenty years older), and some are no longer here. Celebrated writers like Dalton Trumbo, Albert Maltz, or Ring Lardner and others returned to work, and in fact never stopped working since they worked under pseudonyms. There are a lot of actors who no longer work, who we no longer see around here. A career, a work in progress or in development, or a work whose development was interrupted by this period—even if someone's life didn't end here—provided no assurance that his career is viable any longer. Victims of war are not just soldiers. . . . Obviously, as I told you, people continued to work underground in one way or another. The blacklist, you know, was directed at paid work, not free labor.

Cahiers: Do you think it is possible and useful to do a fiction film on blacklist?

Polonsky: I don't know; I doubt it. Not useful, but possible. I don't think the subject interests the studios that make films destined to be shown worldwide and all across American screens. I think this film should be done, but it would be difficult. It would have to be a very self-critical American work. Of course, there are and were critical American films. . . .

I wrote a book on the blacklist—a novel—*The Season of Fear*, which has no precise relationship with cinema but more generally poses the problem. I like it; I'd like to film it some day. During the period in question, I couldn't get it published by anyone. Finally Angus Cameron, who published the books of blacklisted writers, formed a publishing house with Carl Marzani, and they published my book. It didn't get reviewed except in *The Daily Worker*, which didn't like it! In this book, I tried to say all that I thought about this problem. The blacklist is a much more complicated phenomenon for those who are its victims than those who institute it. The victim's problem is twofold: he wants to survive, and, at the same time, he wants to preserve his rights and opinions that landed him on the blacklist. Gradually, however, as time passes, the hateful reasons why all this started become acceptable; you adapt and start to forget why you're on the list. You end up becoming a stranger to yourself, like someone who has a secret disease. The people—the world—do not realize it. But try to be yourself, and you realize that you can no longer do things that you normally should do. If you're weak, you believe that it's your fault; if you're strong, you hate everyone, which really makes you very weak. So, it's very difficult to be on the blacklist while remembering why you got there and staying human. It's very difficult for the victims. For the executioners, by contrast, it's very easy. They put you on the list and forget you. . . . And then there are those who earn their living and do business by denouncing others . . .

Business, you know, like science, continues from one generation to the next. I tried to show all that in my book, which tells the story of someone who *isn't* on the blacklist but thinks he can easily be. How prophetic! In the sense that it can happen to all of us. . . .

Cahiers: How do you judge those today who wanted to continue to work at that time and were allowed to compromise?

Polonsky: It's not a question of judgment, or even of knowing that they were wrong. To pose the problem differently: there's a way to explain why people change their political views. If today I believe in a political system, and if tomorrow, I *sincerely* believe in another political system, I have the right—I need—to change my views. What do you do then? Decree, declare to all those that believed as they did yesterday, and continue to believe, that I no longer believe what they do today, and that they're my enemies? This is called civil war, and it always existed between men and the societies they formed. It's very difficult to bring universal judgment about how people should behave in a period of political change because they generally act horribly. In a way, maybe they have the right to be horrible, but then they turn horribly on themselves. As to the question, "What do you think of the people who really haven't changed their political views or who changed them to work?" the answer is obvious. It depends on what you attach importance to. It's as if you ask me: "What's worth living for?" If a man is or believes himself to be an artist and wants to continue to make films that cost a couple million dollars; if, therefore, he needs to support the studios, and these people tell him: "Do you want to make this film? Change your politics"; if you answer "Okay" and make it; if you think it's more important to make this two-million-dollar film than to have your own political convictions—the real problem is all of that. Not that of whether, frankly, you truly have the right to change your political opinions, but whether you are able to deny them without having changed.

Cahiers: Do you think that's the case with Kazan?

Polonsky: In Europe, we admired him so much that people were very disappointed in his attitude and they wrote defamatory things about him. Here things do not happen as easily. I don't know Mr. Kazan; I never met him. I know that, like many others, he was at the point of changing his political views; the Communist Party was a very difficult organization to live by, like it is to belong to it today. It represents a whole. However, there are several things to distinguish betrayal, as I told you earlier. If you say, "You don't believe in communism. Make a film and tell us why," that's one thing. (Besides, these films, despite all the hopes placed in them, never made a dime.) But if you said, "Prove to us that you really changed your political views. You must give the names of your friends who still belong," who believe or no longer believe in this doctrine, that poses ethical problems for some. You ask me what I think of Kazan. I don't know. I could not have done what he did, that's all. I did not do what he did, and I would not do so today.

Cahiers: What truly was his public behavior?

Polonsky: He went before the Committee and said, "This man, this woman, this someone was a member of the Communist Party."

Of course, this wasn't a secret, but it's like joining a religion. Do you believe in God? Good. Prove it. The means of proving it will then decide who should go to hell. You were asked a horrible thing, not information that one would not have had, but the act of inquiry was a public act, and the consequence of that act was to make life impossible for some people in society—unless they're doing the same as you. Some people refused to do so, whatever their political views. Similarly, if I were German, I'd have refused to be an officer in a concentration camp. I would have been able to survive under Hitler's regime; but I would never have wanted to be personally responsible for a gas chamber. The Committee asked you to be responsible for a gas chamber. . . . If you're capable of sending someone to the gas chamber, then that proves that you really did change your views. Indeed, what greater proof is there than that?

Kazan was not content to change. He said, "To prove to you that I am not a Communist, I will even name the names of those people you already know were party members, I will tell you publicly." This is no reason to condemn him forever, because we all commit horrific acts all the time. But we mustn't forget the nature of the act. We mustn't forget that killing someone and then asking for their "pardon" is a decisive moral act. In the case of terror, coercion, or purposes of personal motive, you simply say one thing: "I don't care what happens; I have nothing to say." As the German generals used to say. Of course, Kazan never deeply changed his views in his films. Maybe he changed their endings, but he was always very critical of society. He's more likely to offer endings in keeping with the spiritual or sexual zeitgeist of the moment. Sex can be used in any manner psychologically. In other words, I believe that to talk to him about revolution would be to consider it only from a psychological perspective. Kazan has always had outrage toward American society, but, one day, he's the one who committed an act of moral outrage.

Cahiers: In Europe, *Splendor in the Grass* appeared to us as one of the greatest films on a repressive society, mainly regarding sex. . . .

Polonsky: Of course. When someone has done something wrong, we'd like to believe that he has also lost some talent in the process, but this isn't true. Kazan just made a mistake. He has a lot of talent—destructive, corrosive; but, nevertheless, at a time in his life, he committed this wrong. I think that, without a doubt, he has regretted it, and all of his films since bear the mark of a bad conscience. But that's not the question. Besides, everybody does wrong at one time or another. . . .

(Interview taped by Michel Delahaye on the last day of the filming of *Tell Them Willie Boy Is Here*, in July 1968 in Los Angeles.)

Notes

1. J. Parnell Thomas (1895–1970) was a New Jersey Republican member of the House of Representatives from 1937 to 1950. A staunch anti-Communist, he was appointed to head the House Un-American Activities Committee (HUAC) in early 1947. Under Thomas, the "Hollywood Ten" were convicted for contempt of Congress for refusing to answer the Committee's questions by invoking their First Amendment right.

Journalist Drew Pearson exposed Thomas in 1948 of taking salary kickbacks from a staff aide. Indicted, he invoked his Fifth Amendment right but was found guilty, and, in a bizarre twist of fate, sent to Danbury Prison, where Lester Cole and Ring Lardner, Jr., two of the "Hollywood Ten," were serving time because of Thomas's witch-hunt of the film industry.—AD

Interview with Abraham Polonsky

Michel Ciment and Bertrand Tavernier / 1970

From *Positif* 114 (mars 1970): 14–23. Translated by Andrew Dickos. Reprinted by permission.

Abraham Polonsky: My film [*Tell Them Willie Boy Is Here*] isn't a fable. The word "fable" creates confusion in people. If you use the word "myth," everything becomes clearer. A fable is a story that has moral significance, while a myth is a story that is part of the life of a people, whose meaning is both clear and dark, without giving a lesson in what the cons are, the way a fable does with its moral ending. The myth is very American, and it functions on several levels depending on the recollections and time when it happens. In America, we have many myths, and many modern novelists, like Faulkner, use it. What attracted me to this story is that it really happened; it was a moment in our past and, at the same time, it had the value of the myth believed by the people at the time.

Q: So you reject symbolism?
Polonsky: Yes, like allegory. Very often symbols are present in your work without your knowing it because thought is abstract and symbolic, as we learn through the study of logic. The analysis of modern thought is called symbolic logic. But I tried to have in my film as few symbols as possible. Nothing is something else, but there are many things in this story. This is an authentic western, which belongs to a genre that I love very much because I'm American. It therefore contains the myths of the West, but also the counter-myths. In fact, it has more myths of the West than does a film by John Ford because John Ford embodies these myths while I am outside them. John Ford feels the West in a very profound way; he says the truth to the extent that he knows it (leaving aside his style, which is admirable) is limited to the world in which he lives, the

West that he created and whose myth he helped perpetuate and which the world has adopted.

There is a myth of the West for Americans, a Lost Paradise; for the American Indian, it's genocide. An American beginning to accept the idea that the lost paradise was a massacre of the Indians causes the myth to disappear, and he can begin to see the West as it was: the conquest of lands by strangers who took everything that they could find and effaced the identity of the native inhabitants. This is an extraordinary story, don't you think?

Q: Before 1960, American Indians on film were merely puppets to be shot down, then with *Devil's Doorway* and *Broken Arrow*, the Indian appeared as the noble savage.

Polonsky: Ford never made this mistake. He does not hate Indians; he loves them. In *The Searchers* they're fierce, and in *Cheyenne Autumn* he takes their side. To see the Indian as a savage beast or as a noble savage is in both cases a racist attitude. People said that Katharine Ross doesn't resemble an Indian playing the role. That's racist. They should ask me why I hadn't chosen an Indian to play the part—that would be a valid question. But what do they know about the Indians in 1909? They were mixed. Some resembled whites, had blue eyes. I was also told that Katharine Ross didn't have the air of an Indian because of her blue eyes, when in fact they're brown. They want an image that corresponds to their preconceived image—squat, fat, flat-nosed, dark complected—but there are also Indians that resemble gazelles. If you take photos of all these young Indians from the high school and put them next to that of Katharine Ross, you can't tell who's an Indian and who's not. These images are of an incredible variety. Indians were mixed together with the cowboys and Hispanics.

I prefer John Ford to the filmmakers today, whose hearts bleed for the Indians, always shown noble and tortured. They're not so. They are like you and me. They suffer a serious problem: we've taken their land and their resources, and now we love them a little more and give them a white-man's education which they don't want because they don't want to be more integrated but Indian again. And whites feel insulted because they're offering them the best gift on earth: "To be like us." But they refuse. All that was on my mind before making the film. This is why I started with an ordinary story, because if it were extraordinary, you'd never see the myth.

Q: You refer in your film to the marriage by capture. . . .

Polonsky: Lola's parents, who live on the reservation, also live in a desert oasis and commute, as the Navajos do today. Lola's parents are very Spanish because this part of Southern California is the location in America where the Indians really were reduced to slavery in the missions and evangelized. Other Indians were simply decimated. This complex history is in their minds, but they never abandoned the heritage of their society. When a young Indian wants to marry a girl, he asks her father's permission. If he refuses, the young man has the right to remove the daughter, and the father can track him down and kill him. But once the young man has rejoined his tribe, the father can no longer touch him, and the two are married. The father's murder was an accident in Willie Boy's particular case, and the mother tells her daughter to flee because her brothers will continue to chase them. But the brothers are too young and three Indian policemen take their place in the chase because the reservation was under the surveillance of an indigenous police force, which could not stop the whites but only the Indians. This is why at the start of the film when Liz exclaims, "You sell whiskey to *my* Indians!" she also says to Coop that the police can do nothing because the seller is white. This detail is important, otherwise I would have cut it like I did many other things.

Q: One critic also told you that Robert Blake spoke like an American.

Polonsky: It's always the same kind of remark. Indians speak like Americans. Of course, in very remote areas, some very elderly Navajos do not speak English. You'd be surprised at the authenticity of their accent! Your idea of the Indians' appearance or way of speaking comes from your personal cultural notions about them and the stage that you've reached in freeing your mind of these misconceptions.

Q: Why did you choose Katharine Ross?

Polonsky: Because she runs like a gazelle and had to cross the desert running. Doesn't she run like a bitch?! I also chose her because she has a youthful air. Lola's situation was very interesting: a white woman who's inspired by a true character and in a sense adopted this young woman who's destined to become a teacher. And Katharine Ross has all the looks of a young American woman who wants to be a young American woman. And this is why I chose her. Because when a girl like her acts exactly like an Indian at the end of the film (something she doesn't understand herself but which is imposed by events), I'm just touched. To be an Indian, that's what an Indian wants, even if now he kills that. Blacks wanted to be integrated in America. We told them no. Then when there was unrest all around, we told them, good, integrate, and blacks refused, because when they started to move they understood that they didn't want to be white. They had discovered their negritude and their identity. Why give it up? And that's what always happens, as people try to free themselves from the idea others have of them and that they themselves have often adopted. Indians don't think of themselves as Indians, but they think what whites make them think of themselves. And isn't that the worst form of slavery?

Q: Another detail of Indian customs: Willie Boy takes his father's shirt.
Polonsky: This is something that you cannot know: the film isn't a documentary; it doesn't pretend to deliver such information. In fact, at the end of the nineteenth century, there was a big revival movement among whites in America that also happened among the Indians. In the Paiute tribe where Willie Boy comes from, a religion called the Religion of the Ghost Dance developed. It professed that one day God would remove all the whites from the Americas, and that all the dead Indians would be resurrected and could start to live again in America. This has united Indians. They then started wearing their clothes with these motifs, which I saw in museum collections and had reproduced in exact detail. And they believed no white man's bullet could pierce them. The last Indian massacre in the United States, officially, occurred in 1890 at a place called Wounded Knee, where two hundred Sioux Indians wore their shirts. The American cavalry killed them; the bullets went through their shirts! Then they fought harder because the aggression against them took the character of a wanton act of violence. Indians wanted to reclaim their land. They were brutally suppressed. So this shirt is buried in the mound with a weapon and a few dollars so he can save himself. He puts it on the moment after Lola's death knowing that he will face Cooper, and that it will not stop the bullets. But he does this like his father and his father's father before him. . . .

Q: And the coyote's death?
Polonsky: The coyote is a totemic animal for the Paiutes. You can say that when they kill a coyote, it symbolizes the death of Willie. I did not mention that this was a totem animal of the Paiutes because I didn't want to use it symbolically. But if you know it, it's information: Willie is going to die.

Q: Does Willie have a death wish?

Polonsky: No, he committed suicide. Indians do not commit suicide when they're in good health. They pounce on the enemy that kills them. This is what makes Willie Willie. He has no interest in killing Coop; there are a hundred million more whites to kill. It's ridiculous. I don't know if Willie killed Lola or if Lola killed herself. Indians offer two explanations: on the one hand, she so loved Willie that she was a burden to him and he could not save himself without her. He returned, but she came back and killed herself. She had lived too much in those days to return there under the protection of being his wife. She'd have no future. She killed herself and liberated Willie. Willie saved himself. A grin slowly appears on his face when Coop tells him he can return; this man is not surprised. And Coop knows this too. On the other hand, if Willie had killed Lola—which is the other theory—he has a right to do so to keep his wife from falling into the hands of the enemy.

Q: Coop believes that he has a chance left.

Polonsky: Yes, but he sees that he hasn't taken it. He believed he played his role and he did not play it. Coop is beaten by an Indian. Liz too. She does not know which way to turn. She wants to help the Indians and she causes the death of two of them. Anyway, Coop didn't give Willie a chance; after all, he's a professional. In a western, there is never a chance. It's always a lure.

Q: The tradition is of great importance. And you said that you need to kill the past.

Polonsky: When you want to keep what you love, you also keep what's bad in society. But they can't understand it. There's a very good drawing in *The New York Times*. A conference is being held right now in America on air pollution. One man standing in front of factories says: "I thought we were going to die tomorrow; we have thirty-five years left. That's fine!" Thirty-five years. It's an eternity. . . .

Q: Liz smiles when Coop returns. . . .

Polonsky: She's happy that it's him and not the Indian. . . . One might criticize me for that. But she loves him!

Q: Your attitude toward knowledge and education is very modern. The teaching is never objective: Willie tells Lola that she'll teach lies. Liz is an anthropologist and searches for objectivity, which is impossible.

Polonsky: She says "my Indians." Anthropologists did that during those years. They recorded the customs they liked, but they were also reporting the death of a civilization.

Q: No one, as an individual, feels himself guilty.
Polonsky: The guilty individuals are difficult to find in this world. As we become more aware, the guiltier we feel. But if someone talks too much guilt, I have doubts.

Q: The parallels underscore a bit those of sexual relationships in society.
Polonsky: I didn't want to focus primarily on the sociological side. It would have interfered with the story.

Q: The fact that no one is guilty is important. Because if someone had been responsible for Willie Boy's death, it would have permitted the spectator to escape into the film.
Polonky: Exactly. It would have been the end of the spectator's connection with the film. He would have treated the character as a son of a bitch and that would have been it. This is why the menace of President Taft's possible assassination has great importance. They invented the idea that Willie led an Indian revolt. The farmers started to abandon their ranches and alert the National Guard. But in the legend—in the real legend— there are no guilty parties. They say it's fate that makes us act as we do. In fact, fate is a conspiracy between us to believe these myths and not face them. This is our fate to us.

Q: This is the environment that provokes the death.
Polonsky: Yes, when events begin to unfold, if we have a conception of life that we automatically accept, then one event inevitably follows another event because we are already committed to the end. I want the public to know that he lives what he sees and must leave. But of course this is not a message, is it? One identifies with the totality of history rather than a particular character. He may have sympathy for both Indians, but also for Cooper and Liz.

Q: It feels like you've done a great job of selecting from the initial scenario.
Polonsky: I don't accept your definition of my work . . . but of course there's truth in what you say. What happened is pretty funny: when I started to write the screenplay, there was a lot more about Willie in this

city at the beginning. Willie went to the photographer and the décor was an English castle. It was a very funny scene. The producer Waxman laughed out loud listening to a reading. When he saw the final script, he asked me where the funny scenes were, and I told him that they diverted attention away from the story and I didn't need them. I removed as much dialogue as possible and all the scenes that had no relationship to the totality of what I wanted to show. And I tried to have the actors play so that nobody can say "What a magnificent interpretation!" I wanted everything a tightly woven fabric.

Some friends have criticized me for not having shown more life on Indian reservations, but I answer that this is not a film against racism or on the life of Indians in America. All this is too complicated for only one film to address. This is a film about Americans. And I give you enough to inform you there. A *Times* critic also said that I always kept my composure, but at one point I was losing it and showing my politics. It was in the saloon scene, when a man makes a speech about America. Well this character is not me; I took it from *Huckleberry Finn*. It's the man on the river that speaks of democracy. The dialogue in the film was carefully written to be said; it's very smooth, and when it's spoken, it's spoken without a splash. In this dialogue, no one answers the other. There are no exchanges except in one scene between Liz and Coop in the room when they quarrel, or so we have that impression at the moment they're speaking, because there is no psychological dialogue in this film. I think that literary psychology is a lie. It's a model we created to live with each other, but it doesn't explain why one acts a certain way against others. I didn't use it in *Force of Evil* either, because it didn't interest me.

Q: How do you see the character of Liz?

Polonsky: She's a liberated woman of her time, at the forefront of feminism. She could have done her studies with Gertrude Stein. The real character was an anthropologist who was coming to this reservation with feminist intentions. She fights with Coop because she doesn't want to accept this new role that she began playing as nothing more than his wife, and he doesn't want to accept her. She accepts more about him when they're on the reservation than when she's among her equals in the hotel scene. When she shows herself openly vulnerable, he can no longer play his role, and this is why he leaves. In France, such a scene can make you laugh because the French have a different view of these problems; in America, it makes you cry. We are more sentimental.

Q: Why the dead animals?

Polonsky: Why not? America has plenty of dead animals. There are all the horses Willie kills and that the vultures come to eat. America is full of the dead: the whites, the redskins, and we've also destroyed our natural landscape. We've created this marvelous new society. If you want to join it, you're welcome!

Q: But if you suggest the violence of American society, you don't revel in this vision as Peckinpah does in his film.

Polonsky: Peckinpah uses it as he feels he must: for the simple pleasure of violence. This is as exciting for Americans as American football is. This is the pornography of violence, just as there is sexual pornography, when it's displayed for itself and not as a role in the lives of men. Of course I couldn't do that. However, in my next film, my characters believe in the pornography of violence, and I can show you this and how it functions while remaining outside it. The only thing that prevents you from misusing violence (that is to say, to provoke a spectator to use it) is to have a clear idea of the whole problem, otherwise you'll fall into any traps akin to those in making a war film that's supposed to be against war and which everyone enjoys. I like Peckinpah's film, but I think that he's crazy. I don't agree with his ideas on life, but I don't think he praises what looks to be celebrated in his film. He shares with a lot of Americans a certain cult of virility and a stubbornness to do what you want to do. My friend Sam Fuller and I really like each other. He's been regarded in America as a fascist. He's against socialism, and sometimes even against capitalism; he's an anarchist. He showed me the script of a film about Vietnam. It's a film against our engagement in Vietnam, and he can't find a dime to make it.

Q: To be antisocialist and anticapitalist, this may be the definition of a fascist.

Polonsky: You're right, but his is not that kind of sophistication. He makes films that I dislike and has attitudes that I don't share. But I know liberal filmmakers that I like less because they do more harm with their well-intentioned films than he does with his films.

Q: Does Coop really understand at the end what he did?

Polonsky: He understands one thing, and that is that what happened at the top of the mountain should not have happened. To understand more than that would require him to have a tremendous amount of foresight. We're all against murder, but when we wage war, we kill. However, if, after the war, we say that we are against war, this statement conveys a different value, a much more important one because we are murderers. This applies to all the characters in my film, and to all of us. We don't know what we are before we commit our acts.

Q: Is this an idea shared by other American directors, which explains the importance they attach to the action?

Polonsky: This is not quite true. The analysis of what we do, of what we want to do, and of who we are—these are only virtual, as we've acted on nothing. It's useless to discuss what's possible. These are events that matter because they determine man's nature. We should always discuss the nature of the universe, but this is hardly a virtual world until the real one comes along! This is why things should happen in movies. But a real conversation between men is also a kind of action, because, before and after the conversation, the character behaves differently. Currently there's a refusal of action in film because people who are familiar with modern art require film to imitate the more traditional art forms and pass through the same evolutionary stages. This is behind the destruction of the history of theatre, of figure painting, and all these underground films address this problem. You also destroy the story if you do something symbolic because nothing happens, each event represents something else. When you kill someone symbolically, nobody dies. I have no objection against such films. I don't always defend traditional art. I love complex searches. But I go my own way.

I want people to know that I also understand that all things aren't so simple. For me, simplicity is a means, just as for them, complexity is a means. Is it effective?—that's the whole problem. If obscurity is clear enough, then go with the obscure! It's only a means, not a solution to the problems of the universe. So, too, I'm a bit interested in metaphysical anxiety, and I don't think that evil is at the center of the universe, because then we disavow all responsibility—we can no longer suffer!

Q: You wrote once that the ancient epics were a model for a new kind of screenplay.

Polonsky: I have indeed considered the screenplay as an independent form of literature. This would be as a poem, not something merely reduced to a series of tips on shooting the film. It should stand on its own as a creative work. This is not the film per se, which would be a poem, but an assemblage of editing possibilities from which thirty films could be made according to the filmmaker's interpretation. We can treat the various elements of a film like mathematical sets, which exist in themselves, but not in relation to others (unless they're being placed in a unique system). We can have an ensemble of dialogues, an ensemble of images, an ensemble of actor's movements, with each element treated independently. That's what I tried to do in *Force of Evil*, while in *Willie Boy* I tried to do everything. As for the fireside stories that men tell or which belong to religions, they're stories that no one really invented; they're waiting to be invented by people and they contain a simplified nature society that existed at that time. They're ways to describe world events and how people behave in this world. That's what myths and religions are. We've come to reject sophistication in the arts as being more of a conversation dealing with the life we live. If we pay attention to these ideas that are all our myths, perhaps then we could change our life goals, which we have so much trouble doing.

Q: If you were being critical and you needed to compare *Force of Evil* and *Willie Boy*, what would you say?
Polonsky: I would consider them closely and come to the conclusion that they were made by the same man!

Q: You are for the auteur theory?
Polonsky: One cannot escape it, yet it would be interesting to do a collective film. When I showed my film at universities, a young man asked me if I believe in the necessity of propaganda films, and I said yes, if they're presented as such. Film is a means of teaching.

Q: How do you see Cooper's decision to kill Willie?
Polonsky: He decides only to trap him. But Willie challenges him. It's a traditional situation, face to face, of equal chances. The Indian would throw his gun, but Willie forces Coop to kill him. The Indians believed in myths without knowing that they were myths. We, we believe in myths and we know that they're myths, and we conduct ourselves accordingly.

Q: Your film uses many signs.
Polonsky: Yes, of course. For example, the two women in the beginning are in white dress. But be careful with the use of signs. If everything is connected to everything, if everything signifies something, nothing has meaning.

Q: How was it working with Conrad Hall?

Polonsky: We talked before the shooting and did some tests. I know from experience that daylight in the desert is not faithfully rendered by the camera, which shows vibrant colors. I also wanted the colors, clear at first, becoming darker as the film became richer. So I chose scenes that were happening at different times of the day and at sunset when the colors are deeper.

Q: The line about the time for the train for El Paso appears to be the only outdoor reference.

Polonsky: It isn't. Willie makes an appointment at midnight with Lola. When his friend tells him that this is a special train that passes through, he answers him, "Do you have a cover?" Of course there's a reference: Are you familiar with the American song "Midnight Special"?

Q: Why did you choose Barry Sullivan to play Calvert? He didn't have the age for the part.

Polonsky: No, but he gives the impression of having this age, and he also looks like Carlyle with his beard. He was a forerunner of fascism. These are private jokes, just as the character is called Sam Wood, the name of a far-right film director.[1] Calvert is a civilized man. He has a car, a new suit, and an orange grove. He speaks of the good old days of the massacres. He looks a lot like those old veterans you often recognize. If you tell the truth, it's true for everyone; if you lie, only some can understand it.

Q: Did you consider, at some point in your work, to give more importance to the President's visit?

Polonsky: I have two additional scenes that I haven't filmed. In the first, a caravan of a dozen cars pass by, and everything we see is a cloud of dust, people waving flags, a man in a tree who is hostile to Taft, and a firecracker exploding on the road. In the other scene, Taft (who we still don't see) is addressed by a man dressed in Indian attire and waving a sign that reads "Down with President Taft!" I told myself that I transformed my movie into a comedy, and I eliminated the two scenes. Mixing these concerns was not my concern in this film.

Q: What are your plans?

Polonsky: A film whose screenplay is already written. On a contemporary subject, *The Old Man's Place*, a story that starts with the return of three veterans from Vietnam, who continue to fight the war at home. I still don't fully understand this story, but I'm discovering its meaning with every corner I turn. My second project, *Sweet Land*, is set in Mississippi two months before the Civil War. It's a gothic romance, a small family comedy. My third project is a science-fiction film based on a novel by Arthur Clarke on the biological future of man. It'll be a very expensive film if I can ever do it.

Q: What influences do you recognize in your work?
Polonsky: I think people we imitate are not those who influence us. We imitate the ones in style when we're young and learning. We really don't know those who influence us: they are what we will become. Maybe it's *Chanson de Roland* that influenced me—I don't know.

The kind of discussion we're having now is eventually turning into a game. We're taking pleasure in talking together—and you know that every director is an actor, with the only difference being that he's too intelligent to put himself before a camera!

He prefers that it be others who make the mistakes.

Now your work is cut out for you, to organize all this confusing chatter and give it a little order. . . .

Notes

1. Wood was a conservative Hollywood film director from the 1920s through the 1940s, who testified before the House Un-American Activities Committee.—AD

Interview with Abraham Polonsky

Jim Cook and Kingsley Canham / 1970

From *Screen* 11.3 (1970): 57–73. Reprinted by permission of Oxford University Press.

Jim Cook: What was the attraction of Communism for American intellectuals in the thirties and forties?

Abraham Polonsky: Well I think it would be wrong to say the attraction of *Communism* for the American intellectuals—it's the attraction of radical political activity—because a great many intellectuals became followers of Leon Trotsky—a great many intellectuals became radical socialists, and a great many more became attracted to standard Communism. They were all attracted to some form of Leftist activity. I think you've missed the point to say just Communism—because that's the way the McCarthy committee talked about it—you've got to get the spectrum that was going on. There were several obvious reasons—one was the Great Depression which proved that Capitalism was a disaster when it didn't work. The most important thing was the appalling lies of fascism and the terrifying notion that there was only one country that would ever fight them—the Soviet Union—the feeling was that the others were going to sell out all along the line. And for those American intellectuals who were Jewish—there were the Nazis' concentration camps, for which they were destined obviously at some point—either by American Fascists or German Fascists. If that didn't drive people to political activity nothing will.

Cook: How much of this concern was reflected in films of the period?

Polonsky: It was reflected in all the films, especially in the films of those who weren't radicals, because they were freer from self-censorship. I think a lot of radical writers pick an attitude that you might call progressive or democratic and encourage democracy in good relations and good feelings—because they know that you can't get any radical activity in films. People who aren't radicals don't know that; so they had the tendency to push stuff in, Frank Sinatra did anything he felt like—and he's a conservative—or John Ford might do something tremendous, as in that film based on Steinbeck's . . . *Grapes of Wrath.*

But it would be a lie to say that American left-wingers didn't do pictures with radical activity. They did pictures with humanist content and the flavor of democracy.

Cook: Why did the 1947 hearings of the Committee of Un-American activities last only two weeks and end after only ten of the nineteen witnesses had been called?
Polonsky: Because at the beginning, the whole of the film industry decided to resist the attack by the House of Un-American Activities Committee. A committee in Hollywood was formed called the Committee for the First Amendment, and its chairman was John Huston. He, Willie Wyler, and Philip Dunne gathered the full strength of the Hollywood community against the committee, so when these nineteen were subpoenaed and summoned to Washington, a planeload of Hollywood stars including Humphrey Bogart and Danny Kaye and many others went to see that these people had a fair hearing. It became such a row that the hearings were called off.

Cook: The Committee for the First Amendment had issued certain statements after John Howard Lawson said in court that it was America that was on trial and not the ten people involved in the hearings. Do you feel that anybody connected with the Committee was in any way using it? Were there any Communists involved?
Polonsky: Well the only left-wingers involved were me—maybe a few others. If we hadn't associated with the Amendment, we wouldn't have been subpoenaed. The Committee for the First Amendment was ripped asunder when the thing exploded in Washington. General Beadle Smith was sent to Hollywood owners. A policy was laid down to call these actors and directors off—the important ones. Pressure was put on them through their agents and the whole thing melted in about two weeks. I finally went to a meeting of the Committee of the First Amendment and Humphrey Bogart turned around and looked up a half empty room; the first meetings were held at [motion picture agent] George Chasen's and you couldn't get in—it was like opening night at the opera—everybody wanted to be in on this. Anyway Humphrey Bogart looked around this room and said: "You don't think I'm going to stand up there all by myself

and take a beating—I'm getting out too!", and he said, "But you ought to be ashamed of yourselves," and he walked out of the room. Then Huston said, "Well, it's hopeless, fellows," and went to Europe. The final meeting was held and the only people present in the room were Willie Wyler, the permanent secretary, myself, and one other. Wyler said, "Well I think we can use our time better than this!" And it was true.

Kingsley Canham: Why the predominance of Hollywood writers in the ten? Nine were writers.
Polonsky: Accident. Of the three hundred people blacklisted, there were some actors and some directors and some producers and a lot of writers, because the writers are the heart and soul of the industry.

Cook: From a public relations point of view, was the blacklist inevitable once the Committee had started smearing names?
Polonsky: It was inevitable once the Committee for the First Amendment was destroyed. Because there was then no support for these people. A blacklist exists only if no one opposes it and if the only ones who oppose it are the people who are blacklisted then whoever opposes the blacklist becomes blacklisted too, which happened to many New York writers who are not even incidentally connected with politics. Ira Wolfert who wrote the book from which they made *Force of Evil* is a newspaper journalist, and by no stretch of imagination can he be called anything but an ordinary American with ordinary American attitudes. I might call him populist from time to time—but he's a very fair kind of fellow. He signed one of the advertisements that appeared in the *New York Times* protesting against the blacklist and then discovered he'd lost all his military security clearances for his newspaper work. It took him nearly two years to get it cleared up because you can never find out who's blacklisting you. I'll go further. His son—more than twenty years later—was about to be hired by the United Nations and found out he couldn't get security clearance, and when it was traced and found out, it went back all the ways to the first one against the father. That's the way the blacklist operates. That's the secret of it—it has no end.

Cook: Was it fear of blacklisting that led people like Sterling Hayden and Robert Rossen to publicly recant before they'd been called?
Polonsky: No! They were already blacklisted—they knew they were going to be called, and they recanted before they were called because that was part of the deal they made with the Committee. Actually Rossen was

one of the nineteen—he resisted the Committee—went off to Mexico— made speeches against it and so on. It was some years later he came back and became an informer. And Sterling Hayden had been in touch with the FBI long before he was called by the Committee.

Cook: Do you think that pressure groups such as the Motion Picture Alliance for the Preservation of American Ideals contributed to the 1951 hearings reopening?[1]
Polonsky: All those kinds of pressure groups contribute and play a role in it—not necessarily everybody in those groups, but the group as a whole, or whoever runs the group, because they're in touch in hearings with the people they're blacklisting.

Cook: What was the function of the Grey List set up by the American Legion, whereby people wrote letters instead of appearing publicly?
Polonsky: One you have a blacklist, you have a whitelist—that is those people who aren't on the blacklist. People you can't tell what they are— they're on the Grey List. Now these people who are on the Grey List are very often people who really aren't on the Grey List—they're on the whitelist—but they're unsure of themselves, and if they don't get jobs for a certain amount of time, they begin to worry that maybe they're on some list. (You never doubt your talent, you doubt your ability to get the job for some strange reason.) So these security clearances were set up not only by the American Legion, but by all kinds of private operators who wrote and read little magazines and little newspapers and so on. It became a very important business—for instance names were sold, back and forth. When there was any kind of meeting or anything of a good cause of which they approve—they put everybody's name down. These people might find themselves in trouble and *Red Channels* would write "Would you like to clear yourselves?"[2] They would charge and so it became a racket—one of the biggest rackets in America. It occurred in the unions, in the schools, in the entertainment industry, and with government jobs, and so there were official blacklisters and unofficial blacklisters.

Cook: How do you feel about the witnesses who did cooperate, such as Rossen and Kazan, giving the names of 324 people who were working in the industry, and how were you yourself immediately affected by the blacklisting?

Polonsky: Well, the second part first. The moment I was called before the Committee I was blacklisted. It traveled with the speed of light. I was working for 20th Century-Fox. Before my name even appeared in the newspapers, I was called up. "Hey Polonsky! What's going on?" And I told them, and it was suggested to me that I should cooperate with the Committee. I said I wasn't going to. But 20th Century-Fox was extremely fair—they didn't fire me. And even after I didn't cooperate they still didn't fire me. They only fired me after several weeks of editorials in Hollywood papers, and especially in the *Hollywood Reporter* saying "What's Polonsky doing—still working at 20th Century-Fox?"

I think all the studios would have resisted as hard if they hadn't been smashed from much higher pressures. Paramount could have resisted, but there were people at Paramount who were on this Motion Picture Alliance. There was nobody at Fox I don't think—Darryl Zanuck was very independent. He said "I'd like to keep you, I'll try—but when the pressure gets too tough I have to let you go, because I can't take it."

Canham: About the witnesses who did name names to keep working in the industry or for other movies?

Polonsky: I think it was unfortunate—for them, not so much for us because we'd been named so many times by so many different people. Robert Rossen's ability as a filmmaker and Kazan's is not affected by the fact that on this one occasion both of them acted in what I consider a very hard way. I'm indifferent to them—that's all I can say. One of them is dead—I can't be more indifferent than that; Kazan is still alive and I'm still indifferent to him. I've been asked about him many times—I wish him luck. He needs it.

Cook: In the light of what you were just saying about Fox—how true is Trumbo's remark in *The Nation* in 1957 "that the studios hedged their bets and whilst operating a blacklist were in the market purchasing plays and other material without crediting the authors."

Polonsky: Well, by 1957 it was widespread. It wasn't true in 1950 and '51. It began to be true about 1953 or 1954—suspicions spread in Hollywood, some of the top writers were winning awards for studios under fake names, and at that point the black market price rose considerably and there was great competition for certain of the blacklisted names—so by 1957 Trumbo was telling the truth.

Cook: Do you feel that fear of Communist infiltration was ever genuine, if paranoid, on the part of the members of the Committee—or was it, from the start, a fairly cynical witch hunt?

Polonsky: Don't know the members of the Committee—I can't say, but Parnell Thomas turned out to be a crook—so I would assume it was cynical on his part, although crooks can be paranoid; maybe that's why he got caught. Congressman Velde didn't get reelected the next year. I would say that even if you weren't paranoid about the fear of Communism, by 1952 or 1953 you would be—even if you were normal—because you heard nothing else. America was about to be destroyed from within and from without, and somehow this all happened while we were taking over the British Empire.

Canham: Even in 1950, about July, magazines like *Time* and *Newsweek* were saying McCarthy's a crank. . . .

Polonsky: *Time* thought him a crank from the beginning, but what happened to America in general on a large political scale is what happened to the Hollywood motion picture companies on a small scale during the time of the Committee of the First Amendment. The first reaction was to fight it off as being motivated by out-and-out reactionaries. But when they saw the wave of power that came down they backed off from it. That created a void into which all the victims fell, like Satan in Heaven into the depths of Hell, endlessly day after day. As they began to realize that this witch hunt was based on a fatal misconception, on which was the Korean War, and as McCarthy became more paranoid and started to surround himself with wilder and wilder specimens of American futility, like those two characters [Gerard David] Schine and [Roy] Cohn that worked for him (Cohn, by the way, has just beaten another felony rap for being a crook), he began to attack General George Marshall as a Communist and Eisenhower as someone highly Communist in the government. The government struck back and wiped him out. Of course, by then, Murrow had delivered his very famous television broadcast, but simultaneously with the tapering off of the cold war, as America and Russia began to stabilize their fears of each other. It was no longer hysterical, it became like it is today. I mean, we all expect to be destroyed but it's pretty ordinary. In those days they thought it was extraordinary, and were frightened.

Cook: In view of your blacklisting, why have you remained living in the United States during the past twenty years?

Polonsky: Well, I got blacklisted in the United States and they lifted my passport, so the only way I could leave the United States was to steal out and become stateless. It never occurred to me to try and get out once they took away my passport, because I had no personal fear of anything happening to me, like happened in Fascist Germany, because the United States at the very height of this whole period was a remarkably free country. This contradiction and paradox has to be understood, otherwise you don't understand Americans. Anyone who stayed in Nazi Germany and didn't either join the underground or run is an idiot. The United States wasn't like that. We've fought against them openly all this time, never stopped. No one arrested us—no one went to jail except the ten—and they were caught on a technicality. It had to do with them taking a wrong position, by accident, in front of the Committee. They were held in contempt of Congress and knocked back by the Supreme Court which later reversed its position. But then it was too late, they'd been to jail.

Cook: Do you consider yourself a political person, like Lawson naïvely was, or say, Godard is today?
Polonsky: I don't know whether Lawson's naïve or not. He is a political person of some sort and Godard is a political person of some sort and I fall between them. I consider life as a political action. But I don't think politics is systematically and structurally as narrow as Lawson might be considered to have thought. I don't think he thought of it that way but he was considered to.

Cook: I used the word naïvely because he tended to make his views public—and loudly public.
Polonsky: Lawson, like a great many people, always thinks he's speaking for the rest of us. Everybody would be much better off if we just spoke for ourselves. He's a very brave man, Lawson; he's to be respected for that and he was once—he's a very old man now—a marvelous writer—and created the whole school of playwriting of which Clifford Odets is the flower.

Canham: Could you describe the process of "ghosting"—ghost writing? Are you normally approached by the credited writer—or the director or the producer or the company?
Polonsky: In the early stages of it, you used your friends to get you introductions to guys who were already using blacklisted people, or you would go to people who know you very well and who would be tempted

to help you and would want to use you and are not too frightened to do so. Later, the producers started going to the writers. All the writers whose names you used, if they were real writers, usually did it just as a friendly favor and courted disaster. The work that appeared under their name wasn't theirs, so no matter what happened, good, bad, or indifferent, there was a psychological problem for them. Blacklisted writers created lots of problems that way—I know I did. It was much better to use a pseudonym, but sometimes you couldn't. We worked on everything we could work on. One film I did has been recognized. When I was in Paris someone said, "Did you write that picture?" I said, "How did you know about that?" He said, "Well, the director told somebody in Hollywood."

Cook: How did your work on *Madigan* and *Willie Boy* come about, and did any personal organization argue against your employment on those films?

Polonsky: I'll tell you one mild report I have on some opposition, I don't know if it's true or not, but I might as well tell it to you since it doesn't concern me whether they like it or not. A man—a Hollywood producer—at Universal, by the name of Frank Rosenberg, who was the producer of *Madigan*, approached me about two years before *Madigan* and asked me to write a television pilot based on the work of the Office of Strategic Services in France and Germany and so on. I didn't waste much time and said I wouldn't do it, because I thought he meant I should do it under a pseudonym, and I was working in the movies under a pseudonym and it pays much better. So he said, "You can put you name on it," and of course I accepted, especially as it was at Universal which was the major studio in Hollywood at that time. If I got cleared at Universal then I was cleared for everyone. I know I was still blacklisted because my name was suggested for two jobs by Martin Ritt and turned down in both cases. I was turned down on the grounds that you should get somebody else who would be better. Now I hear that when my name was submitted to one of the networks by Rosenberg, the network did not turn me down, but said: "Why don't you find someone else who's more familiar with TV and stuff like this; as far as we know Polonsky has never done any TV." Of course I had done a considerable amount at that time including *Seaway*. TV at that time was under the jurisdiction of Jennings Lang who picked up the telephone and called up this network and said: "Look, we're going to use Polonsky anyway. You do what you feel like!" I came out to California to work on it and was greeted very warmly by both Lang and Rosenberg, so they obviously both had something to do with it. I went to work and did this TV pilot. I went home. I was working on something else and Rosenberg called me and said: "Could you do a rewrite on *Madigan*?" I found out that an acquaintance, Howard Rodman, had worked on a first press, and naturally I called him up and said: "What's going on?" and Rodman said: "I don't talk to him and he doesn't talk to me—if you want to write it it's O.K. with me, because I'm not going to work on it any more." Not only did Rosenberg get me to do the script, but he got me the same salary that I was getting the day I quit in Hollywood which was considerable.

Canham: Did you work with Siegel at all on the script, or did Siegel just take the final script to shoot?

Polonsky: You, of course, have seen Siegel's pieces on his experiences with Frank Rosenberg. Now Rosenberg was the man who got me cleared of the blacklist, so I think he's a fine fellow. But he did have difficulties with Siegel. Now the difficulties with Siegel came from the fact that Siegel was trying to make a movie and didn't care who the producer was. He thought it was his movie to make. But Rosenberg had been working on the project for several years and considered he was the producer in an old-fashioned Hollywood way, and that was what the problem was. Rosenberg also likes to write a little bit, and that was the real source of the difficulty, because obviously when Siegel saw the script, which I had rewritten, it was obvious there were some parts which I hadn't written. There's some parts still in it which I didn't write. Siegel got uptight about it and said: "Let me get to work with Polonsky, and we'll get to work on this thing," but Rosenberg didn't want that. That was the source of the difficulty.

Canham: Were these the sections featuring Henry Fonda?

Polonsky: Mostly, because Frank Rosenberg's idea of the Commissioner is somewhat exalted, and Don Siegel's and mine is less exalted, and it would have been better.

Cook: What are your views on the underground and/or political cinema like *Newsreel*?

Polonsky: Imagine making like forty films a year—two reels and one reel—I don't care what they're about any more, at this point, and since it's mostly propaganda reportage on actual events taking place in the United States, some of the longer ones are marvelous like the Columbia one [*Columbia Revolt*], some of the shorter ones are hair-raising—I think it's just wonderful—it's genuine cinema. . . . When I was at the University of Southern California, I showed them *Willie Boy*. One of the questions that came up right away from the four hundred to five hundred students was: "Do you think a propaganda film can be a work of art?" and I thought that was a foolish question to ask because the answer is: "Yes, of course—obviously." There's no exclusivity in any of this except bad films which all fit the same category.

Canham: Is the blacklist still operative?

Polonsky: Not the blacklist that I was on, but the new blacklists, which I probably am on too, are fully operative, but they're not operative in the movies. They're mostly operative against very young people, who protest in peace movements and are physicists or chemists and then try to get jobs with the government or in some of the large industries—all of whom have war contracts. They can't get security clearance and it may prevent them from getting jobs in certain universities—I don't know whether that's true or false. They're also operative against all Nobel Prize winners who find their name on blacklists in the Department of Education and Welfare [the Department of Health and Human Services since 1979, with the establishment of the Department of Education]. There are security offices in every organization in America. What do security officers do? They make blacklists. They say these people ought to be trusted—those people ought not to be.

Canham: Could you comment on your connections with Orson Welles in radio? Were you connected with the Mercury Theatre, for instance?

Polonsky: I was not, but a friend of mine, Bernard Herrmann, the composer, was doing the music for Orson Welles, and I was not writing for television or anything. I considered myself a serious novelist about to come to birth, and Herrmann introduced me to Houseman, and they asked me if I would do a show for them—that's the way it started.

Canham: How did you actually come to enter films in 1939?

Polonsky: I didn't enter films till after the war, but I signed the contract before the war was over. I'd received a number of inquiries about me coming out to Hollywood, and just before I went overseas, I received another such inquiry from Paramount. I accepted it on the grounds that it might be a good thing to have when I came back. That's how I got into the movies.

Canham: Were the novels written in a naturalistic frame, similar to Odets?

Polonsky: They were not. They were very classical.

Canham: Are your films preconceived and prerehearsed or does the image-word-actor tie up result from the editing process?

Polonsky: The film scripts pretty well suggest the kind of film it's going to be. The style that I use in *Force of Evil* is not my habitual writing style, but one that I thought was appropriate for that film. It's partly based on the way the book is written, but it's different also. What I did was have Wolfert write the first draft screenplay after we had discussed it. I wrote the second draft myself and asked him how he liked it and he said: "Great." You can recognize my style as a writer whether I'm writing essays or something else, *Force of Evil*, or the non-dialogue I have in *Willie Boy*. After all, repetition, like metaphor and things like that, is a technical device, and technical devices sometimes become so much a part of the writer or director or painter that they become identified with his content and even his nature. But I think my range is much wider than the range of *Force of Evil*. The director must edit his film. Obviously he must edit it with an editor. In Hollywood you have to because of the union and sometimes you have to because you don't know the technique, but the film is the editing too. I can't imagine that you'd turn your film over to another and say: "See what you can make of it, old boy," and go away. I work very closely with the editor; I take all the suggestions and consider them, but then I take the suggestions from everyone who works with me—my cameraman, my actors especially, obviously, my costumer, my make-up man and art director. Everybody is very creative and full of talent, but it's my film they're making, and in that sense I think the editor is part of a director's filmmaking process.

Canham: *Force of Evil* wasn't a commercially successful novel. Presumably your producers must have had some fears about handling this as a first film on your part?

Polonsky: Fear is the wrong word. Absolute terror. However *Force of Evil* was a terrific hit. I thought it was a good gangster picture and they went along with it. Bob Roberts, who was the actual producer, wasn't frightened. It was the financiers who were slightly terrorized, but I had the support of the man and I had the background of *Body and Soul*.

Canham: I think there's ambiguity that's represented in the roles of your heroes, for instance in *Body and Soul*, where William Pechter has said Garfield is a combination of tough cynicism and urban dreaminess without awareness, and in *Force of Evil* there's the same combination, yet he has an awareness so this becomes a perversion of strength, and then in *Willie Boy*—Willie Boy is a combination of natural skill and cunning, and he has an awareness of white attitudes, and also of a ritualistic element of his position with regard to his own people.

Polonsky: Well, first of all, I probably have a natural tendency which is impossible to escape. I present the contrary in every case, and that lends an air of suspicion to everything I do. In *Willie Boy* unlike *Force of Evil*—it's not deliberate. *Force of Evil* is bathed in ambiguity; in *Willie Boy*, the whole thing is bathed in clarity in order to trap you in the ambiguities; it's a different technique, but it's only technical, the difference, I would say.

Canham: The score in *Willie Boy* is especially prominent. I don't remember it being as prominent in *Force of Evil*. Could you comment?

Polonsky: When I made *Force of Evil*, I must have made the whole thing in a blind frenzy. Bob Aldrich reports in some kind of interview he gave in *Sight and Sound* that in *Body and Soul* I was a pain in the neck, because I was around trying to get everybody to make this movie correctly, and he would have thrown me off the set. But, of course, Rossen couldn't throw me off the set. I was his boss, since I became partners with Garfield. Now what happened in *Force of Evil* was that Aldrich was my assistant, as was Don Weis, so I was surrounded by plenty of talent. Richard Day was the art director, but Bob Roberts tells a story about that: he hired Richard Day to make sketches of the shots and so on but Day was sitting in a chair and I was making sketches of shots. I worked in a kind of strange way in *Force of Evil*—I didn't know what was going on. I told the composer what I wanted, and left it up to him. Raksin's score is excellent, but it's not my idea of what music should be in films. It's what people who like movie music like. I mean people who really like it for good qualities. In *Willie Boy* it was demonstrated when I went off to Paris with Jennings Lang on some business and I talked to a composer suggested by them. I wanted Dave Gruson to begin with, but he was busy doing another film and they suggested another composer—here nameless—and I told him what I wanted—and I left him just the way I left Raksin, the only difference is that the Polonsky who came back from Paris is not the Polonsky who walked in on *Force of Evil*. Polonsky knew what he wanted by now. I listened to the score and it was terrible because it was telling me about the movie and that's not the role of music in a movie. It had already been recorded, and this cost about $71,000. I raised my complaints, and they just took it away. They'll use it in some other picture I suppose, because in Hollywood you can always find a use for music. Then I got Gruson. I sat through the film three times with him—and he went and composed a few themes. We discussed the orchestration and the role of the music in the film and had ten electronic musicians, carefully selected by Gruson. He handed them bits of paper, and they practiced a little, and then we ran the film and then he would improvise along with them along with the film, and I would be sitting there saying: "Too much—No! Very good! It sounds too much like music!" Gruson is totally conscious of what his music is doing. He worked out all kinds of effects and strange things. You've heard the recorder before, but have you heard it with a girl soprano singing in unison? That's what makes that queer sound—that's Gruson's contribution to it. I was the audience who if he didn't applaud had his way. That's the difference between the two scores. Raksin's score is absolutely first class—I like it; but Gruson's score is part of the picture.

Canham: The women in your films play a catalytic role rather than functioning as totally central characters. . . .
Polonsky: It happens because it's the men's roles that dominate, but if I were to do two other films I have written—where the woman's role is central—it may be different.

Canham: Why did you choose a Western?
Polonsky: It was partly accidental in a sense that Philip Waxman had come to me with this historical study before I even thought of directing a picture, and I was about to write it for Martin Ritt. When Jennings Lang said: "We'd like you to direct a film for us, Polonsky"—it was supposed to be a television film by the way—I could have suggested anything. I had several suggestions, but I was already working on this one. One of the reasons it attracted me was this whole question of how we live in America. We live by myths—well all countries live by myths, but we live by myths too, and the sweetheart of America is the Western myth. All our best movies are made like that. Our kids dress up like that. Like all paradises lost, it never existed, that's the best paradise lost of course—those that didn't exist.

Canham: This is the idea of the desert wilderness turning into a Garden of Eden?

Polonsky: Our Paradise Lost is the Indian's genocide. It had a different approach to him. It was this American mythology that had turned me into an exile, the way they wanted to see the world—which wasn't exactly like that. I said I would take this myth—the actual incident, which is a true incident, has a resonance with the assassination of John Kennedy—and McKinley had been assassinated only a few years before. Here, they thought that Taft was about to be assassinated by this renegade Indian who's leading an uprising in the desert. None of those are facts. Strangely enough, I probably chose, with a tragic certainty, the exact myth to be treated, because while I was shooting the riverside scene, Bobby Kennedy was assassinated. We were living in the myth, not only telling about it.

Canham: About *Force of Evil*—to whom were you referring when you said "the people are merged except where I agreed to wrong casting"?

Polonsky: Well there were several characters—the wife of Tucker for instance, Marie Windsor was wrong. She was suggested by Ironfell who said: "Come on, what difference does it make?" She was surrounded by considerable actors and she couldn't carry it. She doesn't give the effect and that was wrong casting. There were several others but the major casting in the film was pretty good, not all chosen by me. Beatrice Pearson was suggested by [lawyer and Broadway producer] Martin Jurow. He became a producer and had a very good eye for people, he knew about her. She was absolutely perfect though she vanished after making a couple of films. She had personal psychological problems.

Canham: Could you comment more fully on your recent description of a film set as a more complex writing experience?

Polonsky: I think that all directors are writers—all, without exception. Now some of them can't write unfortunately—as a matter of fact they can't write as a matter of technique, as a matter of control—but they are writers. They take writers and bash their heads together and pull scripts apart and push them together and get other writers. I start out with the assumption that the writing experience is continuous with the directing experience, from the director's point of view. But that's not true from the writer's point of view because there are writers who are probably not ever going to be directors, although almost all of them should want to be. But say a lot of them are not going to be directors, they won't be able to handle actors. So I would say that all writers are not directors, but all directors are writers. Unfortunately, most directors are bad writers, but they must write, because that's the only way you can make a film. The directors were also writers in silent films, but they don't have to be such a good writer as you have to be when the people talk to each other, because the ability to write dialogue is a specific gift. You either have it or you don't. So a director may not have it; he's going to have to get someone to write dialogue, but he's going to push that stuff around, he's going to mold it and twist it and bother everybody and drive everybody out of their minds. And there are directors who are uncertain of themselves and actors write lines for that reason. They don't know where it should come from and they don't trust writers. Directors don't trust writers. Directors who don't write don't trust writers. Directors who can write will trust them because they understand the process. I think that's what I meant.

Canham: Could you talk about your relationship with [cinematographer] Conrad Hall? The photography of *Willie Boy* seems to be particularly tightly constructed in its use of lighting, and the light around the actors.

Polonsky: Universal hired him—I didn't. I got him to be my colleague. He was in the South Pacific working with [film director John] Boorman, who is, I think, one of your best directors. I expect great things from Boorman. [Cinematographer and director] Haskell Wexler said: "Get Conrad Hall." I'd seen Con's work, so I looked at it again. I called him as he was about to do *The Arrangement*, and I talked him out of it! He was on a ship some place, and we got together when he came back. Kazan was having some problems with Brando at that time—I don't know what problems—but anyhow I got Conrad Hall to do my film. Then Conrad Hall comes with his own whole crew you see. That's why his stuff is so proficient and lovely. We did two weeks of experimental shooting in the desert, he read the script and agreed with it and was very cooperative. He had been making experiments on his own because he's a creative cameraman. He's going to be a director now. He's preparing *The Wild Palms* by Faulkner. Connie worked out a system of using very fast films— which you use anyway—but he overexposed it all about two stops, and this would differentiate during the course of the day, as more or less light, more or less color, because daylight destroys color in the desert. The printing process was to desaturate the film—of color. Now this is a complex process from which you balance out the colors on all the different angles and shots and so on, which they do for you. The whole two-thousand-foot roll has to be saturated, which changes all the balances and relations of the color. It's a long and difficult process, which Technicolor resents bitterly, and the studio resents bitterly because you stay there for months—in my case four months—and I sent back eighteen prints before I agreed on this one, and the one you're seeing here which is very, very good is still not right—because the only one that was ever right was the one I made. So that goes for the daylight stuff. Secondly, all the night stuff was either the day for night, or night for night.[3] It's treated in a separate kind of way. The film was not only desaturated, but all the day for night stuff had black and white prints made and they were printed one upon the other, which gives it the quality that you see. There is also a systematic development of the use of light throughout the whole course of the film, and if you leave out the night stuff, you will find that the progress is from intense light to evening, and the scenes are selected to play that way.

Canham: Yes. The final shot in the mountains, was that done in the studio?

Polonsky: It was done in the mountains. And those were real rocks, but Conrad Hall stretched canvases over the top, and black cloth. He brought more gear into the desert than he uses on the stages. We had a machine out there—we could have lighted up a city I think—a generator.

Notes

1. The Motion Picture Alliance for the Preservation of American Ideals (MPAPAI), formed in 1944, was an organization supported by conservative members of the film industry who, several years later, were willing to testify publicly before the House Un-American Activities Committee (HUAC) against a possible Communist infiltration of the Hollywood film industry. Prominent members of the Alliance included Gary Cooper, Clark Gable, Ginger Rogers and her mother Lela, Leo McCarey, Ronald Reagan, Adolphe Menjou, Morrie Ryskind, King Vidor, Walt Disney, Cecil B. DeMille, and John Wayne.—AD

2. *Red Channels: The Report of Communist Influence in Radio and Television* was an anti-Communist tract published in the United States at the height of the Red Scare, by the right-wing journal *Counterattack* on June 22, 1950. The booklet names 151 actors, writers, musicians, and broadcast journalists purportedly manipulating Communist sympathies in the activities of the entertainment industry. Some of the 151 were already being denied employment because of their political beliefs, history, or mere association with suspected "subversives." *Red Channels* effectively placed the rest on the industry blacklist.—AD

3. Day-for-night is a technique of filtering and processing film stock to give the appearance of night.

How the Blacklist Worked in Hollywood

Abraham Polonsky / 1970

From *Film Culture*, nos. 50–51 (Fall–Winter 1970): 41–48. Provided courtesy of Anthology Film Archives. All Rights Reserved.

Polonsky directed his first feature, Force of Evil, *in 1948, when McCarthyism was beginning to terrify Hollywood. Blacklisted for years and forced to work under pseudonyms on fifteen feature films, Polonsky at last has returned to directing, after twenty-one years, with* Tell Them Willie Boy Is Here. *The following is a transcription of a tape-recording of Polonsky, taken from an interview conducted by James Pasternak, former UCLA film student and Preminger production assistant, now free-lancing in New York, and Prof. William Howton, Chairman, Department of Sociology, City College, New York.*

I never paused to consider compromise. When you start to ruminate, you get into trouble. If you start to ruminate on the question of betrayal, you are very often in the process of betraying. You don't necessarily have to do so, and you may not, but then you have a lot of self-punishment and self-pity going on all the time. And that's the worst form of punishment that the enemy can inflict, I would guess. To make you think, "My God, how good things would have been, if I'd only cooperated with the Committee!" What a lifetime of punishment that must be!

Regarding those who betrayed, I don't meet them socially today, since my return to Hollywood. I don't meet them professionally. If they're around, I may pass them—I can't help that, because I don't control the street.

There is the common assumption about the blacklisted writers that, having refused to cooperate with the Committee, from then on these men did nothing but work on rotten material under pseudonyms to make a living. But in my case I wrote books. I wrote articles. I carried a picket-sign against the Korean War. I continued to live in my general way, as I do now. The blacklisted life wasn't that narrow and sterile. A whole life went on at the same time, in every sense of the word. In the same way, that's why you just don't make a film, you live it, too. You're making a film and all the while you're watching to see if it happens.

For the blacklisted writer who remained active in the industry but under cover, there were two kinds of pseudonyms. But more accurately, if you use someone's real name, that's not a pseudonym; it's *your* pseudonym, but it's his real name. That's one of the main reasons, for not discussing this whole subject, because someone who was kind enough to let you use his name in order for you to make a living, he also had to take, but without remuneration, all the rewards, good and evil, that came from his having his name on your film. In no case that I know, among my friends, did any of these people do this for money. The loan of one's real name, so that a blacklisted writer could keep working, was done out of the best good will. In such cases, the producer paid that person the full amount for the script, which he in turn paid in full to us, and in our turn we paid the whole income tax. We were always very careful never to take any deduction for anything. The government knew this all the while, of course. That branch of the government is not interested in how you make your money, but only if you pay. In this regard, the blacklisted people had this in common with the gangsters.

During the blacklist period, I did possibly fifteen film scripts under various names. One or two are not bad. Major Hollywood directors were involved in some. One of these Hollywood directors opened his mouth inadvertently in Paris last year, because when I arrived there some journalist knew of the films I had worked on, but I think it is pretty well concealed again.

It might not be damaging to me today to name the films I worked on during this blacklist period, but I think it's up to the persons who lent their real names to this purpose to name the films, not me. I don't see why they should do so. There would probably not be any harm, except to them personally perhaps. I mean it's a very difficult thing to be a writer, who's writing, and occasionally someone else writes something but your name is on it. That's the greatest sacrifice you can demand of a friend. And to say later, "I want to distinguish between this and that" seems to be absurd, because I don't think there are any great major works of art now going under false pretenses.

But perhaps as history the exact credits are important. If the situation were reversed, I don't know what I would do. I wouldn't do anything, I guess, unless I felt it was a bad thing that I was keeping something from someone, but that's because I'm an old Puritan. But in general I don't think the inaccuracies of these credits, due to the blacklisting, is a bad thing. I think it's better to let the past be the way it is. And instead let us writers make our usual claims that we wrote all the good pictures and everyone else wrote all the bad ones. In that way the guerilla warfare continues. Don't you think so?

Some people think that history has claims on men, but it's the other way around. Perhaps man has claims on history, to suppress it or alter it to survive. The thing is to get rid of the past, when it is objectionable. That includes getting rid of some good things, too. After all, they're only accidental correlatives.

It has been remarked that with a little opportunism the characters I created in *Body and Soul*, *Force of Evil*, and *Tell Them Willie Boy Is Here* could have adapted and survived. And so, with a little opportunism, we all can. That fits into blacklisting. Compromise was offered to everybody. Everybody was offered that, including John Howard Lawson, the spokesman of the Hollywood Ten. Everybody got that offer. People who were more profoundly involved in radical politics than John Howard Lawson made the switch, and these people often appeared before these committees as what were called "expert witnesses," and they made a career of it. A career of being expert witnesses.

I'm sometimes asked—"What would you have been required to do? And what difference would it have made in your development." Well, I don't know what difference it would have made in my development. "Iffy" questions are hard to answer when you deal with character. But I was offered—they asked me if I would give the names of people I knew who had been involved in certain radical activities. And if I would just give them those names—they didn't want too many, just a few to establish the fact that I was cooperative—why then I could just go on doing what I was doing, I could have continued to get directing offers, of course. They guaranteed them. I might have made a whole series of Kazan pictures.

But compromise never occurred to me as a possible action. I never thought of doing that. It never even occurred to me as a possibility. I mean, I knew compromise existed as a possibility, because it had been offered to me, and I had seen it operate around me, but it never occurred to me, the same way that it doesn't occur to me to hit someone on the head and take his purse. I mean, it just doesn't occur to me that that's a thing I should do. Now, of course, someone might ask, "What would you do if you were hungry and starving?" Well, my reply is that nobody was hungry and starving in that time because it wasn't that kind of situation.

I know from experience and from knowledge that lots of people were forced to talk about their friends when they were captured by the enemy in Germany, Italy, maybe even Russia, too. Some talked. Some didn't. Just what the limits of resistance are in those cases are doubtful; we don't really know. We just know that some do and some don't. We know that some last longer, and some don't. I myself don't take any moral position on that because I think that's an ungenerous attitude toward the problems of living. Life can be extremely difficult, and at certain points people survive under any circumstances they can. It may not be worth surviving, but that's a kind of *post facto* decision that people make, you know. I don't believe that's a serious judgment to be made on people, when you know all the circumstances of it, even in the case of the people who talked before the Committee. My feeling towards them is that they did what I consider a bad thing, I'm sorry they did it, and I'm not interested in being their friends or anything like that. But people do that in life. People live a long time, and they act badly very often. But that should not upset our general attitude toward what should be done. As for yourself, what you do is do what should be done, according to how you conceive how things should be done, if that's the kind of thing that interests you. And when some fall off, they fall off, that's all. That's the way it happens. I mean, in the general biology of humanity it's a very common occurrence. Maybe that's the way evolution works. I don't know.

Hollywood's left-wing in the late 1940s, after World War II, when the witch-hunts began, was an amorphous, but really existing, grouping among writers, producers, directors, actors, some back-lot workers, and so on—people who were interested in politics. Politics were significant at that time, because earlier, during the war, they had had a Hollywood Writers Mobilization whose job it was to make war propaganda of the idealistic sort for the United States government. Most of these people who were in that were allies of one kind or another. So when I came to Hollywood after my war service, I came right into a situation with which I was familiar. I knew most of the people or got to know them very quickly. Bob Rossen, who directed my first script, *Body and Soul*, was one of these people. I followed that film with *Force of Evil*, which I wrote and directed.

This political grouping of Hollywood workers they were not "radical artists," because that means their work was radical, and that's not true. They were a group of social radicals, with a rather wide spectrum of opinion with the—I suppose—more traditional Communist Party attitudes as the center of it in some kind of way, with all kinds of variations all around it, with liberal democrats, socialists, and so on. That was the community and it was significantly involved in politics at that time, and had been in both state and city politics. I merely dropped right into it like I was at home, since I'd been a politically aware person to begin with.

But in any community there is a group of conservative people—there always is. Because the studio represented the same spectrum of American life you find elsewhere. There were conservatives, liberals, radicals, and so on. But there were more radicals than usual in that particular small Hollywood community, because of the people who had been drawn on for the motion picture industry out of the New Deal times. That was the reason for it. In normal times, it wouldn't be that way, because I don't think that artists are politically more radical than other people in general. They sometimes think they are, but it very often turns out they're not.

But in that particular time, because of the theater and books and the role that had been played in the New Deal and in the vast union organization. I would say that artists of that time, —*especially* the writers of that time—were more significantly left *en masse* in Hollywood than later, and even before.

We must also remember that the writers had been the leaders in the struggle with the producers in unionization for the writers' union. It's been written about before in books and in novels. They had been beaten several times and finally they won and had a great deal of coherence among themselves. So they were important in the community.

Regarding whether this political grouping in Hollywood in the late 1940s was also an artistic *movement*—I have just received a letter from Penelope Houston asking me to write an article for *Sight and Sound* about that period; and in France and in England, Stockholm, and Amsterdam recently, I was asked—everybody wanted to know: "Was there really a social film movement going on among certain writers and directors that was cut off by the McCarthy movement?" And the answer is yes.

But it wasn't an aesthetic movement, in the sense of surrealism as an aesthetic movement. Instead it was a generalized political awareness in one way or another when they had an opportunity to do so. But that opportunity in Hollywood is very limited, and probably the most socially aware films are often made by what should be called conservative directors, like Frank Capra. Because what we consider socially aware in

America is a sentimental attitude toward the goodness of man, and getting together and working things out right, and getting rid of injustice. That's a political attitude, of course, but it's generalized, like breathing as opposed to not breathing. It could hardly be called a definite political attitude.

I don't know what themes this movement might have brought to the screen. It's impossible to predict, because what cut off the movement was something that was happening elsewhere in the U.S. on an even larger scale. Many progressive trends were cut off in the entire nation—which is what we mean by the McCarthy period. It must be remembered that the main political fight that took place in the country—about this time and towards the last years of the war, and right after it—was a struggle in the trade union movement, within the CIO, ending in the destruction of the left-wing leadership. That struggle within the unions was enormous and its consequences were fatal, because that made it possible for McCarthy to operate against people who had lost their allies. Because the main allies of this artistic, intellectual movement had been, of course, the organized trade unions, built up during the founding of the CIO, with all the alliances around that among the bourgeoisie, so to speak.

Really and truly, the triumph of McCarthyism was, in effect, the cutting off of a generalized social movement that had been begun before the war, that had identified itself with the objectives of the war. As the war changed, when it was over, then the battle was now drawn between the two victors—the U.S. versus the U.S.S.R.—so that social movement came to an abrupt halt, as the U.S. foreign policy changed and as the internal life of the country changed.

So the picking on the Hollywood people in the witch-hunt was, in a sense, a consequence of that generalized defeat. It received a lot of attention because everybody knew who these stars were. But nobody knew those little trade union leaders, district organizers, school-teachers, and all those anonymous people who never get into the newspapers unless they get run over or get held up or die, and then someone takes an ad out as they die. But the small McCarthy victims never get into the newspapers, whereas all the Hollywood people were well known, or they could easily become well known by just mentioning their names and some pictures they were in.

My first film as director, *Force of Evil*, was made during the first main rush of that period. It was an expression of the fear of this movement, an expression of this conflict. The Hollywood Ten had already been in trouble, and we were already conducting campaigns for them. The Committee for the First Amendment had been destroyed. I was then making *Force of Evil*, based on Ira Wolfert's novel. I worked closely with Ira on the screenplay. Wolfert's book in a sense reflects this period, too. And I assume the film reflects it very deeply, perhaps more than most films of that time. That was maybe one of the reasons people today still look at *Force of Evil* and find something in it, aside from whatever aesthetic pleasure they find in it.

The technique was to attack all the films written by these people, regardless of what kind of films they were. They sometimes picked out lines that occurred in the films—like a certain line in a Dalton Trumbo picture which he had Ginger Rogers say—but mainly they picked on the films made during the war period that said "We can get along with the Russians, they're not too bad," films like *Mission to Moscow*, which starred Walter Huston and Ann Harding, those were the kind of pictures that were picked on. *Mission to Moscow* was written by a man who was not even a radical, Howard Koch. But he was blacklisted because of that. I mean he wasn't a reactionary or a conservative, he was a man identified with forward-looking things, but he was a kind of typical, good-willed American and he became one of the main objectives of the attack.

There was an anticipation of the McCarthy attack. By the time the war was over, the Hollywood Writers Mobilization had begun to harden its attitudes, too. People who were in it began to drop out. They tried to make films about the returning veteran, his rights. But no one was too interested in that. And they tried to repeat again the objectives of World War II and the promise of humanity which had been in that, all the usual things, the political hangovers, you know.

But the attack had already started because it was going on in the union and then, as if to crystallize it in Hollywood, a strike went on which was led by the Conference of Studio Unions, which was an attempt to shake off the leadership of Browne and Willie Bioff, some people like that, IATSE union politics and so forth. And that was a very devastating strike, because it destroyed almost all the good unions in Hollywood, like the story-editors union, I mean the story-analysts union, whatever they call that. That was a bad strike. The Screen Writers Guild, in effect, sided somewhat with the Conference of Studio Unions, and when the strike was lost, the leadership in the Screen Writers Guild changed, too.

What I'm trying to say is that you're not dealing with an isolated event in American life, but merely with the focus of such a national event as it happened in Hollywood. It was very characteristic of what was going on throughout the country. And the fight was lost. It was lost the day that

Churchill made his Iron Curtain speech at Fulton, Missouri, when he declared the Cold War. That was the day it was really lost because thereafter the full strength of the American government was thrown into this Cold War, and there was no hope. No hope—because the gains of the New Deal had not really created a true left-wing, labor-oriented mass organization in America. And where that spirit did exist, in some of the big CIO unions, it had been destroyed in the internal struggles within those unions.

Hollywood's first reaction to the blacklist when HUAC subpoenaed the Nineteen, of whom the Ten were a part, was to react furiously against it. Hollywood formed the Committee for the First Amendment, which had almost every single writer, director, and actor in Hollywood on it. But by the time the first hearings were held in Washington, by the time that plane got back with them to Los Angeles, the Committee for the First Amendment was in a state of absolute disillusion. I went to the various meetings of the Committee, of course, but no one was there by the second meeting. I remember Humphrey Bogart walking around the room saying to everybody, "You sold me out! I was in Washington and you sold me out!" He said, "The hell with all of you. If you don't want to fight, I'll take care of myself!" and Bogart stormed out of the room.

When I made *Force of Evil*, I wasn't a member of the director's guild. I would have joined—I don't remember if I did or not, it's hard to remember—I certainly didn't keep up my membership, because I didn't make any more pictures. I became a member, however, of the Screen Writers Guild. After McCarthyism really socked in hard, all the guilds put in those loyalty oaths, as the screenwriters did. I was rather amused recently when I got a notice from the Screen Writers Guild in which they had just passed a resolution condemning the Soviet writers association for casting out a member whom the association called disloyal to the Soviet Union. Our guild thought that that was terrible, but they were forgetting that they did that same thing themselves.

The Screen Writers Guild itself in time just quietly got rid of its loyalty oath. In the same way, the Academy of Motion Picture Arts and Sciences, without calling attention to it, got rid of their ruling that denied Oscars to film people who were uncooperative with the HUAC investigators. It's kind of an irony that the screenwriters have never fully rehabilitated themselves, so to speak, except by *quietly* rehabilitating themselves. But those ironies are so consistent that it's hard to call them ironies. I would call them the rule.

I joined the Screen Writers Guild when I got my first open job in Hollywood, an open job under my own name. Before I directed *Tell Them Willie Boy Is Here*, a producer from Hollywood named Frank Rosenberg came to me and asked me to write a television pilot about the OSS, the Office of Secret [Strategic] Service[s] because I'd been in it during the war. Rosenberg knew who I was, of course. By then the blacklist was no longer operating with a fury, but it was operating like a cultural lag, so to speak. A number of writers were already working under their own names, although I hadn't yet. I refused the OSS writing job until I found out my name was going to be on it, then I accepted the job, went out and did it, and then Rosenberg called me in to do the re-write of *Madigan*, directed by Don Siegel, with Henry Fonda and Richard Widmark. Following that, I made the deal on *Willie Boy* with Universal.

The directors union had that same loyalty oath problem. The East Coast directors union, called the Screen Directors International Guild, never reacted with the same obedience to the investigating committees, as they did on the West Coast in the Screen Directors Guild, because the eastern directors were not as closely integrated into the Hollywood mentality, so to peak. The two have now merged. I wouldn't be able to join the directors union now, and direct, if they had retained the loyalty oath, because I wouldn't sign it. The U.S. Supreme Court has ruled, of course, in a number of cases that the oath is illegal. When the oath was taken out of the passports, when Leonard Boudin, my old classmate, won the fight in the Supreme Court, I was able to get my passport back. That, in a sense, was the beginning of the end of the loyalty oath. By the time McCarthy met his fate on television at those Senate hearings, fundamentally the old blacklist was over except that by now the blacklist had spread into many, many, private organizations and had become a business, a business with people trading in names. There were security officers in every bakery and every corner shop and everywhere. So the blacklist went on long after McCarthy was defeated. It was only the John Henry Faulk case that really stomped on the blacklist, but even then someone had to hire you and take the chance that the blacklist might not work in your case. For example, the case of Albert Maltz, one of the Ten who went to prison—Frank Sinatra tried to hire Maltz, but Sinatra finally gave up trying to make the picture because there was such a hue and cry. Yet by then Dalton was already working under his own name, with Otto Preminger.

Preminger, of course, had always had a very strong position against the blacklist. As a matter of fact, throughout the entire blacklist period, Preminger kept someone employed who was officially on the blacklist. But Preminger said to hell with it. I really shouldn't mention the name of this employee. It's up to Preminger or to the person to reveal it. But there was someone there, and Preminger wouldn't fire him.

Although the old blacklist, over the years, was gone with the wind, there was a cultural lag. I mean—"Why use *him*? If you just wait a few more years, you won't have this problem." That was the attitude. But if the studio wanting the blacklisted person took a strong attitude that said, "No! We're going to use him anyway," why then the blacklisters backed down and said "Of course." Because by then, years later, there was really no struggle over that anymore.

Of the Ten who went to jail, Sam Ornitz is dead, and Maltz has finished a film for Universal called *Two Mules for Sister Sarah*, directed by Don Siegel. Maltz is working on other films elsewhere. Ring Lardner, Jr. wrote *M*A*S*H*. Waldo Salt, one of the original Nineteen, wrote *Midnight Cowboy*. The reason Salt was never called before the Committee was because of the work done by the Ten in breaking up that whole Congressional hearing. So Salt never got called, he was never indicted, never was on the stand. But he was blacklisted thoroughly like all the other 330 and some odd people from Hollywood.

Walter Bernstein, the writer, was blacklisted because he was the instigator of an ad in the *New York Times* protesting against the blacklist. So he found himself blacklisted. And now Bernstein has recently done *The Molly Maguires*, directed by Martin Ritt and starring Sean Connery and Richard Harris, probably one of the first working-class pictures ever made in America. Bernstein is associate producer as well as the writer. James Wong Howe shot *The Molly Maguires* and years earlier had shot *Body and Soul*, which I wrote. Even James Wong Howe found himself moderately blacklisted, just for having been associated with these desperate characters.

I'm often asked—didn't writers during the blacklist sometimes have to do hackwork beneath their dignity, to work under pseudonyms? Aren't those conditions corrosive to one's art and self-respect and to one's country? My answer: it certainly is. But of course. I, Walter Bernstein, and Arnold Manoff—he's now dead—we gained control of one of the most important CBS series called *You Are There*. In fact, we did all of it during that period under pseudonyms. This was a very good show on television and it was probably the only place where any guerilla warfare was conducted against McCarthy in a public medium. That was in the 1950s during the height of the McCarthy period. Sidney Lumet directed all our shows and we worked under pseudonyms. It was known to some people who we were, and every once in awhile the pseudonym would be revealed, so we would just use another one, because they would blacklist even a nonexistent writer. Aside from real names, there were fictitious names on the blacklist, too. I shouldn't say now what names we used, because then they would know who wrote what shows. Except that one of the shows, by Arnold Manoff on Socrates, has been put in the archives of, I think, the Museum of Modern Art, with credit to him on it. We did Socrates, Milton, Galileo, shows like that. When everybody was afraid to say anything, these shows were talking about the things that should be said. We also did Savonarola, who burned the books and artwork. And we did the Wright Brothers, whose diaries are magnificent

After I did *Force of Evil* in 1948, I went abroad and wrote a novel called *The World Above*, published by Little, Brown and Company, which reflected in some ways the Committee's operations—but not with writers, of course. Then I returned to the U.S. and did a screenplay at Twentieth Century-Fox, *I Can Get It for You Wholesale*, and I used the money from that to return abroad and try to set up a film adaptation of *Mario and the Magician*, by Thomas Mann, which I was unable to do. When I couldn't set up *Mario*, I came back again to the U.S. But by then the blacklisted people were being called before the committee. I knew what to expect, but I returned in any event. I never lived abroad for a long period as a blacklisted writer. I returned, knowing I would be blacklisted. That was the one discussion I had with my wife—we had only that simple discussion. We were then in the south of France, living there, and we knew I'd get blacklisted if I came back. We thought about it awhile, and we decided that we should be in the U.S. So we came home.

But I don't think that that was better or worse judgment necessarily than remaining abroad, because the fellows who remained abroad, had just as hard a time as those that returned to the U.S. Joe Losey couldn't direct for years and years. He had to direct under pseudonyms. Jules Dassin couldn't get a picture to do. But finally—when the blacklisted people started to work here in the U.S.—the blacklisted Americans living in Europe started to work there, too. That's all that happened.

We must remember that Nixon was one of the main McCarthyites. It was Nixon, as a California congressman, who redbaited Helen Gahagan Douglas out of her job in Congress, and he made his career in Washington as such a person. And now he is President of the United States. He's just changed his advertising agency, that's all, not his opinions. It's very clear.

I came into Hollywood in the late 1940s when McCarthyism was beginning. Now after more than twenty years, I'm coming back just as a new version of the McCarthy period may be starting. That doesn't strike me as ironical. It strikes me as significant. I feel like a gyroscope pointing directions.

I agree with the New Left, I think there is a wider blacklist now than existed then. Agnew's attack on the media is characteristic of such a period, and the fact that the networks are laying down in front of it is very recognizable to me. As a matter of fact, as an English instructor I'd already seen our own form of McCarthyism in the Rapp-Coudert Committee[1] at City College in New York, which years before, in the late 1930s, did the same thing at City College when they fired some instructors accused of being Communists. As I recall, it was the same hearings and so on. Rapp and Coudert were then state legislators in Albany.

I remember reading an editorial in the *New York Times* while I was in Europe recently, on the existence of a blacklist in the Department of Health, Education and Welfare. When I was on the *Johnny Carson Show* [*The Tonight Show* with Johnny Carson] recently, they asked me about the continued existence of blacklisting and I told it to them there. We discussed it for fifteen minutes. It's obviously true that if you're in the peace movement today, if you get arrested, they take your picture. If you're a physicist or a chemist or something of a scientist, you can't get a job with any company having government contracts. I assume all that is true; I assume the blacklisting exists today. The only difference is that magazines and newspapers are exposing the blacklisting and getting out the information on it.

Regarding this question of creating an identity through action and commitment—it's very hard to take some thirty-five million young people and generalize that they represent this or that attitude. But I would assume that many students today who are directly involved in meeting some of the problems I think are significant, in the end they are adopting this existential attitude in one way or another, no matter how they may explain it. Whether they're conscious of choices and commitment, in terms of the philosophy that our generation is familiar with, is irrelevant. Because to have that attitude is not necessarily to speak about it or even to know what it means philosophically.

But when a sufficient number of people become committed to action, then you begin to see that it's a movement or a meaning. It's one of the possible attitudes toward human life. All the other attitudes are present all the time, too. There will never be a totally existential society. The more complex the society is, and the less ritual there is available for acting out how life should be, then the more they'll be driven to that existential attitude. When you have a smaller, more compact society whose relationships are deeply ritualistic, they don't have to make those decisions, because to do what is unexpected is almost impossible. But in our complex society, everything is possible. Almost, it seems. Which is our fate.

Notes

1. The Joint Legislative Committee to Investigate the Educational System of the State of New York, referred to as the Rapp-Coudert Committee, conducted inquiries from September 1940 through December 1941 on the extent to which subversive influences (Nazi, fascist, and communist) penetrated the public education system in New York State. More than five hundred faculty members, school administrators, and students were interrogated in the process and encouraged to name suspicious individuals, and over fifty professors and administrators were dismissed for their political affiliations. One of the first acts of the Committee was to subpoena the records of the New York Teachers Union and the College Teachers Union. The subpoena required anyone who was mentioned more than twice as a Communist Party member to come before the Committee. Students were not allowed to have their parents or an attorney present at these proceedings.

The Committee was chaired by two Republicans, attorney and future congressman Frederic René Coudert, Jr. (1898–1972) and assemblyman Herbert A. Rapp (1891–1964).

The Committee's activities were attacked as undemocratic and part of a political witch-hunt that very much presaged the HUAC investigations of the McCarthy era ten years later. On the fortieth anniversary of the Committee's final hearings, in December 1981, those faculty and staff members persecuted were given a formal apology by the City University of New York for the injustice done them.—AD

Making Movies

Abraham Polonsky / 1971

From *Sight and Sound* 40 (Spring 1971): 101. Reprinted by permission of the British Film Institute.

Up to *Romance of a Horse Thief,* the film I have just finished, such images as I used in my movies originated in the eye, and whatever was visionary, however defined by memory, began with an event, not someone else's memory of an event. Of course, my memory of my memory of an event is already bogged down in the ritual of critical philosophy. Nevertheless, the images of *Romance of a Horse Thief* signify something beyond, because they come by way of the tales my grandmother told me, worked through the stories of the Opatoshus, father and son. It is her voice I hear all through the movie and it was her voice and her face which toured the locations at Vukovar, Ilok, Osijek, Djakovo, and elsewhere in the northern plains of Yugoslavia where we established a Polish border town between Russia and Germany in the year 1904.

Even in *Tell Them Willie Boy Is Here* (Riverside, California, 1909) the Cahuilla Indians were there before me. The times had altered them but they were there, and some had been present at the incident. And that was the landscape, and the places, and the very ranch house, and that orchard, and even an old man who knew that Willie had escaped to Mexico. The details which Harry Lawton had dug out of the old newspapers and from the records in Washington still existed in the events before us, before we made the movie.

But Vukovar, the Vuka River, the Danube, the geese and swine and horses of the countryside, were not in fact Poland, not Malava, not anything like it directly. The Jews were dead except for one old lady who lent us her Sabbath candlesticks, her linen cloth, and her memories of Nazi terror. We were working by way of analogy and bit by bit. I tried to crystallize that antic, continuously imaginary world with which my grandmother entertained me on those late Saturday afternoons when my parents brought me to stay overnight while they went off to watch the vaudeville on the Fox circuit.

I believed my grandmother lived in the city and we lived in the country, but in fact we both lived in New York City. However, it was that kind of journey which in a way her storytelling continued. Everything was imagination in her apartment, including my grandfather who spent his time smiling and praying at home or in the synagogue in a lifelong intimate murmuring with our God.

My grandmother was an atheist, a socialist, and a storyteller and, like her daily paper, believed in education. Each week *The Forward* printed an installment and reinvented it for me. Once, it must have been Huckleberry Finn. I remember Jim as a powerful Russian serf, and Huck sailing down the Volga to freedom. My grandmother felt more at home with her own memories of Russian towns and neighbors, so she retranslated, and years later when I came to read the literature of the world I had the strangest sense of having met all of it before in my grandmother's Russian landscape.

Romance is a fairy tale, pretending to affect an older style but in fact the contrary. It is wrapped around and around with those old memories about a hard and chewy center of the interminable now. We wandered into Yugoslavia looking for the past and found it somewhat surrealist in the present, but not hopeless. Yul Brynner, playing the Cossack commandant, created the bleakness of exile in himself long before the Jews went into their diaspora. The local band from Osijek, weary, sweaty, stagey in Polish peasant costumes, marched up and down in front of the museum converted into the Cossack barracks, and blew quarter-tones out of their instruments. On the Danube the sporting club zoomed up and down on outboards. Cranes, trains, tractors, cars, motorbikes, everything protested against our imagined past. We had a few adventures. The cameraman turned up the day before shooting. The camera sounded like a coffee grinder. There were no lights. We followed the sun. Everything and everyone was a little crazy. We used to walk out in the morning, take a look around and ask, what shall we remember today? Not a bad beginning. I could hear my grandmother's voice everywhere.

In this strange way *Romance of a Horse Thief* is attached closely to the films of my childhood long before I had heard of fine art. For me movies are irrevocably and richly rooted in kitsch, in childhood, in storytelling, in the rubbish of paperbacks and sitting under the streetlights while off in the zoo across the lots flowering with burdock, lions roared out their fantasy of freedom.

Now that movies are being moved into the fine arts and a serious occupation for voices, it was those other voices, casual, inventive, bemused, remembering too, the voices of the Opatoshus, my grandmother, and that enchanting continuously unrolling film refreshed by a weekly visit to the movie house which I wanted to hear in *Romance*. So the camera is transparent, just there, like clear water to let the fiction of the *I* see through, yet somehow like consciousness biased and bent.

It was a great pleasure to make a movie again. Nothing is better; perhaps revolution, but there you have to succeed and be right, dangers which never attach themselves to making movies, and dreaming.

Abraham Polonsky: Interview

James Pasternak and F. William Howton / 1971

From *The Image Maker*, ed. Ron Henderson (Richmond, Va.: John Knox Press, 1971), 17–27.

Question: Tell us about your new project?
Polonsky: I have three. One of them is *Childhood's End* by Arthur Clarke, which Universal bought for my company to make into a film. Another is an original screenplay by me called *Sweet Land*, which Universal bought for my company to do, and a third is one I haven't sold to anyone yet, *Mario the Magician* by Thomas Mann.

Question: You've been working on that property for quite a while now, haven't you?
Polonsky: I got it from Thomas Mann in 1950. He was living, in those days, in California. I've known his daughter for a long time, and I'd already directed *Force of Evil*. I got in touch with him and we had a discussion about my notions of directing it, which wasn't to be exactly the way he wrote it. He gave me an option on it, and I went to Europe to try to set up the project, but was unable to raise any money for it. No one was really interested at that time.

Question: Why?
Polonsky: In 1950 everybody thought fascism was old hat. I think that was the real reason for it. In any event, when I was blacklisted, I had to drop it. So, the first thing I did, when I got to direct *Willie Boy* and had the project set up at Universal, was to get in touch with Erica Mann, and I got it back. But, of course, in all these years my notion of how it is to be done changed. Fundamentally, it's the same discussion I had with Thomas Mann. It was at that time that Thomas Mann said to me that he thought fascism was coming to the United States and he advised me

to leave the country. He said he was going to England, and did in fact go to Switzerland. He had just finished *Faustus*. I disagreed with him and didn't come.

Question: Is *Mario* your most immediate project?
Polonsky: I think it is. My problem, of course, is to get it financed without telling them what I'm doing, which is very difficult to do.

Question: Isn't that easier to do, though, because you're dealing with a classic? It has a kind a built-in acceptance for the studio mentality?
Polonsky: Well, our studios are not impressed by Thomas Mann.

Question: Yes, but it would make it easier for you, an impressive director, to bring in an impressive property. I'm trying to psych out the twisted psyche. . . .
Polonsky: They don't have a twisted psyche! Their psyche is extremely clear. There's nothing twisted about studios: They know what business they're in. They don't understand what business they're in, but they know what it is. I mean, they don't know how to operate very well, because they have a tendency to make money in the way in which they are accustomed to making money, which is, to do again what has already been successful.

Question: You mean to make a film of the film that was a film originally?
Polonsky: It's even worse than that! It's to be immediately up to date with what has already gone out of fashion. It's hard to escape that in the studios, because—to use your words—they're trying to psych out the market. And when the market has changed radically, as it has in the last five or six years, I would imagine for them (it has been changing over the years) they keep insisting that that market still exists out there, even when they say, "no, it doesn't really exist any more," we're going to adjust to it. So, now when they say they're going to do youth films, and in a sense are like the people in *Vogue* magazine who have a youth consultant, that's the youth market, this is what youth likes now, then they do youth films, whatever they think youth loves. "Youth" is, of course, a fiction—their youth, at least, is a fiction. Actually (they) would like to make pictures that appeal to the television market, that is to say, the widest possible market. They would like every film to appeal to every possible audience. And when they get something like that, they're very happy.

Question: I gather you don't endorse the thesis, which is fashionable, that the big studios' dominance of the industry is somewhat passé, that the success of comparatively low-budget films, has been so impressive that the studios are more and more inclined to simply lease out their facilities and not, in fact, the entrepreneurs themselves?

Polonsky: Well, that's going on obviously with some of the studios, especially if they're in the stages of potential bankruptcy. But I would say that the new money coming in will ultimately go back into some sort of studio operation, especially if they want to stay in the television business, where you need a studio operation, since films for television and television series are made under studio control, unless you can't make them for the price.

Question: Isn't that how the property of *Willie Boy* was originally conceived by them, as a television film?

Polonsky: That was a device. What actually happened was that Jennings Lang, a vice president at Universal, who was in charge of the whole television operation, said that if we brought *Willie Boy* in under television, then he, on his own, could okay going ahead with the project. He was certain that if I wrote the script they would turn it into a feature, and as a matter of fact they did at once—the minute I handed them the script.

Question: Mr. Polonsky, could you tell us how you changed you mind? I think you had an original impression of the *Willie Boy* book as being not especially interesting for a screenplay and a movie.

Polonsky: There's no particular reason why I should write a western, or any other genre film, although I'm interested in genre films, but I didn't see how it was relevant to me. Not that you only do films that are relevant to yourself when you're trying to make your living as a writer in the film industry, although they do become so. I talked about it with others a little and I suddenly realized that the events in the story had taken the exact sequence of the western myth: the actual historical events had taken that sequence. That interested me.

Question: Which myth? The myth of the western American movie, or the western myth?

Polonsky: The way I always put it is that the western genre film deals with the Western Myth, an illusion. I'd always enjoyed those films myself as a young man. Now the illusion of the West as a kind of Paradise

Lost—in which for a small period Americans lived in this strange and marvelous world, this frontier in which all kinds of heroic sentiments were generated, and in which an idea of what the American was was most clearly presented: the adventurer in search of the Good Life. But, of course, the Paradise Lost was genocide for the Indians, and, in fact, Ford in *Cheyenne Autumn* had that too in effect. But the very great western directors kind of know that, even as they're dealing with and eulogizing the myth in terms of its excessive nature.

Question: An exploitation of the myth?
Polonsky: Of course. Suddenly, I saw that in fact this myth was still operating—as a notion of American life—and that it was possible to tell the story and set in motion a counter-myth to it. But I wanted the film to have the clarity of a myth and not be overly psychologized, because if you overly psychologize the relation between the characters you destroy the mythic quality in which the events determine what is really going to happen.

Question: Is that why the language is very spare, very lean?
Polonsky: And the remarks are kind of gnomic, so to speak—little balls of words like stones and rocks that I dropped. There are only one or two scenes that are really dramatic scenes in a normal motion picture narrative sense. They just drop these words, and they're not very relevant as dialogue even; in fact, the film could be silent, almost, and still work.

Question: Would you elaborate on the counter-myth theme?
Polonsky: The counter-myth is genocide. Now, of course, some of the critics, even those who loved my picture speak of the scene in the poolroom as representing my political opinion, which is absurd, since it's kind of a take-off on a Mark Twain–Huckleberry Finn kind of scene in which some of the poolroom hustlers and river characters are making the usual remarks they make in a poolroom. They like to talk about democracy a lot and what he's really saying, of course, is very funny. When a character says, for example, "Let's hear a cheer for President Taft, but not to me. That's the inequality in the country. . . . I pay my taxes," and so on—that's supposed to be a funny scene, and hardly represents any political opinions I might *possibly* hold! I included it really in a way to remind people of Mark Twain.

Question: And also, it's there to give a democratic idea when he speaks of what democracy can do for an Indian.

Polonsky: That's right. And it's supposed to be amusing rather than pretentious and important. It's certainly not my idea of what democracy is. I begin to doubt it occasionally. So, the counter-myth is the genocide theme.

Now, the film is embedded in the whole notion of racism, and it's not against it in any kind of way, as if that were the point of the film. It just takes that for granted. What I do is assume that the western myth is fundamentally racist, even though the question never comes up, but just the way the Indian appears in the mythology of American life: an invisible person. They're the original exiles in this country. And, of course, that third factor came into mind when I finally became interested in it because I've been a kind of invisible exile myself, in my own country, for twenty years.

Question: And you, like Willie Boy, refuse to be invisible.

Polonsky: But I was luckier than he was, because I didn't believe in the Indian notion of the earlier days of not committing suicide, because if you committed suicide, you lost your relationship to whatever future there was after death. So what the Indians did was charge into the enemy and have the enemy kill them so that they died heroically in battle, which is exactly what Willie does on top of the mountain, because he could have killed the sheriff Coop, with any of those three shots which is demonstrated in the attack on the posse.

Question: You wanted to, it seems, say something from your generation's perspective to youth of today through this film that has some relationship to you being blacklisted for twenty years. You have also mentioned that you think of this film as a "free gift" of entertainment. How do you relate these two conceptions of *Willie Boy*?

Polonsky: I think it's important to know that, to begin with, I didn't make this film for any market. I assumed in the very beginning, when it became possible to make this film, which was an accident and a miracle of a sort, to get the right to direct a film after twenty years and spend $2.3 million of their money, it's impossible, and when the impossible occurs, it's like a miracle. So I made this film, with the notion in mind that it was probably unlikely that, first, I would ever finish it, because it's possible you might not finish it, and secondly, I probably wouldn't make another film again as a director, because it's very hard to be a director in Hollywood. The director is the most dangerous man in the business and usually he is circumscribed in various kinds of ways; the old producer-supervisor system was set up to control the director.

Question: You mean from the Thalberg days?

Polonsky: Oh, yes, sure. The whole point about it was that the director was an employee, and not the maker of the film. The maker of the film was the producer. Now this has been changing, of course, in recent years, and never was really true; it was true financially, but never was true in the case of the really important directors, because they, in some way, were always making their films, using products, stories, handed to them of which they had very little choice. In a very significant way, they were actually making their films, and there now would be no film history or film classes if they *hadn't been* doing it. You would have had nothing but sociology as a way of studying film. This would have been a product made in those days; it would have had its audience; it was made for this kind of an audience; it was made like the *Saturday Evening Post* stories, or whatever stories were being made then, and when the time passes the product is gone, has been consumed, and can never be reconsumed, because it's so boring, dated, and gone.

Now what makes that not true is the fact that the directors really operated during this period and created the medium as you now know it. Walsh did it, Ford did it, von Stroheim did it, all the ordinary American directors in one form or another did it. In recent years it's been recognized that this is so and now that they begin to speak of film as an art form, why, of course everybody becomes very self-conscious about that, and begins to make films that reproduce the discoveries made in the other arts—to imitate them, so they feel it's more artistic that way—but fundamentally I would say that the contribution made by the older directors is even more significant in that sense, but they didn't think so. It's better to make movies than works of art.

Question: You said that you spent twenty years directing films in your mind. Surely you must have lived vicariously in the films of others. What filmmakers are you interested in?

Polonsky: It's hard for me to remember the films of those twenty years—there are all the American films that were made and all the foreign films that were made. When I made that remark, it was made because I'd been challenged by a peculiar question. The question was in praise of me; it embarrassed me. It went something like this: "How come, after not directing a film for twenty years and having only made one before, this is such a good picture?" I don't know how to answer that question, so what I said was I've been directing films in my mind for twenty years and I've had a lot of experience.

Of course, it's based on another notion which I think I share with some people that being a director is something in your mind and not just a question of techniques. The techniques of directing a film are really trivial, I would say. The techniques are not trivial in the sense that the more experience you have the more valuable your resources are when you begin to approach a subject. That's really true. But you elect yourself to be a director the way you elect yourself to be a writer, or elect yourself to be a revolutionary, or you elect yourself to be a prophet. There's no evidence except the conviction in your own mind and whatever sympathy you feel for works similar to what you have in mind. Having elected yourself, you try to get somebody to let you practice this new profession you've chosen for yourself. If it's a revolutionary, it's a revolution; if it's a director, it's a film; if it's a writer, it's a novel; if it's a painter, it's a picture. Now, there's quite a wasted election from that, naturally, but some are not wasted.

Question: Would you elaborate on what you mean when you say that the technique of directing a film is trivial?
Polonsky: There's nothing trivial about the technique; what's trivial is your control over it. In the commercial picture the fundamental resource is the actor. There is enough resource in the studio, if your election is correct, that you are able to draw upon it very freely, and in terms of what your notion of your film is. In the elaboration of all the techniques into film, you are almost able to assume others' talents as your own. That demands a certain kind of temperament, a certain kind of intelligence, a certain talent.

The precondition of a certain kind of elaborate technical training, like the one that makes you a surgeon, is not the same thing that makes you a director. And somewhere along the line before you elect yourself director or get the job, you've done something in film. In my case, I had been a screenwriter. And being a screenwriter is in effect to do all the things you talk about by assuming that someone would show you how to do it if you had to do it. The screenplay is evidently a strategy for making a film.

Question: So on the basis of two films you've learned on the job and you're ready to make your first film?

Polonsky: On the basis of my past I am willing to say that I am willing to reelect myself on the next occasion. I don't know if this makes it clear, but I really think that you can watch a thousand films, if you're a writer, of course, or an editor and have worked on many films, but being a director is a unique kind of thing, like being a novelist or being a painter, and most of us share that unique ability in some sense, but not as much as others.

Question: You wrote *Body and Soul* before you directed *Force of Evil?*

Polonsky: Right. *Body and Soul* was a situation where the writer turned out to have more influence with the producer and the studio than the director did, which is very bad for the director, Bob Rossen. But it didn't hurt Rossen because after he made that film, he became an important director.

Question: What were your impressions of Rossen? Did you ever agree on an interpretation?

Polonsky: I never interfered, actually, on the interpretation of the movie. We discussed it all the time in the sense that I had opinions, that Rossen had opinions, or anyone else had opinions. That's not interference; it was a normal, healthy situation. The genuine interference that I posed had to do with the fact that Rossen was a writer, and his conceptions of what a scene should be began to alter as he directed the film. He would like to bring out elements that I suppressed, for example.

Question: Like what?

Polonsky: Well, I think he is more sentimental than I am, in the main, and also his force comes from the application of a great deal of energy—unrelenting exercise of energy throughout the picture. He was in an unfortunate position because if I hadn't been there, he would have been able to rewrite scenes to make them happen that way. No one would have objected, but with me objecting, he wasn't able to do that.

Question: Isn't it rather atypical for the writer to have as much influence compared to the director as you described?

Polonsky: Right. And it happened because of the personal relations that had been established so quickly between Garfield, who played the lead, myself, and Bob Roberts, the producer—between myself and Enterprise Studios which is the very reason that I was able to direct there. In other words, I think it was a question of personality, I suppose—I don't know what the words are for this—it was my relationship to the whole project that gave them the confidence that I could direct.

Question: Did Rossen have another ending he wanted to shoot?
Polonsky: Yes. He suggested another ending to the story which was really carrying through my ending which was very ambiguous. Rossen said it should end as a real tragedy, and he wrote such an ending. And we decided to shoot them both because it was the end of the picture. In Rossen's ending Garfield gets shot and rolls through the ashcans, and they fall on top of him, and he's dead among the garbage of history. Then we shot my ending which was more ambiguous, in the sense that Garfield says that everybody dies, and he walks off. He may or may not die, but what's so unusual about that? Everybody may or may not die all the time

So we screened both versions the next day and Rossen got up and said, "We'll use Polonsky's," and that was the end of it. He agreed. So I would say that in the main our relationship was good, although in memory Rossen probably resented it a lot. But people always resent you when they disagree with you, and they don't win. I suppose that's the normal kind of thing. Anyway, if you've been in politics a little bit, you take it for granted; after all, I'd been a teacher and I was quite used to it. And also, to having my way!

Question: Before we get to *Force of Evil*, tell us about the group of radical artists you formed while working in the industry during the 1940s.
Polonsky: "Radical artists" is wrong, because that means their art was radical, and that's not true. They were a group of social radicals with a rather wide spectrum of opinion with the more traditional Communist Party attitudes as the center of it, in some kind of way, with all kinds of variations all around it: liberal Democrats, Socialists, and so on. That was the community and it was significantly involved in both state and city politics at the time, and I merely dropped into it like I was at home, since I'd been in it to begin with.

Question: Was there a hard-core conservative group of people?
Polonsky: There always is. Because the studio represented the same spectrum of American life you found elsewhere. There were conservatives, liberals, radicals, and so on. But there were more radicals than usual in that particular small community, because of the people that had

been drawn on for the motion picture industry out of New Deal times. In normal times, it wouldn't be that way, because I don't think that artists are politically more radical than other people in general. They sometimes think they are, but it very often turns out they're not.

I would say that artists—the writers of that time, *especially* the writers of that time—were more significantly *left en masse* in Hollywood than later, and even before. You must also remember that the writers had been the leaders in the struggle with the producers in unionization for the writers' union. They had been beaten several times, but finally they won and had a great deal of coherence among themselves. So they were important. In the community. Recently, when I was in France, everybody in Europe wanted to know if there was really a social film movement going on among certain writers and directors which was cut off by the McCarthy movement, and the answer is yes. But it wasn't an aesthetic movement. It was a generalized political awareness existing in a number of people who were trying to make films that reflected this in one way or another when they had an opportunity to do so, but that opportunity in Hollywood is very limited.

Probably the most socially aware films are often made by what could be called conservative directors like Frank Capra, because what we consider socially aware is a sentimental attitude toward the goodness of man, and getting together and working things out right, and getting rid of injustice. That's a political attitude, of course, but it's generalized, like breathing, as opposed to not breathing. It could hardly be called a *definite* political attitude.

Question: You say this movement was cut off. What themes would this movement have brought to the screen if it had not been cut off?
Polonsky: I don't know. It's impossible to predict because what cut off the movement was something that was happening elsewhere in the United States on an even larger scale. So that was cut off in the entire United States, which is what we mean by the McCarthy period. You must remember that the main political fight that took place in the United States about this time and toward the last years of the war, and right after it, was a struggle in the trade union movement, the CIO, and the structure of the left-wing leadership. And that movement was an enormous movement in American life, and its consequences were fatal because that made it possible for McCarthy to operate against people who lost their allies, because the main allies in that movement, of course, were

the organized trade unions, and what had happened during the building of the CIO and all the alliances around that among the bourgeoisie.

But really and truly, the triumph of McCarthyism was in effect the cutting-off of a generalized social movement which began before the war, and identified itself then with the objectives of the war. As the war changed, when it was over, and the battle was drawn between the two victors, that social movement came to an abrupt halt as United States policy changed, and the internal life of the country changed. So the witch hunt against the Hollywood people was, in a sense, a consequence of that generalized defeat, I would say, and it's gotten a lot of attention because everybody knew who these people were.

Question: Do you consider *Force of Evil* an expression of the fear of this movement?

Polonsky: Not only that, but an expression of the conflict. Because *Force of Evil* was made during the main rush of that period. The Hollywood Ten had already been in trouble, and we were already conducting campaigns for them. This may be one of the reasons people still look at *Force of Evil* and find something in it, aside from whatever aesthetic things they find interesting.

Question: Was the film specifically attacked?

Polonsky: No, what they did was attack all the films written by these people regardless of content. They really picked on the ones made during the war period with lines such as "We can get on with the Russians, they're not so bad," like *Mission to Moscow*—a film written by a man who was not even a radical, Howard Koch. But he was blacklisted because of that.

Question: Was there an anticipation of the McCarthy attack?

Polonsky: Oh, yes. By the time the war was over, the Hollywood Writers Mobilization[1] had begun to harden its attitudes, too. People who were in it began to drop out. They tried to make films about the returning veteran, his rights, etc. They tried to repeat again the objectives of World War II, the promise to humanity which had been in that, all the usual things, the political hangovers. And the attack had already started because it was going on in the unions. And then, as if to crystallize it in Hollywood, a strike, led by the Conference of Studio Unions,[2] was called which was an attempt to shake off their leadership. That was a very devastating strike because it destroyed almost all the good unions in Hollywood like the story editors' unions. The screenwriters' guild, in effect, sided somewhat with the Conference of Studio Unions and when that strike was lost, the leadership in the screenwriters union changed, too.

What I'm trying to say is that you're not dealing with an isolated event in American life, but merely the focus of such an event that happened in Hollywood. It merely reflected what was going on throughout the country.

Hollywood's first reaction to the blacklist, when they subpoenaed the nineteen (of whom the ten are part), was to react furiously against it. They formed the Committee for the First Amendment, which had almost every single writer, director, and actor in Hollywood on it. But by the time the first hearings were held in Washington—I think by the time that plane got back to them—the Committee for the First Amendment was in a state of absolute disillusion. I went to the various meetings of the Committee, of course, and no one was there at the second meeting. I remember Humphrey Bogart walking around the room saying to everybody: "You sold me out! I was in Washington, and you sold me out!" He said, "The hell with all of you. If you don't want to fight, I'll take care of myself!" And he stormed out of the room.

Question: People like John Howard Lawson were such obvious main targets that his jail sentence was inevitable. Could you have played ball and adapted, and compromised?
Polonsky: Of course, that was offered to everybody, including John Howard Lawson. People who were more profoundly involved in radical politics than Lawson made the switch, and very often appeared before the committee as what they called "expert witnesses," and made a career of it.

Question: A career?
Polonsky: A career of being expert witnesses. They functioned as the main advisors to those committees.

Question: What would you have been required to do and what difference would it have made in your development?
Polonsky: They asked me if I would give the names of people I knew had been involved in certain radical activities, and if I would provide those names—they didn't want too many, just a few to establish the fact that I was cooperative—then I could just go on doing what I was doing.

Question: Then you would have continued to get directing offers?
Polonsky: Of course, they guaranteed them.

Question: You might have made *Funny Girl*?
Polonsky: No, I might have made a whole series of [Elia] Kazan pictures.

Question: There were others, like Rossen and Kazan, who talked. What were your decisions at the time? Did you talk them over with you wife?
Polonsky: It never occurred to me as a possible action. I mean, I never thought of doing that. I knew it existed as a possibility because it had been offered to me, and I had seen it operate around me, but it never even occurred to me, the way it doesn't occur to me to hit you on the head and take your purse. Now, of course, you might say, "What would you do if you were hungry and starving?" Well, our attitude is that nobody should have been hungry and starving that time because it wasn't that situation. I know from experience and from knowledge that lots of people were forced to talk about their friends when they were captured by the enemy in Germany, Italy, maybe even Russia, too. And did. Some did; some didn't. Just what the limits of resistance are in these cases is doubtful; we don't really know. We just know that some do and some don't. We know that some last longer, and some don't. I don't take any moral position on that because I think to do so is an ungenerous attitude toward the problems of living. Life can be extremely difficult and, at points, people survive under any circumstances they can. It may not be worth surviving, but that's a kind of post facto decision that people make, you know.

I don't believe that's a serious judgment to be made on people, when you know all the circumstances of it, even in the case of the people who talked before the Committee. My feeling toward them is that that they did what I consider a bad thing. I'm sorry they did it, and I'm not interested in being their friends, or anything like that, but people do that in life. People live a long time, and act badly very often. But that should not upset your general attitude toward what should be done.

Question: How can it help then?
Polonsky: No, what you do is do what should be done, according to how you conceive how things should be done, if that's the kind of thing that interests you. And when some fall off, they fall off, that's all. That's the way it happens. I mean, in the general biology of humanity it's a very common occurrence. Maybe that's the way evolution works, I don't know.

Question: You were natural and spontaneous; it wasn't a matter of ruminating?

Abraham Polonsky: No, when you start to ruminate, you get into trouble. If you start to ruminate on the question of betrayal, you are in the process of betraying, very often. You don't necessarily have to do so, and may not, but then you have a lot of self-punishment and self-pity going on all the time. And that's the worst form of punishment the enemy can accomplish, I guess. To make you think, my God, how good things would have been, if I'd only cooperated! What a lifetime of punishment that must be.

Question: You mentioned the price paid by the people who cooperated; but didn't you pay a price, too? You referred on another occasion to working on "rotten pictures" for TV or for Hollywood. This must have been an unpleasant experience.

Polonsky: You're assuming that we did nothing else. In any case, I wrote books, I wrote articles, I carried a picket sign against the Korean War, I continued to live in a more general way than just being a writer working in Hollywood, as I do now. So the life wasn't that narrow and sterile. You see, a whole life went on at the same time in every sense of the word. That's why you just don't make a film, you live it, too. You're making a film and all the while you're watching to see if it happens.

Question: Do you find it ironical that you went out of filmmaking, at least in the official sense, at the beginning of the McCarthy era, and now you're coming back with a big bang at the time we seem to be moving into a new period of repression?

Polonsky: It doesn't strike me as ironical at all. It strikes me as significant. What I mean: I feel like a gyroscope.

Question: I'm not sure you want to comment on this, but at present the attacks on the mass media by Agnew, and the deliberate use of the mass media, especially television, by Nixon, suggests to many people that a new version of McCarthyism is building up which will take as its focus of interest the writers and artists and producers in the mass media. Do you see it that way?

Polonsky: You must remember that Nixon was one of the main McCarthyites. It was Nixon who redbaited Helen Gahagan Douglas out of her job in Congress,[3] and he made his career in Washington as such a person; now he's the President of the United States. He's just changed his advertising agency, that's all, not his opinions. I agree with the New Left: I think there's a wider blacklist now than there was then. While I was in Europe, I remember reading an editorial in the *New York Times* on the existence of a blacklist in the Department of Health, Education and Welfare. It's obviously true that if you are in the peace movement today, you get arrested, they take your picture; if you're a physicist or a scientist, you can't get a job in any place that has anything to do with government contracts. I think Agnew's attack is characteristic of such a period, and I think the fact that the networks are laying down in front of it is very recognizable to me.

Question: I find it interesting that both of your films, *Force of Evil* and *Willie Boy*, are derived from the two essentially American film genres.

Polonsky: See, I think genre, like other social habits, speak for us in terms of summaries of the way we see life. We live out the genres as we live out the myths and rituals, because that's the way we systematize our relationship to society and our relationship to other people. I think anthropologically speaking it has very deep connections with the role of religion in life. I would assume that I am essentially a religious person of some sort, at least in the sense that I try to make things signify as if there were some ultimate significance all the time—the ultimate significance sometimes being something that's not so ultimate after all. That's a question of temperament, personality, belief, and so on. I like gravitation—it's the gravitation that operates when I select themes, characters, meanings, and stories. And I am going to assume without deciding on it, that that'll probably happen with everything I do one way or another.

I don't think that the development of genres in the art forms is an accident. I think they're fundamental to the way art operates on our life. I don't think I make works of art in any deliberate sense—like I'm going to make an artistic film. I don't think that way. But, for instance, if I were to make a film outside the commercial media, inexpensively, you know, about some little thing, intended for a different kind of audience, or a smaller audience, it would then adopt a genre of whatever art form appealed to a smaller audience.

So in the long run, they're inescapable. Now, always, of course, as art advances, what you do is destroy the genre in one form or another, and reconstruct it in some other form, ultimately. If we leave out faddism, since by nature I'm not attracted to fads, and reject them deliberately. But genre is not a fad.

Question: *Force of Evil* is essentially a study of polarities. You have an evil man who is a little man and you have an even more evil man who's a big man, and in between you have a fat, heart-aching slob, Leo. Did you mean Leo to be humanity, torn in between and unable to make a decision, helpless in the midst of all these forces at work?

Polonsky: Well, I don't think he's a slob, because I don't think that about humanity, of course. But I do think that most of us are able to work out a pattern of behavior in society in which we can accept a role we don't want to play in general for the benefits we get immediately by not recognizing what the implications are. So, Leo is able to say, "Gee, I just run a small business, I'm good to my help, It's not really a bad thing I'm doing, everybody depends on me, and now you want to get me involved with something big and terrible," because he doesn't realize that that relationship is inevitable. And his brother's superiority to him as a person or as an intellectual is that he knows that you can't be slightly pregnant with evil in this society, you're dealing with it all the time, it's part of your life, and it's manipulating you as you think you're manipulating it. So Joe, in effect says, "Let's manipulate it and let's beat it, and take the advantages," and his brother says, "You'll become an evil man. You'll be Cain. You'll be a murderer." And Joe says, "I'm not the murderer, the whole thing is the murderer and we don't have much choice anyhow, so let's beat it. We have to survive. Let's be on top instead of on the bottom, because on the bottom you're doing the same thing, except it's doing it more to you than you to it." This relativity in values, which to each of the people seems to be ultimate, [they] are fundamentally not ultimates at all, and this relativity of values is coextensive with the entire morality of our society, I would say. And all societies, perhaps—I don't know—except the one we hope someday will come, which will not be like that.

Question: I find it interesting that the flaw in Joe's development as a fictional character is his desire to maintain the sense of family, to protect his brothers, and it brings his ultimate downfall. In *Willie Boy* you have a hero who refuses to participate in the family relationships of, let's say, a tribal society. And this also brings his downfall. What were you saying in 1948 about families?

Polonsky: I've been trying to see some families in 1970. I'm looking very hard, but I can't see any. In the older Jewish environment, the family center was a source of strength, because it formed a cooperative effort in a hostile society. We were able to draw force from it, and allies. The tribal structure of the Indians is a disaster for them today. It's a disaster for the Africans, too, isn't it? Because in the context of modern technology, it has no strength to win. Willie is not a reservation Indian, he's not a white man either, although he's a partial success in the white world. He's a success in the white world by refusing to be white, and he's a success in the Indian world by refusing to be an Indian, and in that sense is able to exist as himself. But the moment the event starts, which he sets off, and he does an Indian thing, he runs off with the girl who's now his wife, now the old rituals and habits of his particular inherited myth, which is disaster for the Indians, begin to operate. And the more he becomes an Indian, the more impossible it becomes for him to live. And when he's really and truly an Indian in the end, he's like all the Indians, he's dead.

Question: One final question: What advice would you give a young writer-director with ambitions to direct a feature?
Polonsky: Don't go to Hollywood. I would give myself the same advice, too!

Notes

1. The Hollywood Writers Mobilization Against the War was a body of Hollywood writers organized to support through various activities America's war effort.—AD

2. The Conference of Studio Unions (CSU) was an association of unions representing set and art directors and related technicians. A six-month-long strike, culminating in a violent riot between CSU members and members of the International Alliance of Theatrical Stage Employees (IATSE) in front of Warner Bros. Studios on October 5, 1945, became known as "Hollywood Black Friday." The event provoked Congress to pass the Taft-Hartley Act in June 1947 and led to the dissolution of the CSU in 1948 and reorganization of its rival IATSE to accommodate their concerns.—AD

3. Helen Gahagan Douglas (1900–1980) was an actress and politician, who became the first Democratic woman elected to the House of Representatives from the state of California. Gahagan Douglas served three terms, from 1944 to 1950, before deciding to run for the Senate against Richard Nixon. Nixon ran a smear campaign against her, using her liberal voting record to suggest that she was a Communist sympathizer; he christened her the "pink lady," claiming "she was pink down to her underwear." She lost the election, but gave Nixon a moniker of his own that stuck throughout the rest of his political career, that of "tricky Dick." She was married to the actor Melvyn Douglas for almost fifty years, until her death from breast and lung cancer.—AD

On John Garfield

Abraham Polonsky / 1975

Introduction from *The Films of John Garfield* by Howard Gelman (Secaucus, N.J.: Citadel, 1975), 7–9.

I met John Garfield when I went to see him and his partner, Robert Roberts, to tell them the story of *Body and Soul*. A new friend, Arnold Manoff, had just come to work at Paramount Pictures, just a few blocks away from Enterprise Studios. Manoff had been trying to make something of the Barney Ross story, but somehow he wasn't getting anywhere, and since he found me numb with Paramount, he suggested that I go over and see what I could do with some sort of prizefighter story for Garfield. But first, we had lunch at Lucey's. The match game was going on all around us, but Manoff was telling me about John Garfield and Enterprise. He made it sound like an ironic dream. It was.

Arnold Manoff is one of the best short-story writers of the depression years. That world of want, poor New York Jews, the Enlightenment, and Utopian Socialism, the Life of Reason haunting the glorious future, was the heart of *Body and Soul*. It is Romance with Rebellion. Clifford Odets, of course, was an electric part of this literary movement, and his plays were their enchanting vision, but Garfield was the star for the whole world, the romantic Rebel himself.

In a way, I found the ambiguity of the movies much like the souls of Odets and Garfield when I got there after the war. John McNulty was at Paramount when I turned up. What was I doing there, he asked me. I belonged back in New York. The racetrack was the only real thing around. The whole place was a fraud. He himself was just hanging in to get enough money to go back to the city, and he cursed Los Angeles, the sunlight, the palm trees, and the movies. He took me onto a set, the first I saw before the Paulette Goddard one, and he showed me Alan Ladd standing on a box for a tight two-shot in a love scene. "This is it," he said. "Go home."

He never went home, but the Blacklist sent Garfield and me back to New York.

The children of rich Jews in those days when they were attracted to the arts had a tendency to become infatuated with the avant garde and the vitality of the irrational, but most poor Jews who didn't join the money system gravitated to socialism, vague or definite; rebellion, moderate or tough; and self-consciousness, harsh or neurotic. Some became gangsters; most joined the establishment of which crime is, after all, as my friend Ira Wolfert says, "the grease that makes things run" (cf. *Force of Evil*, based on Ira Wolfert's novel *Tucker's People*).

As an actor Garfield was the darling of romantic rebels—beautiful, enthusiastic, rich with the know-how of street intelligence. He had passion and a lyrical sadness that was the essence of the role he created as it was created for him. In the hysterical tragedy in which he found himself he became an exile in his own country. That others before him and others after him in every age would play the same role was no satisfaction to him. He was ambitious. The Group trained him, the movies made him, the Blacklist killed him. The popular story, for instance, is (and he may have said so in public himself, for he was obliging in other things besides politics) that he refused the part of Kowalski in Tennessee Williams's play because the woman's part was better than the man's. I read the play when it was submitted to his company, and I know the part was turned down by Roberts because Irene Selznick wouldn't make a proper moving-picture deal on it, so Roberts decided. Garfield was unlikely to turn down anything because a part was smaller or bigger, although he liked to be the star. Everything he did flowed from his magic and frustrating years in the Group. The play was the heart of it. The ensemble was the soul of it. He knew it and acted like that on both occasions when we worked together.

Garfield felt himself inadequate as an intellectual. Most serious actors feel like this. They aren't actually inadequate, any more than intellectuals are, but they feel that way. Being an intellectual and being an artist aren't genetically paired, any more than being an artist and being a good character. Being an intellectual is a full-time occupation, and although it, like everything else, is enriched by other talents, it has its own universe and its own cast of fools. As an actor Garfield was total, and he could play an intellectual with the same vigor and astonishing rapport as a cab driver. Regarding *Force of Evil* he told me before we started that although he really didn't understand some of the meanings, the minute he hung that Phi Beta Kappa key on his watch chain he was in business.

And so he was. He had the true actor's genuine wisdom for the human, and he could play his kind of intellectual just as well as he could play his kind of cab driver. You won't meet either in New York, but you wish you could.

He didn't have the range of an Olivier but then Garfield was a star who represented a social phenomenon of enormous importance for his times and, perhaps, ours too. He lived as a star without contradiction in the imagination of those who loved him for something that lay dormant in themselves, and this was tuned to the social vigor of the time that created him. Naturally, when those times became the political target of the establishment in the United States, Garfield, whose roles, whose training, whose past were the environment of the romantic rebellion the depression gave birth to, became a public target for the great simplifiers. From his dead body and those of many like him, from the hysteria and know-nothing rage of McCarthyism, HUAC, and Nixon, there rose the ominous star of Watergate, which today bewilders us as Nazism bewilders the German people.

Garfield knew on the night he died that Clifford Odets had that day testified before the House Un-American Activities Committee and there, in general, had made the popular derogatory remarks about the left and communism. In addition, Odets said he had been a member of the Communist party in the past.

> Mr. Tavenner: Were any of the meetings held in your house?
> Mr. Odets: No, I don't think I had a home then. I was a very poor man.

And so were the people he named. John Garfield, who wasn't even a fellow traveler, refused to speculate, refused to name names on the grounds he couldn't remember anyone who was a member of the Communist party, not in the Group, not in Hollywood, not anywhere. For years the federal government used their resources to prove he had perjured himself, and for years they failed, but they did succeed in killing him.

The former Mrs. Garfield says, "I believe in fate, and he might have died anyway. But he wouldn't have died so angry. He was so angry."

He had a right to die angry. He had a right to be angry, for he could find no way to free himself from those who were destroying him.

Now, here, on this terrible night, wandering like Joe Morse around New York, talking to himself with a voice from the grave, really with no place to go, rejected, he saw far off on those screens his own face, which had become the face of a generation of New York street kids. I joined those same New Yorkers and we stood across the street from the funeral parlor watching the tumult and fifty policemen with white gloves. Later, the papers said ten thousand people had come, nothing so big since the death of Valentino.

The strangers I stood with, and they were quiet, unlike those who got into the event, were the same I saw forming a great line around the Globe Theatre in New York after *Body and Soul* opened, the same faces, the same figures, the same bodies, and the same life. They understood in terms of the romantic rebel from the streets that even though he was torn and tempted, he could never give in.

The political vultures who flew about him and descended after his death to croak that had he lived one more minute he, too, would have confessed to the committee, have vanished into the ultimate irrelevance. I hope this book [*The Films of John Garfield*, Citadel, 1975] reminds those who love movies of yet another star in a world that charmed the lives of our generation, and in the end Garfield was right to do as he did, right to act as he acted, true not only to his generation but to the country that spawned him. Is it important? I don't know. But it's a fact.

"A Pavane for an Early American": Abraham Polonsky Discusses *Tell Them Willie Boy Is Here*

Joseph McBride / 1980 / 2011

Previously unpublished essay and interview. Archived. Joseph McBride Papers, Wisconsin Historical Society, 1980/2011. Printed by permission of the author.

This 1980 discussion with Abraham Polonsky that I moderated with the audience of the Los Angeles International Film Exposition (Filmex) was actually my second extended discussion with Polonsky about *Tell Them Willie Boy Is Here*, which I regard as one of the great American films. From its original release in 1969 to less than widespread acclaim in this country, I was an admirer of Polonsky's radical, bleakly existentialist Western, only the second of three films he was able to direct in a career riven by the blacklist. When I moved to southern California in 1973, I spent a year living in Riverside, where I explored some of the locations where the "Willie Boy incident" had actually taken place. I sought out Polonsky at his home in Beverly Hills and found him among the handful of most brilliant people I met in the film industry (Orson Welles, Jean Renoir, and Billy Wilder were among his few intellectual peers in Hollywood), as well as a surprisingly droll and cheerful fellow considering his long period of internal exile and the often-bleak themes of his work. Abe pointed out that the film of his that he most resembled in person was *Romance of a Horsethief* (1971), an even more neglected work that defied its Czarist Russian setting to become his most joyous celebration of life.

In 1975, I persuaded Abe to screen *Tell Them Willie Boy Is Here* with me at Universal for the first time since he had made it. We followed that screening with a long and fascinating talk about the film, which is based on a 1960 nonfiction novel, *Willie Boy: A Desert Manhunt*, by Harry Lawton, a predecessor of mine as a reporter for the Riverside *Press-Enterprise*. I mentioned to Abe that one reviewer thought *Willie Boy* was so carefully crafted and constructed that it looked as though he had been mulling it over throughout his two decades on the blacklist. Abe replied with a smile, "They just haven't seen fancy dancing for a while." The motif of dancing pervaded Polonsky's vision for the film and its themes; the intricately rhythmic pacing of the chase (in effect, The Last Western Chase), portrayed by the writer-director as both somewhat absurd and profoundly symbolic, is a major part of the film's meaning as a bitter elegy on the nation's formative period of frontier genocide. Polonsky described *Willie Boy* to me as "a pavane for an early American." The dictionary defines "pavane" (a word of Middle French and Italian derivation) as "a stately court dance by couples that was introduced from southern Europe into England in the sixteenth century." That stately pacing alone made the film out of step with the frenetic *"Easy Rider* era" from which it shines as a rare beacon of intelligence, and *Willie Boy*'s uncompromisingly radical political viewpoint toward American history and its demolition of the Western genre were not calculated to make the film popular in its native land (France, with its tradition of existentialist cinema and anti-Americanism, has always been far more receptive to it; until recently if you want a DVD of the film, you had to order it from France).

Five years after my first talk with Abe about the film, I had an opportunity to discuss it with him publicly when I offered to host a screening at Filmex (I have incorporated in this transcription some of the insights gleaned from the earlier discussion). Although the audience at a Century City theater in early 1980 was attentive to the film and polite to Polonsky, who fielded questions with acuity and his characteristic wry wit, one can sense in some of the questions a certain incomprehension toward the film's most original elements. Some audience members seemed particularly thrown by its subtle and complex view of sexual relations as a lethal battleground (including Polonsky's decision to make Susan Clark's Indian agent a more conflicted figure than the actual historical character) and its depiction of Robert Blake's Paiute Indian Willie Boy as fatalistically expressing his defiance of the genocidal white world through what we would now call "suicide-by-cop" in his fatal confrontation with Deputy Sheriff Cooper (Robert Redford). These deeply disturbing elements in Polonsky's vision of early twentieth-century American history ran contrary to both genre expectations and to the romantic expectations of U.S. audiences in the late sixties and mid-seventies about how women, minorities, and rebels should be portrayed onscreen. The film's challengingly unconventional, starkly unsentimental nature helped account for the largely dismissive attitude it provoked in the U.S. at the time of its release and continued to engender among some segments of the audience. Cooper's comment to a fellow member of his posse that "we better forget about the good old days right now" and his great ending line, "Tell 'em we're all out of souvenirs"—expressions of Abe's own contempt for Western mythology—did not offer a message many Americans wanted to hear even in those days when the genre itself, reflecting the out-of-control violence in the country at large, was taking such a sharply nihilistic turn.

Joseph McBride [*to the Filmex audience*]: Abraham Polonsky will be here in a couple of minutes to talk with us. Abe's blacklist background helps you understand where the filmmaker is coming from, since *Tell Them Willie Boy Is Here* deals with themes of persecution and betrayal and ostracization, but I think to emphasize that totally would limit the film a great deal because it's about much more than that. The themes that are in this film are so rich and complex, and yet the film is so simple. That's what I think makes it so powerful: the spare dialogue—there's not a wasted word—and the extreme precision in the visual style and the refined acting and lack of melodrama. [*Polonsky enters, to applause.*] Would you like to sit here through my remarks or would you want to say something?
Abraham Polonsky: I think I'll sit here and listen.

McBride: I was just pointing out the lack of melodrama in the film, which is what I think distinguishes it from the ordinary Western and helps make the themes work. Most people who see Westerns superficially talk about "the good guys and the bad guys"; that's why they don't like them, because they think they're shallow morally. I don't think that's true of the great Western directors, such as John Ford, Howard Hawks, and Anthony Mann.

It's interesting to compare *Tell Them Willie Boy Is Here* with another great American Western from the 1960s, Ford's *The Man Who Shot Liberty Valance*, which was made in the beginning of the decade, in 1962, before the John F. Kennedy assassination, which I think was the dividing point in that decade. The country was not the same after that. Then came *Willie Boy*, at the very end of the decade, after we'd seen the assassinations and the black riots and the campus upheavals. As a matter of fact, the scene in *Willie Boy* in which they discuss the 1901 assassination of President William McKinley [Sheriff Frank Wilson, played by Charles Mc-Graw, tells the press that they don't want a repeat of that as part of the Willie Boy incident] was shot the very day Robert Kennedy died when he was assassinated here in Los Angeles in June 1968. The news of his death was brought to the set, and the whole cast and crew broke into tears. The Martin Luther King Jr. assassination happened two months before that. That was one of the worst periods in American history.

Liberty Valance is thematically related to *Willie Boy* because it's also about the fabrication of a myth. It's about a man who builds his political career on a murder he didn't do. *Willie Boy* is about a myth of an Indian who gets involved in a personal fight, but because of the proximity of the visiting President William Howard Taft, whom you don't even see in the film—only the enormous chair awaiting him at Riverside's Mission Inn—the event gets magnified out of all proportion to a ridiculous charade in history, which, in fact, is the way it happened. The film generally is quite true to historical events, although it adds the character of Deputy Sheriff Cooper [Robert Redford], for example, and Calvin, played by Barry Sullivan. In the real history of the event, there were many people chasing Willie Boy. And it was even more farcical than it is in the film: A bunch of buffoons chasing this poor Indian, and the press running around blowing it out of proportion. It's the classic case of the rumor in which somebody says there's an Indian running around shooting people, and then somebody says it's three Indians, five Indians, a hundred Indians—you know, the Indians are trying to take over the United States. So even in its time this was seen as a symbolic event.

This was the very end of the Western frontier period, 1909. Right around then, the last states were entering the Union and the Old West was dying. And the commentators at the time saw this event as a parable of what was happening in the West, the death of the Indian. The newspaper editor in the Ford film—though not Ford himself—argues that myths are good for the country, even though they're false ["When the legend becomes fact, print the legend"]. *Willie Boy* says that myths are bad for the country, and this is precisely what we have to destroy and get rid of, this kind of mythological crap that we carry around with us. I see it as a film that shows how individuals are determined by history and how individual behavior is conditioned. For example, the sheriff's father was a sheriff, so Sheriff Cooper behaves the way his father behaved. I see the sheriff as the protagonist of the film, not Willie Boy [Robert Blake], because the sheriff is the only person who changes to some extent. To me, he is the modern American. Like all of us, I think, to some extent, he is living out a life pattern which doesn't have much relevance to him. But he's forced to do this: He's the American carrying around the legacy of the past and he's acting out this history without much conviction. Redford gives a great performance, I think it's the best thing he's ever done. Robert Blake is magnificent as well. So you have these two people, and the sexual themes relate to this in many ways.

Mr. Polonsky, would you want to say anything about the film, having seen it for the first time in, what, several years?

Polonsky: I haven't seen it. I didn't stay to watch it. I couldn't stand it. [*Audience laughter*] Well, then, I never can stay to watch, so it's not unusual. What do you want to ask me?

Audience Member: The role of the women. I'm curious about the time when both women were crying, both at the same time [the questioner refers to a sound-bridging transition between them]. First it shows the doctor [Dr. Elizabeth Arnold, played by Susan Clark] crying, and then it shows the young Indian girl [Lola, played by Katharine Ross] crying. Was that symbolic in some way?

Polonsky: I just made that point. It's not symbolic at all. It's the fact that's occurring. And it doesn't stand for anything but what's going on at that particular moment. Now that in turn, of course, is related to everything that's happened in the film up to that moment. So that merely culminates in the relationship between them that I try to establish very early in the film when you first see them, they're the only two people in white, for instance, in the opening scenes. I think what you try to say about this—the sexual point about the relationship of the woman to the men and the women to each other—that's more complicated, and that is not symbolic either.

Actually, there was a woman anthropologist [Indian Agent Clara D. True] who was in charge of that reservation that day [superintendent of the Malki Indian Agency at the Morongo Indian Reservation, Banning, California]. This woman tried to defend Willie Boy and tried to prevent these things from going on, and she was fired off the reservation from her job and went to become the head of another reservation elsewhere and then lost her job there too. In the course of doing research, we were able to unearth the report made to the Indian Department on her and her arguments. And in a sense this film embodies all of that. Now, the part that Susan Clark plays in this film is *not* that woman. In other words, this woman [Dr. Arnold] *wants to change* the Indians, in fact wants to make this Indian girl a little white girl. The real woman in the case was not like that at all and was a very unusual character in the time. However, the white woman in this [film] story is of course an advanced, sophisticated, intelligent anthropologist who at the same time is carrying on her personal story in terms of her relationship to Coop. She thinks that by separating a young Indian girl from her relationship to the Indians from which she comes, and turning her into a little schoolteacher, that she will liberate her and make her a woman of the present. In fact, it's what kills her. As it always does. So, therefore, the sexual relations, for instance, between Willie Boy and his wife, according to Indian custom, and of the sheriff and Susan Clark, the anthropologist, are part of the fugal little game that we play, which in the end releases what is suppressed in both their natures and makes it obvious to the audience, I hope.

McBride: Could you tell the audience the story you told me about the ending of the film where Redford improvised and changed the meaning of the film?

Polonsky: In shooting the final scene of the film, we decided to shoot in what we call the "magic hour," which is just after the sun goes down but before it sets, because of the extraordinary relationship of the light at that time. That lasts for about an hour, and therefore we scheduled two evenings for that—and that was during the fire sequence and so on. Now, in the way I originally set up the scene, Redford remains at the fire. He doesn't participate. He remains and watches. And when we were shooting it on the first night, he suddenly started to walk off away from the fire, and that's when I nudged my cameraman [Conrad Hall] and told him to hold the camera on Susan Clark. So that startled look on her face, which is so integral a part of the finale of the film, is therefore an accident. After that was shot, I asked Redford why he walked away, and he said he thought the film should end with these two people separated. Although they're not really joined in that scene, they're just there. And he wanted the film to end with him walking away. Susan Clark was of course terribly upset by that. I already had seen the end of the film now, despite this conversation, so we argued most of the night in the parking lot before the next day, and then I shot the scene the next day during the magic hour, shot a thousand feet of him walking away, and then didn't use it. Because the film had already ended, you see. That's how it happened. That's based on my theory that a good accident is always better than a good intention any time in art.

McBride: You told me that you thought the look on her face was the point of the film.

Polonsky: Yes, it was the very point of the film. I couldn't have *told* her how to do it, nor would she have been able to formulate it, but she was absolutely *bewildered* by what had happened, and lost, and torn, and not knowing what to do, which is precisely what her position was, although it was generated by a different scene entirely. But, of course, everybody who deals in film knows that what you look like when you're doing it depends on how you orchestrate it or surround it by other elements, and that no faces have real looks on them until you surround them with other elements of the film. Then looks have significance. Otherwise, all looks are neutral; they mean nothing. You don't know whether it's agony or bliss. *We* tell you. [*Audience laughter*]

McBride: It's my feeling, also from having read the book by Harry Lawton, that the character of the woman in real life was much more sympathetic than Susan Clark's character. I think one of the reasons for that change is that Dr. Arnold is your attack on liberals.

Polonsky: Yes, that's why I tried to make that point.

McBride: Early in the film, when Dr. Arnold objects to liquor being sold on the reservation, she causes a wagon to go dangerously out of control through a crowd of peaceful Indians. I told you earlier that I thought that was a visual metaphor for the trouble you experienced with liberals during the blacklist era.

Polonsky: It's worth making pictures for you, because you see things.

McBride: Did it come out of your blacklist experience that you portray liberals so unsympathetically in this film?

Polonsky: I thought they behaved very naughtily during the blacklist period. They were very naughty. [*Laughing*]

McBride: Worse than that.

Polonsky: Well, they were real lousy. The liberals were the worst.

McBride: Orson Welles said liberals in Hollywood sold out their friends to pay for their swimming pools [his actual quote, from a 1964 interview with Spanish film critics, was, "What is so sad about the American Left is that it betrayed in order to save its swimming pools"].

Polonsky: Well, I think we should forgive them [i.e., Hollywood liberals] because they didn't win. [*Audience applause*] But otherwise I wouldn't.

McBride: You portray Dr. Arnold as a woman who causes havoc for the Indians.

Polonsky: Yeah, but the thing I wanted to accomplish, and I thought Susan did very well, since she is really a liberated person herself and understood very well . . . what I wanted to get the feeling was that she, really, *deeply*, was sympathetic to the Indians, and in everything in her culture and in everything she wanted to accomplish, she felt she was bringing them into a world that was so much better than the world that they had come from, even including the fact that this world had been caused in fact by the white people who had conquered this country. And at the same time, she was selling them out. Of course that was exactly the position of all the blacklisted people with their liberal friends at that time. I don't mean all liberal friends, but the liberal movement *as such* in that time was deeply involved in the Cold War and therefore deeply involved in the blacklisting of the blacklisted people. As a matter of fact, as we discovered recently, one of the directors of the ACLU [the American Civil Liberties Union] was handing information to the FBI at that time about the members of the Communist Party who happened to be in the ACLU.

[The actual Indian agent involved in the Willie Boy incident, Clara True,] was a real first, before her time—a real first-rate anthropologist who understood that the problem in dealing with the Indian was not to turn the Indian into the beginning of a white man, [but] to make him enter the twentieth-century civilization *as* an Indian and in terms of as much of his culture as he wanted to possess. She was extremely sympathetic to Willie Boy when everybody was against him.

McBride: Let me repeat an audience question: She said she liked the film, but she is bothered by the fact that we identify with the white, blond sheriff, presumably the representative of the oppressive culture. [*To the audience member:*] Why would you? Do you identify with him? A lot of people identify with Robert Blake's character.

Polonsky: I think Robert Blake gives an extremely good performance in this picture. And so does Redford. I thought the white blond sheriff was the white *blind* sheriff [*Audience laughter*], and that, fundamentally, being the son of a father who was a victor in the past because the nature of the circumstances were such that he had to be a victor, because that's who finally ran the country, he had no real role to play. By letting himself become involved in this and finally turning it into a personal question of his own, as I demonstrated I hope in that scene on the railroad tracks between him and Susan Clark, we find out the reason why he must persist in his choice. I think that the very opposite effect is the key. At least that was my intention, of course. I mean, our intentions always don't come out the way we want them to. If they did, how impossible this world would be!

But I thought in this particular case that I had succeeded, or hope to have succeeded, in making his killing of Willie Boy his *defeat*. Because Willie had no bullet in his gun. Now, actually, Willie Boy was surrounded by a posse, and Willie shot out and then had no bullets left, and they assassinated him. Then they cut up his body and took pieces of it and pieces of his equipment and brought it back, in the actual story. I have a photograph of them all standing around the body of this Indian. I felt that that would not tell us anything except what we know. The important thing was to find out what that *meant*.

So in creating a fictional ending in a sense, which is still based on the facts that occurred, I tried to make what that event signified become clear rather than the mere brutality of the event itself. So that the killing of the Indian is a brutal event and not intended by this man [Sheriff Cooper] who was willing to take him a prisoner, but Willie will not be a prisoner. Also Willie could have escaped and refused to escape. Because by then he had determined to live a different life, at that particular moment. Many of us who were involved in the radical political movements of that day [i.e., the blacklist era], but less heroically, were often in this position, and very often had to take such stands. And many did. More people did not betray their friends than those who did betray them. That's the fact. Do you see?

Audience Member: How did the project come about? Was it a script that you came up with, or did Universal bring it to you?
Polonsky: No, no. It had nothing to do with Universal at all—except that they made the picture, of course, which was their last charitable act in this world. [*Audience laughter*] I'm on good terms with them in that sense, but that doesn't mean I don't understand what happens. [*Audience laughter*] [Producer Philip A.] Waxman came to me with this project and asked me if I would write the screenplay. Then in the process of trying to get the thing made, we finally ended up with Jennings Lang [an MCA executive who produced the film with Waxman], and Jennings

Lang said, "Look, if you want to make a movie out of this, I have to get an okay from Lew Wasserman [the head of Universal's parent company, MCA Inc.], and he may not okay it. But if you pretend, or go along with me, that we just want to make a long television show out of this, then I don't have to ask anybody's permission because I'm in charge of that. Then you'll write the script and we'll see if we can force it through as a picture." At which point, Waxman got very nervous, because you don't get much money for television screenplays. But I talked him into it. I also gave him my share of the profits. That helped.

Then I wrote the screenplay, and they liked the screenplay so much, they told me that they would make it into a film if I could get one of eight actors to play the part of the sheriff. They had all the stars, starting with Warren Beatty, who had just made *Bonnie and Clyde*, all the way down, and Redford was the number eight. They knew, though, he was going to be a big star. He wasn't one yet. But they knew it and wanted him very badly. It was through Waxman that we met Redford. Redford read the script and immediately wanted to do it. I made a joke once and told him he could play the Indian too if he liked. [*Audience laughter*] He considered it.

McBride: Didn't somebody actually try to get you to cast Redford or Paul Newman as the Indian?
Polonsky: No, no. That was just a joke I made, and later on the press took it up and thought it was serious. [*Audience laughter*]

McBride: Could you tell us about how Robert Blake got the part of Willie Boy?
Polonsky: We were having great difficulty finding someone to play— first we tried to find an Indian to play it who would be acceptable. At that particular moment there was no young Indian actor we could get in this picture. Except for the parts of Katharine Ross and Blake, all the Indians are played by Indians, most of whom are members of the Cahuilla tribe where this took place [the characters in the film are Paiutes; both tribes have lived on the Morongo Indian Reservation]. The people from that reservation cooperated in this film, and they're all over the picture, as you can see. Redford recommended Blake to me. And Blake came in. I called up Jennings Lang, who happened at that time to be in Rome. I got him in a restaurant, and I said, "I just found someone who seems to be very good for the picture." He said, "What's his name?" I said, "Blake." He said, "No, he's just a small crippled guy." Because he had seen *In Cold*

Blood. [*Audience laughter*] He said, "Forget it. Get some tall, more interesting fellow." Well, Blake went out into the desert and lived there for two weeks, went out with his truck and got very muscular and very dark. And then he came to the studio dressed as he is in the picture. I sent him up to Jennings Lang. A minute later, after he was in, the phone rang, and Jennings said, "Well, he's taken shape, and we'll take him." [*Audience laughter*] But a lot of that was due to Blake's workout in the desert. He really got himself until he looked like he does in the picture.

Audience Member: Did you have to make many political compromises to make this picture for a major studio?
Polonsky: Did you notice any? [*Audience laughter*] Because if you did, I'll tell you if it happened.

Audience Member: Well, I was thinking more of a scene that might have been cut out?
Polonsky: No, no. The only compromise I had to make was a question of money. The picture was about $200,000 over budget before we started, and I was told I had to get that out. I had a very interesting scene in which a party of white farmers who were against Taft dressed up like Indians. They attacked President Taft's automobile as he came by on the road. I had to eliminate that. I was able to shoot a scene when they raided the hotel, but it didn't work very well. It got very boring, and it was so obvious a point that I finally decided to drop it. So I can't think of any compromises I made.

The only compromises were theoretically in terms of the cast. At a time like this [1980], it would be better—at that time [1968] I already was aware of that—to use Indians to play Indians. Not because Indians are better actors. In an absolutely free world, it wouldn't make any difference who played what as long as you were good enough for it. But it seemed the useful thing to have them in, but I couldn't find them at that time. And also [Universal] wanted four so-called "stars" in the picture. So that was the only compromise. It was either that or not make the picture. I was very pleased with how [the actors] did do the job. I have no complaints about that. But I don't think you could make a real Indian film today—I don't think I would anymore—nowadays I would think I would insist in a picture dealing with the liberation of the Indians or their problem, or the blacks, or anyone else, that they should play their own parts. You know, when our world is freer, anybody can play it. But at that particular time . . . well, it was earlier than now.

Audience Member: Could you discuss the striking visual style of the film?

Polonsky: There were two interesting things that we tried to do in this film. The photographer, Connie Hall, really stretched the saturated color to its limits. We scared the life out of the studio because they were afraid nothing would show up on TV. And they brought some pressure on us to change that. That was one of the things. The other thing was that since we were using Panavision, because it was desert and all that, I didn't want to concentrate the characters toward the center of the screen, because I wanted to use the entire Panavision frame. So a dialogue might take place between two characters one at one end of the screen and one at the other, some hundred feet away, and that would not show up on the TV screen. So those were the two technical problems we had with the studio. But they gave in on both of those. I really didn't have any trouble with them. They protested, but they gave in. The studio cooperated completely in making this picture.

McBride: Jennings Lang really went to bat for you.

Polonsky: Yes, he backed me all the way.

Audience Member: [Inaudible question about the climactic confrontation on Ruby Mountain between Sheriff Cooper and Willie Boy and why Willie has no bullets in his gun, allowing himself to be killed.] . . . Why did you compromise in that sense?

Polonsky: Well, I didn't consider it a compromise at that time. Maybe after discussing with you I will, you know? My mind is open to my errors. But the situation that occurs on the mountain is very clear. The sheriff is willing to take him as a prisoner. Willie is not going to be a prisoner. Therefore—he's not armed—he does what the old Westerns do: They're going to have a gunfight. But there is no gunfight. A gunfight is a *fraud*. Now that scene is better to do in terms of what we know in this particular picture than to show the scene where he would just be shooting and shooting and shooting and then, finally, they would kill him. Because they'd been doing that for hundreds of years. They've done it in every Western film. And it has no particular moral significance. It only has moral significance if there's a moral *issue* involved. The moral issue in this case is in terms of what happens to the sheriff who realizes, for a moment, that it's time to start to stop looking at the past and how we act, that we don't need any more souvenirs from the past. It's about time we *forgot* this dream and stop pretending to learn from it, and just changed our lives. Now he doesn't go that far, but that's all implied in the scene now, that's why I did it. It may have been better. The genocide which has been part of American history with relation to the Indian is a common fact. The isolation of that into this particular act, I think, makes it better for the picture. I don't know. That's what I thought then.

McBride: There's also a sense in which the entire chase is absurdist— Blake is chasing Redford more than Redford is chasing Blake.

Polonsky: Well, yeah, he played this game with him all the way through the thing, which actually happened.

McBride: If he'd wanted to get away, he could have easily gotten away. But he wanted to make a statement.

Polonsky: Ah, that's what I thought.

Audience Member: What is the meaning of the scene in which Redford puts his hand into Blake's palm print in the mud?

Polonsky: I don't know. Maybe we all come from monkeys. I don't know what that means. Maybe really they're brothers after all, you know. Even if they're going to kill each other. I mean, that's been our lives constantly, hasn't it?

McBride: There's also one tiny change you made from the book when Redford goes into a cabin and eats from a can of peaches. Blake says that there's a place where I can get some food, and then you see Redford appear there. Redford eats the food that's intended for Blake, which, again, symbolizes their kinship. But in reality, the whole posse ate the food . . .

Polonsky: Right.

McBride: . . . but you just made Redford do it.

Polonsky: Yeah. Well, the picture is very complicated in that way, you know, it's not only full of the intentions you have when you begin to make a picture, it's full of the intention you discover as you make it.

Audience Member: What eventually caused the film to be revived theatrically?

McBride: A couple years ago they did bring it back, because Blake and Redford are both much bigger stars now than they were at the time.

Blake was not very well known in 1969, but now he's done *Baretta*. And Redford has gone way up. It did play around again.

Polonsky: And they got a television version. One of the things that happens in the desert is that you have flash floods. I shot a scene like that. But after I saw it with the rest of the film, I decided that it broke the dryness of the film and I didn't use it. But when they made the TV version, they put it in, because it was quite a big scene, you know, it was very good. So I was pleased to see it on television, at least.

McBride: Seeing this film many times, you notice the great care Abe puts into the symbols, such as ones of sterility: there's a lot of emphasis on dust and rocks, small touches which add up to this tremendous feeling of the wasteland in the film. And the costumes—except for Sheriff Cooper's cool blue shirt and Dr. Arnold's light-blue dress when she goes to meet President Taft—are mostly earth-toned. It's a very somber, austere film.

Audience Member: Why was Susan Clark crying in the bedroom scene with Redford?

Polonsky: I felt like crying myself, but I . . . you mean the scene where she finds Redford in her bedroom?

Audience Member: Yes.

Polonsky: She thought that she was being humiliated by her own passion for this man. And therefore she wept as she was beginning to give into it. Because she really had this profound sensual relation to this man, and she was driven by it. But she had never wept before. She always attacked him before, as you saw in the previous scene. But in this scene, after what had gone on before that evening, she started to weep. And at that point, Redford walked out. He walked out for the same reason that he was only his father's son. What he should have done is taken advantage of her, of course. Because it shouldn't make any difference to him whether she's crying or not. After all, she's still human and therefore can be used. Right?

And so I felt in a way that—I mean, *Susan felt that*. I didn't tell her to cry. She started to play the scene, and she started to play the scene with anger, as usual. Then suddenly she started to cry, so we kept on shooting. And it was much better. I think if you can learn from a woman, you should. [*Audience laughter and applause*]

Audience Member: I have one question about the character played by Katharine Ross. Are we to assume that Lola took her own life? She was found in the wedding dress . . .
Polonsky: Yes.

Audience Member: . . . in order to free him?
Polonsky: Yes, so he would be free to run. Without it, he would be caught. Therefore she took her own life.

McBride: Don't you think there's a real ambiguity about that in the film, though?
Polonsky: Well, naturally, I made it so you couldn't tell. Because in the real story, he may have shot her himself, actually, when they were very closely pursued, because he wasn't going to let his wife—she was his wife by then—fall into the hands of the posse. So he killed her. Then he himself, instead of getting away, made a long turn around and came back and faced them. And see, not that he knew he can win, but he felt that that was what he had to do. I thought by leaving it ambiguous, in this particular case, it made it more relevant to *our* situation rather than their situation.

McBride: In real life, she was shot in the back, wasn't she?
Polonsky: Yeah, yeah.

McBride: Which means that he had to have done it?
Polonsky: Yeah. But at that point he was just fulfilling something in himself. And I thought it would be much better if she participated in some way in that action, or at least she might have participated in the action. Therefore their relationship became more interesting, I thought, and more real.

McBride: I thought of a line that Dalton Trumbo said a few years ago—another blacklisted screenwriter—this line caused a lot of controversy—but I think it could apply to *Willie Boy*. He said that during the blacklist there were no villains or heroes, there were "only victims." And he implied that the persecutors were victims too and . . .
Polonsky: Ah, yes, but different times. Just the way that the Nazis were victims too of history. But you know, everybody's a victim of history. It depends which part of the camp you're in. I never agreed with Dalton when he said that. I mean, I don't feel viciously towards them anymore

because they're too far away, like the Greeks and the Romans. *Of course* we're all victims of history. But we're all actors in history too. And we're different kinds of victims. There are the victims who are the victors and there are the victims who are those who are destroyed. So I don't agree with him in that way. It's always better to be the kind of victor who's a victor, isn't it? Those are the ones who run history. [*Audience laughter*]

McBride: Well, time vindicates.
Polonsky: Time vindicates everything, Joe.

Interview with Abraham Polonsky and Walter Bernstein

Robert Siegel / 1993

From *The NPR Interviews*, ed. Robert Siegel (Boston: Houghton Mifflin, 1994), 62–67. © 1993 National Public Radio, Inc. NPR news report titled "Blacklisted Writers Reflected Upon" was originally broadcast on NPR's *All Things Considered* on June 14, 1993, and is used with the permission of NPR. Any unauthorized duplication is strictly prohibited.

Walter Bernstein and Abraham Polonsky talk to Robert Siegel about writing the early CBS television program *You Are There* when they were blacklisted during the McCarthy era. The two men, together with the late Arnold Manoff, submitted scripts through fronts, individuals who lent their politically acceptable by-lines to the banned writers' works, to the producer Charles Russell, who was in on the ruse. Polonsky's long-unacknowledged *You Are There* teleplays were assembled and published by California State University at Northridge.

Polonsky: It's very bad and very sad that Arnold Manoff and Charles Russell are dead. It's very sad that all the scripts, the wonderful scripts, that Arnie wrote shouldn't be made available with the name of the proper author on them. His show on Socrates, remember, Walter? I think that was picked up by the Museum of Modern Art as one of the better shows that they had, right?

Bernstein: Yes.

Polonsky: They got some prize of something. So I think these things should be made known. Walter and I can defend ourselves with lies, but he can't.

Siegel: Walter Bernstein, what did you do as the outside man?

Bernstein: I had been working in television. It was then live television, before Abe and Arnie Manoff came from the coast. I had had certain credits under my own name and I knew certain producers, like Russell, so I was able to go to Russell in particular, and say, "I have these two friends who are here and they are very good writers and how about using them on the show?" He was very amenable to it.

Siegel: Did he know that you were blacklisted?

Bernstein: He was the one who told me when he was the producer of *Danger*, which was the show before *You Are There*. Oh, yes, he knew we were all blacklisted.

Siegel: Your friends from the coast? He knew that when you were speaking of Polonsky and Manoff that they too were blacklisted?

Bernstein: Oh, I told him that, and his concern was only that he be able to tell his bosses upstairs that there was a real, live person whom they could see on demand.

Siegel: So the three of you would be able to write this new television program, *You Are There*, provided that you each had a front who would be the body?

Bernstein: Yes, that was an absolute requisite.

Siegel: Did the three of you meet frequently?

Bernstein: As often as possible. We would meet in Steinberg's Dairy Restaurant of Broadway.

Polonsky: And don't forget Max the waiter.

Bernstein: We had a waiter named Max who couldn't figure out who we were because we looked like bums but we would occasionally throw around big numbers and money and things like that. We would be talking about scripts, but he wouldn't know. He came to us one day and he said he had finally figured out who we were and what we did, and we said "What?" and he said, "You're in the wholesale fruit business."

Polonsky: [*laughs*] That's right.

Bernstein: [*laughs*] I don't know how he put that together.

Polonsky: Because Arnie looked like he worked at the produce market.

Siegel: Arnold Manoff?

Bernstein: Yes. But we would meet regularly, usually there or at one of our houses.

Siegel: For people who don't remember this program at all, for those who are too young or who didn't watch television at the time, we should say that after an introduction by Walter Cronkite [who was not yet the anchorman of the evening news], CBS news correspondents like Mike Wallace and Bill Leonard would cover an event as if it were a live television event. One of them was "The Crisis of Galileo." That's in your collection of screenplays, Mr. Polonsky. Did you choose that subject?

Polonsky: It came up in a discussion probably at the restaurant one day and I got it because I knew who Galileo was. The others weren't quite sure.

Bernstein: That was not a subject that CBS would have chosen.

Siegel: Yes, tell me about writing Galileo for CBS.

Polonsky: I understood his scientific importance and I understood also the moral problem involved in his life, which was very similar to the moral problems involved in the lives of many people around us at the time. So it was historically accurate, even though it was told in terms of the nature of those times, and I did not move away from what happened historically. Nevertheless, it was significant at that moment in terms of what was going on in the United States. The significant event in his life was when he was challenged by the church to say he didn't believe in his own theory and that he would report anybody to the church who in any way violated the rules of the church about the nature of the universe at that time, and Galileo said he would do that.

Bernstein: After they showed him the instruments of torture, I believe. Do you remember that?

Polonsky: In the original script I wrote, they threatened him, but Charlie Russell, the producer, when he had the show written, he ran down to the Catholic Church headquarters in New York and said that it was too violent or something.

Siegel: You mean they ran the script past the archdiocese to see if they would object to your depiction?

Polonsky: Bill Dozier did, the executive producer, and then told Charlie what he had done. Charlie got around the problem by having the conference take place in front of the instruments of torture. So it was obvious what was going to happen to Galileo if he did not change his opinion.

Siegel: When you wrote a program like that, you must have been consciously, if in a muted way, protesting against the McCarthy era of the day.

Polonsky: I would characterize our writing of all those scripts as the only guerilla warfare waged against McCarthyism at that time on television.

Siegel: Three of you, blacklisted, working through fronts in cahoots with the producer Charles Russell.

Bernstein: And the director, Sidney Lumet.

Siegel: You were able to write in "The Tragedy of John Milton," or Arnold Manoff in "The Salem Witch Trials," about many a historical incident that was equally about the 1950s.

Polonsky: Walter did too, a great many of the shows.

Bernstein: "The Death of Socrates" we did. What Abe said was essentially true. We were very consciously trying to say something about the period we were living in.

Siegel: How did this system come to an end?

Polonsky: Walter, you tell him.

Bernstein: It came to an end when two things happened, mainly. They moved the show to California and put it on film; our shows were live. Lumet was no longer associated with it, nor was Russell, and we remained in New York, where we lived.

Polonsky: Bill Dozier, as a matter of fact, Walter, was going to the West Coast.

Siegel: He was the executive producer who took it out to California?

Polonsky: Yes, it was for a big job at CBS out there. He wanted to take one of the shows with him and he wanted to take *You Are There*, which was a prestigious show at that time, but the CBS executives in New York didn't want to let him do that, so Dozier said, "Well, these shows are being written by blacklisted writers." He knew that all along, as a matter of fact.

Bernstein: Yes, he always did.

Polonsky: In fact, I think it was on the jazz show, he once told Charlie, "That's a good script Abe wrote." I don't know how he knew that.

Siegel: But you are saying that he disclosed that so that he could get the show moved to California with him.

Polonsky: They were eager to get rid of everybody connected to the show and go out to the West Coast, and then Dozier discovered out there that it wasn't so easy doing the show.

Bernstein: No.

Polonsky: He also discovered that the best thing was not to treat any subject that had any significance whatsoever.

Bernstein: This show was not successful out there, once it moved to the coast, for a number of reasons.

Polonsky: The main reason was they abandoned the subject matter.

Bernstein: They wouldn't deal with historical conflict; they wouldn't touch anything.

Siegel: For many of us growing up after the war, *You Are There* was the program where we first encountered Walter Cronkite, reading an introduction and a conclusion to every program that summarized what it was about.

Bernstein: Abe wrote that final marvelous thing that Cronkite said at the end.

Siegel: Which I would like to hear the true writer of read for us in a moment, but first, did Walter Cronkite know, Abe Polonsky, that you, that a blacklisted writer, were the author of these immortal words?

Polonsky: I don't think he knew. He may have suspected, but it was better not to know. That was the age of it being better not to know anything.

Siegel: Abraham Polonsky, could you read for us the line that Walter Cronkite used to say?

Polonsky: I would be happy to read, but I don't have it here, but let's see if I can remember it. "It was a day like all days, filled with . . ."

Bernstein: Excuse me. He started by saying, "What kind of a day was it?"

Polonsky: Thank you, Walter. "What kind of a day was it? A day like all days, filled with those events that alter and illuminate our times . . . and you were there."

Interview with Abraham Polonsky

Paul Buhle and Dave Wagner / 1997

From *Tender Comrades: A Backstory of the Hollywood Blacklist* by Patrick McGilligan and Paul Buhle (New York: St. Martin's, 1997), 481–94. Reprinted by permission of the authors.

Abraham Lincoln Polonsky, the son of a Jewish pharmacist, grew up in New York and graduated from City College and the Columbia Law School. He taught at City College and started writing for radio, scripting episodes of *The Goldbergs*, during the mid-1930s. By the end of the decade he was also writing for *Columbia Workshop Theatre* and Orson Welles's *Mercury Theatre of the Air*. As he continued working on plays and fiction, he visited Hollywood for the first time in 1937. But instead of immediately attempting a career there alongside so many other left-wing writers, he made a political choice. For two crucial years when the American labor movement was at the apex of both its influence and its collective idealism, he operated as educational director and newspaper editor of a regional CIO union north of New York City.

Right before World War II, Polonsky had a novel serialized in *Collier's* that attracted renewed attention from Hollywood. But military duty took precedence. After serving with the Office of Strategic Services [the OSS, the wartime precursor of the Central Intelligence Agency], at times behind the lines in France. Polonsky returned to Hollywood at last, in 1945. After a disappointing start at Paramount, he became the leading scenarist for Enterprise, the best of the new, small production companies. With the hit boxing film *Body and Soul* under his belt, Polonsky then wrote and directed *Force of Evil*, considered by critics to be one of the best films noirs of the era, an intensely poetic, radically stylized work that nonetheless managed to observe the conventions of the crime genre. A script for *I Can Get It for You Wholesale*, produced while Polonsky was out of the country, rounded out his Hollywood life before the black-list drove him out of the industry.

Polonsky had better luck than most of the blacklistees. In collaboration with Arnold Manoff and Walter Bernstein, he pseudonymously wrote the great majority of the scripts for one of television's "quality" shows, *You Are There*. In 1959, he wrote, without credit, a caper film for Harry Belafonte, *Odds Against Tomorrow*, the first of what was intended to become a series of projects with African American stars and themes but which, like so many other blacklistees' projects of those days, failed to materialize. His "comeback" film, *Madigan*, directed by Don Siegel, is regarded as a classic cop drama, the model for Clint Eastwood's Dirty Harry series. *Tell Them Willie Boy Is Here* was one of the most unusual westerns of the late 1960s. *Romance of a Horse Thief*, which Polonsky took over as both scenarist and director in mid-production, offered a radical version of *Fiddler on the Roof*, the pre-Holocaust Eastern European Jewish saga as only an unbroken Marxist could tell it. Although they have their bright moments, his last two credits, *Avalanche Express* and *Monsignor*, were poorly received; in any event, both were impersonal jobs over which Polonsky exercised little control.

Question: When and why did you join the Communist Party?
Abraham Polonsky: I joined the Party very late, after I got out of college, around 1935 or 1936, at the time of the Spanish Civil War. It was kind of funny, because I wasn't "joining" in the usual sense—I was already meeting with some of these people, mostly other instructors at City College, who were all members of the Anti-Fascist League. I myself taught English literature at City College from 1935 until the war started.

I came from a family of Socialists. Philosophically, I was always a materialist and a leftist. And I never felt alone. I came of age in a country that had come to a standstill, with fifty million people unemployed and the banks closed. I voted for FDR, and the New Deal was "left" enough for many of us.

Question: What effect did your work in the Party in the thirties have on your development as a writer?
Polonsky: It didn't shape my artistic goals at all, because I had already taken a position of wanting to do socially significant art. The theoretical work of Marxism that everyone was talking about then I had already done. That kind of discussion with other Party members gave the po-

litical work around me some kind of intellectual basis. But we quarreled with the Party leadership, right from the beginning, on the various issues of writing. In our branch, anyway, at least among ourselves, we isolated the Philistines.

Question: Let's go straight to Hollywood. When you arrived, you were already under contract.

Polonsky: Little, Brown published, as a book, a serial I wrote, *The Enemy Sea*. It was a potboiler which I wrote in three weeks. But it was a good story. I had been to sea, briefly, as an ordinary seaman when I left school, and I knew the subject. Paramount signed me to a deal which gave me fifteen or twenty thousand dollars on the rights and a job as a writer on staff. However, even before I received the contract, I went overseas to serve in the OSS [Office of Strategic Services].

When I got back, I took a military plane and went to see [producer] Bill [William] Dozier at Paramount. His secretary was Meta Reis. He kept me waiting, and I started calling him all kinds of names—to her. Either she told him what names I was calling him or he overheard me. In any case, when he finally called me in, he said, "You may have a contract, but you're not going to work here." I put a letter from [OSS director] Bill [William] Donovan on his desk, saying that the OSS was going to issue a story covering my new career in Hollywood, which it did. Dozier had no choice. My job was protected by a law that had been passed to preserve the jobs of GIs when they returned from the war. But behind my back Dozier said, "Fire that son-of-a-bitch as soon as you get a chance."

Question: How did you learn to write screenplays?

Polonsky: I didn't have to learn how to write screenplays. I took one look at them and knew. That's not quite true. When I went to Paramount, I made sure I saw every movie they had in stock. On the other hand, I really didn't know how to direct. But I didn't come out to Hollywood looking to become a screenwriter or a director. I came here because I had a job waiting for me.

Question: But you had a longstanding interest in movies.

Polonsky: I had an interest going back to childhood. In the Bronx, where I spent part of my boyhood, the Saturday movies influenced our daily play for the rest of the week. I grew up with movies.

But I started out in radio. The first time I visited Hollywood was in

1937, as a guest of Gertrude Berg, when I was writing for her radio show [*The Goldbergs*]. I was met by a *New Yorker* writer who asked me, "What the hell are you doing here? I'm trying to make enough money to get back to New York." He never could make enough money, because he drank it all up. He told me, "I'm going to show you how terrible everything is here." He took me on a set, and it was terrible—to him. He complained, "You see? This is what it's all about—chaos." But my reaction was, "This is wonderful!" All the small, marvelous details of film production I loved.

Question: Your first film credit was at Paramount, with *Golden Earrings*, a wartime romance with Ray Milland and Marlene Dietrich. Everyone remembers her line "I luff you, English."
Polonsky: My script was about how the Gypsies became the first victims of the Holocaust. The studio cut all that out. They made it comic.

Question: Then you moved into a much smaller, independent operation, Enterprise, where you got the assignment for *Body and Soul*. Wasn't the story based originally on the life of the boxer Barney Ross?
Polonsky: Arnold Manoff, who was also at Paramount, had been working on the Barney Ross story for six months. But Ross, a famous Jewish boxer, was a drug user, and even though he was also a war hero, the studio eventually decided that they didn't want to make a movie about him.[1] Whatever Manoff wrote the studio wouldn't accept. So finally, one day, he was about to leave Paramount, and I happened to be visiting him in his office. He said to me, "Abe, I'm going back to New York. I can't stand this. They never make anything I like." And then, "By the way, do you know John Garfield?" When I said, "Yeah," he said, "Let's go over and visit him at Enterprise."

Enterprise was two blocks away from Paramount, and while I was walking over I was also thinking of a boxing story for Garfield. And here comes the story that is *Body and Soul*. I got to Enterprise, and I told it to Garfield and his producer [Bob Roberts], and they loved it. Immediately they called a meeting of the heads of the studio and of production, and I told the story again. Now, since I'd had about an hour to think about it, I had a complete story.

I started to leave, and Charles Einfeld—he was the second in command—said, "Where are you going, Polonsky?" I said, "I'm under contract to Paramount; don't you know that?" Einfeld said, "What should we do now that you've told us this story?" I said, "Get a writer; I'll make you a present of this story." And I left. I got to the gate at Paramount, and a guy stopped me and said, "They want you in the main office."

Question: So you were loaned out from Paramount.
Polonsky: From then on, I was a two-thousand-dollar-a-week writer, even though I only got one thousand of it. Paramount got the rest. That was a lot of money. *Body and Soul* turned out to be a tremendous success. My script is the fundamental reason it turned out the way it did, although it was a wonderful job that James Wong Howe did. He had decided to use cameramen with experience at the battlefront, who had learned how to use hand-held cameras, in order to get some really unusual shots. That made *Body and Soul* kind of special for the time.

Question: Enterprise didn't have that many hits.
Polonsky: Right. And no matter where you are working in Hollywood, there's nothing like having a hit. I went to see *Body and Soul* the first time it was being shown to the public at a preview. During the last part of the movie, the audience got up and started taking sides. People were arguing about Garfield's character, Charlie, when he faced the big decision of his life—"He should do this"; "No, he should do that"—as if the real thing were happening before their eyes. I never saw anything like that in a movie theater before. The head of the studio, Arthur Loew, turned to me and shouted, "It's a hit!" I said, "Maybe it's just a lot of noise." He said, "No, no, it's a hit!"

Question: Robert Rossen was, of course, the director. How well did you know Rossen?
Polonsky: He was a good Warner Bros. writer; he made their kind of "social" pictures. He had that idea of himself.

Question: His pictures frequently seem a mishmash of blue-collar melodrama and art film, as though he had always wanted to do both types of films and constantly mixed them up.
Polonsky: You have him down cold.

Question: Was your script so tightly written that you were virtually codirecting?
Polonsky: No one codirects with Robert Rossen. You keep trying to prevent him from spoiling the picture, and writers hardly ever win those

fights. We made Rossen promise that he wouldn't change a line of the screenplay, and then we found out he was handing out pages on the set, anyway. That was in his character.

I made sure he wouldn't change the picture in any substantial way. I was able to win a big fight about the ending because of my relationship to Garfield and [producer Bob] Roberts. Rossen wanted Garfield to go out and be killed, with his head stuffed into an ash barrel or something like that, which was just crazy. We shot both endings, his and mine.[2] When Rossen saw them both, he said mine was better.

Question: People say that when Rossen, one of the original Hollywood Nineteen subpoenaed by Congress, didn't make the cut as one of the Ten, he was outraged. He thought that he was the great Hollywood Communist artist.

Polonsky: You wouldn't want to be on a desert island with Rossen, because if the two of you didn't have any food, he might want to have you for lunch tomorrow. The Communist Party was for years the best social club in Hollywood. You'd meet a lot of interesting people, there were parties, and it created a nice social atmosphere. He loved that. He was the kind of a guy who would go to public left-wing meetings and get up and say, "I donate a thousand dollars!" He never paid the money that he pledged. But he always got the applause. He was talented like Elia Kazan was talented, but like Kazan he also had a rotten character. In the end they both became stool pigeons. I figured all along that Rossen couldn't be trusted, but no one asked me.

Question: Although Enterprise was not purely a left-wing operation, it relied heavily on various talented leftists, including you, Garfield, Rossen, Roberts, Manoff, Carl Foreman, and John Berry. Did that give you extra leverage to do projects your own way?

Polonsky: At Enterprise I was God, thanks to *Body and Soul*. I was the only one who had made that much money for them. Therefore, they thought that I could fix anything for them. For instance, one day Einfeld came to see me and said, "Ginger Rogers wants a picture made, and she says she'd like to talk to you." And Garfield insisted, "Go up and see her!" So I did. She wore a fur bikini outfit, and she took me down to her cellar and made me a black-and-white ice cream soda. She was very affable and nice. Since for those particular two seconds I was the most famous writer at Enterprise, she wanted me to write her picture. She had some book, and I took it and sketched out a possible story line for her. But I didn't do any real work on it. I didn't want to work on a Ginger Rogers picture. I already knew that I wanted to direct my own picture.

Question: It's surprising that she would pick you, given that she was well known, along with her mother, for expressing conservative political views.

Polonsky: There's no vehemence against good writers working on a script. The vehemence comes before and after—before because "I can't get you," after because "You didn't do what I said."

Question: How did *Force of Evil* come about?

Polonsky: Garfield said, "You want to direct? So direct!"—with him as the star, which would make it possible. "But," he said, "it has to be a 'melo'"—pronounced "meller," that is, a melodrama. We never called it a "melodrama"; we always said a "melo."

I knew a novel, *Tucker's People* by Ira Wolfert, which was about the numbers racket. I got Wolfert to come out here, and he stayed at Donald Ogden Stewart's house on the beach. There we broke the story down into what it needed to become a picture. I said to Wolfert, "I have to write the final screenplay, but you draft one and we'll see if there is something in it that we can use." Then I gave him coscript credit even though I didn't use anything in his screenplay except the lines from the book.

Question: The book and the film show that it is an illusion to think that honest liberals and conservatives are going to clean up crime and make society better.

Polonsky: Here's a story Wolfert told me: he happened to be riding up in an elevator in the New York Supreme Court building with Governor Thomas Dewey, who had just arrested some big politicians and supposedly cleaned out the numbers racket. Dewey was getting ready to run for president in 1948 and boasting about his great victory over organized crime. Wolfert said to him, "If you promise in advance that you won't do anything about it, I can teach you something right now." Dewey accepted the offer. Then Wolfert asked Dewey, "How much would you like to bet on a number? The elevator operator right here will take your bet." The policy racket had simply moved the elevator operators to different locations. Nothing had changed.

I'm the son of a pharmacist, *il dottore*, from a Sicilian neighborhood on the East Side where we lived after the Bronx. The Sicilians didn't teach me about organized crime; it was part of everyday neighborhood life. If your kid couldn't get a job, you went to Tammany, but you needed to have an old man with you. This old man was part of the organization. Thanks to him, you got a job pushing a cart someplace. It wasn't much, but you were working. According to this ethic, you had to take care of everybody. Meanwhile, the alderman made his visit to every store for a donation. Part of the money went to Tammany, part of it went to the organization.

Question: Did you have any feeling that *Body and Soul* had been compromised by Rossen, and that *Force of Evil* offered a second chance to reach the same blue-collar audience with a more sophisticated message?
Polonsky: When you talk about the political problems of film production, it was not just Rossen, it was the whole system. You have to talk about what it means to be a radical working in a conventional medium, with certain kinds of aesthetic interests forced on you by the studio and certain kinds of aesthetic interests that you utilize out of the studio material. You also have to realize that we were in the film business not to change the world but to make films. To change the world we were involved in other kinds of things, like the labor struggle in Hollywood, against the studios and against the right-wing union, the IATSE [International Alliance of Theatrical Stage Employees].

Question: You have described *Force of Evil* as an avant-garde work. Is it avant-garde in the same sense as the postwar European movies?
Polonsky: I mean avant-garde in the full sense of any modern art. And it is avant-garde. Garfield put up with all of that. He was marvelous. I did almost everything but cast the film. I was trying for one unified expression, and I got it! The film's moral standards are completely different from other films' standards—every act of love is also an act of betrayal.

In writing the script I was constantly thinking, "Am I pressing forward, getting a different view of everything?" I was afraid that once I was finished, they'd throw me out of town; they'd never let me make another movie. Of course, I didn't succeed completely, and I had all this trouble with the Hays Office all the way through the picture. And they did throw me out of town, anyway, but for other reasons.

Question: The film certainly breaks rules. Nothing is "right" in the standard Hollywood sense of making criminals pay for their actions. What problems did you have with the censors?
Polonsky: I was breaking every single rule that the censors had. We

went full out, and it drove them crazy. They constantly said, "You can't do that." The biggest problem the censors had was that the Garfield character, the syndicate lawyer, doesn't want to improve humanity; he just wants revenge! I had to leave out the word "revenge," because according to the official rules you couldn't want "revenge"; you had to want "justice." I made it about as ambiguous as I could make it.

Question: Did you have any difficulty directing actors for the first time?
Polonsky: Two of the principal actors, Tommy [Thomas] Gomez and one of the actresses, were gay; they both had their lovers on the set. Even so, Gomez and this actress couldn't act together. They hated each other. I asked a friend, "Are all homosexual actors that way?" No gay people that I knew were like that at all. He said, "No, these two just don't like each other." Then he explained a John Ford trick to me. You shoot one of them, and then you shoot the other. When you join them on film, it looks as though they're acting together in the same scene. As actors the two of them were marvelous—but alone, not together.

Question: What kinds of discussions did you have with the cinematographer, George Barnes, about shooting the film?
Polonsky: We shot one day to see what the footage was going to look like, and I realized that for years George had been shooting all these female stars who were too old to be glamorous; they were fiftyish, and his job was to make them look thirty-seven. He was using a lot of diffusion and soft focus and stuff like that. He had started to shoot the same way for our picture. I said, "No, this is all wrong." He asked, "So what do you want?" Remember, he was famous, and I was new. I went out and got a book of Edward Hopper's Third Avenue paintings, and I brought it to him and said, "That's what I want." He said, "Why didn't you say so! Single-source lighting!" [Laughs]. And that made the picture look the way it does,

Question: How involved were you with the score? The film's composer, David Raksin, was one more left-wing coworker who would later become a friendly witness.[3]
Polonsky: Before I made *Tell Them Willie Boy Is Here*, I didn't have the nerve to challenge the scoring. I knew that the music in *Force of Evil* was wrong, but I couldn't do anything about it. At the end of the story, the music soars, although the picture is going the other way. That is when I realized that musicians are stupid—like actors, soundmen, everybody.

Everybody but the director is stupid! [Laughs] All Hollywood composers try to tell the story of the picture, as they understand it, through the music. But it's not always the director's idea of the story.

A few years later, at the time of the HUAC hearings, Raksin asked, "Would you mind if I used your name in my testimony? Everyone has already named you, anyway." I told him, "If you want to be a rat, you have to be a rat." He also offered me something as a consolation: "I can lend you money, you know." He wanted to bribe me, in a friendly way. I never forgot that.

Question: Let's talk for a moment about one of the most famous scenes in the film, the so-called million-dollar-ruby scene. It takes place in the back of a taxi, where Garfield tempts his girlfriend—played by Beatrice Pearson—with an imaginary jewel. He expects her to reach out and take it, even though it represents a life of crime. It is a light, very seductive scene. Then, suddenly, it turns very dark. Garfield begins to contrast her willingness to be tempted for pure pleasure with his brother's refusal to join the numbers syndicate, to accept his share of the profits.

Let me just read these few lines of Garfield's as he stares out the cab window: "To go to great expense for something you want—that's natural. To reach out and take it—that's human, that's natural. But to get your pleasure from not taking, by cheating yourself deliberately, like my brother did today, from not getting, not taking—don't you see what a black thing that is for a man to do?"

This, to me, sounds a lot like William Blake when he said, with poetic hyperbole, that not to act on a wish is worse than killing a child. This logic is entirely contrary to what liberals—and Socialists and Communists—have always preached about revolutionary self-sacrifice.

Polonsky: That's right. It sounds like Blake, but it's really Polonsky. Garfield tries to win this brother over to being part of a bigger syndicate. He promises him, "I've come here to help you. I'll put you up in the clouds." Gomez won't listen to it and replies, "No, no, no." Gomez was great in that scene.

Incidentally, that was my whole attitude toward the Communist Party and its lack of understanding of what makes people tick. When I was a district educational director of the CIO, and we had to run a union election against the right-wing faction, we offered jobs in return for votes. After we won, the Party officials congratulated themselves, "We won because we're right, not because we could buy votes." I was brought up around the Tammany Hall machine, so I knew that wasn't true.

Question: In the conclusion of *Force of Evil*, in a remarkable sequence of shots, Garfield walks all the way down from the bridge, on a series of stone staircases, to the rocks along the river, to recover his brother's body. It's an incredibly effective montage, figuratively showing Garfield descending deeper into his own guilt, taking responsibility for the murder of his brother. Some people think this sequence is inspired by similar scenes in *Battleship Potemkin*. Is there any sense in which this was an homage to Eisenstein?

Polonsky: It's my homage to Polonsky, who knows his own streets—my city and my bridge and my steps, the most normal thing in the world for me to write about. Eisenstein would have enjoyed it, just as I enjoy Eisenstein.

Question: The film doesn't present any hopeful alternatives. Unlike most other films, there isn't a single character to articulate the ideals of humanity.

Polonsky: That's right. The film is unrelenting, hard-boiled all the way through, and very well shot for that purpose by the cameraman. By 1948 lefties knew this social change was not going to happen so simply; the old straightforward plan of working-class triumph wouldn't work anymore. Of course, the Communist Party went on repeating the old words, like a religion. Even when things didn't work out the way they had planned, they kept the words.

But something new was needed. It had to come. We needed to learn not from economics, which repeats the past, but from biology, from the biological innovations in nature which go in new directions and never repeat. Socialism had to be a biological invention, in that sense. Otherwise, everything, all history, became just the story of a bunch of crooks—as we've learned from all the defeats and disappointments since.

Question: Let's move on to *I Can Get It for You Wholesale*, for which you wrote a screen adaptation. The novel was a best-seller about the needle trades in New York, a satire about a Jewish labor organizer who takes union members out on strike and then cynically forms his own company and breaks the strike. The satire traded pretty fiercely in stereotypes. Zanuck is supposed to have said to you, "Fix this into a movie. The book's anti-Semitic."

Polonsky: He didn't say it to me; he said it to [producer] Sol Siegel. The studio brought the author, Jerome Weidman, to Hollywood, and Zanuck asked him, "Can you change it?" Weidman said to Zanuck, "But I sold it to you!" Zanuck didn't give up: "Can you change it?" Weidman said, "Not me—but why not make the lead a woman?"

I was just about to leave for France when they called me in to do the script. I knew the book, of course, and I said, "Let's make it on the woman question," this is, on the issue of women's equality. So we made the lead a woman. She was played by Susan Hayward, a very fine actress who was perfect for the part.[4]

Question: The Sam Jaffe character, the old tailor who runs the shop, doesn't appear in the novel at all. His appearance seems unmistakable as the film's conscience and the means by which you confront the anti-Semitism of the novel, through a *zeyde*, or grandfather, figure who speaks with an obvious Yiddish accent. Where did he come from?
Polonsky: Everything is meant to blunt the anti-Semitism of the novel. There's no anti-Semitism in the film. The Sam Jaffe character was my invention—the voice of experience. That character came from my own life. I had a grandmother like that; we all had grandmothers like that.

In fact, there's where I first learned to tell stories. I heard from my mother's mother all the stories that I would someday need. She used to get the stories out of the [*Jewish Daily*] *Forward*, stories that were translated into Yiddish to educate the Socialist readers.[5] Later on in life, I realized that I had learned from her the stories of Tom Sawyer and Huck Finn, who happened, according to her version, to be Jewish boys on the Volga, with a Russian serf in the role of Jim, instead of gentiles on the Mississippi. I probably heard twenty percent of the *Arabian Nights* stories that way, and even two George Eliot novels. She read all this stuff, then told me all these stories in Yiddish. Incidentally, she wasn't the only one in the family to vote Socialist, so did my father. And my aunt, as I wrote in my novel *Zenia's Way*, actually went back to the Soviet Union after the Revolution.

Question: Susan Hayward in the film is trying to fit into a man's world. There is a crowd scene with Dan Dailey in which he confronts her, insisting that she subordinate her career to his. Susan Hayward makes a speech that is considerably more feminist in your draft of the script than in the final film. Did you know the script was being changed, and did anybody consult you?
Polonsky: At the time, I had left Hollywood to write a novel. I was in the south of France when the film was shot, although I had some control through Michael Gordon, the director, who was blacklisted briefly

before he turned "friendly" in front of the Committee. The ending in particular had to be suitable to Zanuck. Despite all of her resistance to Dailey's courting of her, which she sees as an attempt to push her out of the business, Hayward still has to go for Dailey in the end.

Question: Wasn't there a vast canyon between theory and practice in the Communist Party in Hollywood?
Polonsky: Certainly, it was unsafe to jump across. But those who tried it were a rather large group, considering the small size of the Communist Party within the United States at large. Many of the Hollywood Communists had been attracted to the Communist Party because of the Russian Revolution earlier on—as a memory of childhood, so to speak—and the Depression, plus the Spanish Civil War, had made them feel that it was important to be a Communist. In that way, and in that way only, could people overcome what they felt was the major thrust of political action in the world, which was becoming Fascist.

Question: Although progressive people in Hollywood became Communists for idealistic reasons, the working situation demanded a political and artistic synthesis that very often turned out to be elusive.
Polonsky: There's nothing unusual about that. Communists in New York and elsewhere often said that coming to Hollywood and writing films was a sellout. Why would anybody in his right mind write stupid pictures about ideas that he didn't really possess, when what he really and truly wanted to do was make a revolution and bring Socialism to the United States? Even many of the Hollywood writers who were Communists also thought it was a terrible or at least questionable thing to be a Hollywood writer.

However, you can't possibly explain the Hollywood Communists away by saying, "They came to Hollywood for the money," although indeed they did. You can't possibly say that they came for the glamour, although some did, in fact. If they had come only for money and glamour, a lot more of them would have become stool pigeons—to hold their jobs, to continue making money and doing pictures. But only a small percentage of them became stool pigeons.

According to Marxist theory, no decent pictures could be made in Hollywood. In the meetings of the Hollywood clubs—a word we preferred to "cells"—one of the great discussions that used to go on all the time was: Should I be in Hollywood, and should I be writing movies? Or should I, say, do documentaries? Or should I try to make films apart from Holly-wood that would in some way deal with the theoretical basis of why we are in fact in the Communist Party? This dilemma was not solved, and it couldn't be solved, because it was artificial and didn't exist. Filmmaking in the major studios is the prime way that film art exists. That doesn't mean that film, as an art form, doesn't exist apart from the studios. But when you want to get into making movies, and if you're fascinated with movies and care about movies, then there's only one thing to do: you try to make feature films for studios. It may not be the best solution to an artistic problem. It may end in the total defeat of every impulse that the writer, the director, and the actor has. But the fact of the matter is, that's the only choice, and that is why so many people who became Commu-nists in Hollywood didn't rush to go elsewhere.

The left-wing writers took themselves the most seriously, fighting within the industry for content. They had the tendency to confuse aes-thetics with content, which was normal. Meanwhile, the high-toned discussions of literary people about film made matters still more con-fused. Arguments in the high-class magazines were based on criticism of the other arts, distant from film. Film is a unique medium. There's some-thing extraordinary about seeing someone of a screen, and if you don't understand that it's extraordinary, then you don't understand how films are made or the strange effect that film has on people—that is to say, film's "magic."

Question: How well did the Hollywood left understand its efforts in theoretical terms, that is, in terms of Marxism?
Polonsky: The Party was a kind of social club here. A lot of people talk-ing about Marxism were certainly not Marxists. They took the ideas seri-ously, but they didn't understand Marxism in any sophisticated way, and so there was a gap in all their lives and work. I'm not criticizing them; it's just a fact. Albert Maltz, in particular, was funny. He came to dinner years after the blacklist and said to me, "I didn't have to become a member of the CP. I could have done all the same things without being a member." I said, "Done what? You wouldn't have thought that way at all. Your tal-ent resides in the fact that you embraced a political philosophy that you still don't understand." I wasn't trying to hurt his feelings. It's like the effect of religion on artists—you don't have to understand your religion in order to get the effect; you just believe. Albert joined, and he was a believer, but he was never really a Marxist.

Question: Are you referring in part to the famous 1946 meeting, in Morris Carnovsky's basement,[6] where only a handful of you in the Party supported Maltz's[7] position of artistic freedom against the New Masses editors? Party leaders had demanded the submission of artists.

Polonsky: Right. When Albert wrote that article in the New Masses, and the fools in New York came down on him, Johnny Weber and Arnie Manoff and I decided to support him. We didn't know that he was about to go downtown to Party headquarters and make his peace with them and agree to take back his opinions.

Question: That sort of typifies the limits of the Communist Party's creative contribution to screenwriting—from above.

Polonsky: The Party style of Marxism didn't have a chance here, or in New York either, among intellectuals. The leadership's behavior violated the whole intellectual life of Marxism, and the Party itself also did that constantly. Look how they ran their magazines and newspapers, with such a heavy hand. I had my fights with them.

Question: What would happen when the Party's cultural commissar, V. J. Jerome, or one of the others came out from New York to lay down the line?

Polonsky: He would raise hell with about eleven people. We didn't give a shit. The cultural leadership obviously didn't know what they were talking about. We ignored them out here, and we did a lot of wonderful things despite them.

Notes

1. Eventually the Barney Ross story was made as *Monkey on My Back*, directed by André de Doth, in 1957.

2. In Polonsky's ending, the corrupt boxing promoter (played by Lloyd Gough) threatens Charlie Davis (John Garfield) after he wins a fight he earlier agreed to throw. "What makes you think you can get away with this?" he asks. Davis responds defiantly, "What are you gonna do, kill me? Everybody dies." In Rossen's ending, the promoter has Davis gunned down in an alley in revenge for not throwing the fight.

3. David Raksin (1912–2004) was famous at the time for writing the score for Chaplin's *Modern Times* and the hit mystery *Laura*. After he testified before HUAC in May 1952, when he named eleven Communist Party members, he scored *The Bad and the Beautiful* and *The Big Combo*, among many other films. In the ending of *Force of Evil*, Raksin's principal theme,

titled "Regeneration," optimistically climbs a major scale even as the character played by Garfield, driven by grief, descends a series of staircases under the George Washington Bridge to find the body of his murdered brother.

4. *I Can Get It for You Wholesale* was later made into a Broadway musical starring Barbra Streisand and Elliott Gould. What made Polonsky's version memorable was its extraordinarily tough female protagonist, a character who was nonexistent in the book. To get rid of the problems with stereotypes in the original book, Polonsky changed the protagonist from a Jewish labor leader to an Irish-American dress designer. Even so, her more fiery speeches were rewritten at the studio's behest.

5. The *Jewish Daily Forward*, the largest-circulation Yiddish-language newspaper in the world, was generally Socialist in its early decades but was also full of literary translations and original fiction. Later it became ferociously anti-Communist.

6. Carnovsky was a stage actor and Hollywood character actor (1897–1992) who appeared in several classic films noirs during the 1940s and 50s. He was married to actress and acting teacher Phoebe Brand (1907–2004), and both were original members of the Group Theatre and belonged to the American Communist Party during the 1930s. Stage and screen director Elia Kazan knew them during this period (from his own membership in both) and named them in his testimony before the House Un-American Activities Committee.

7. Albert Maltz (1908–1985), author and Hollywood screenwriter, was blacklisted as one of the "Hollywood Ten."

Selected Sources

The following citations are for books and essays on Polonsky's work and career and essays written by Polonsky. The published interviews with him appearing in this book are also cited.

Brinckman, Christine Noll. "The Politics of *Force of Evil*: An Analysis of Abraham Polonsky's Preblacklist Film." In *Prospects: The Annual of American Cultural Studies*, vol. 6, edited by Jack Salzman. New York: Burt Franklin, 1981. 357–86.

Buhle, Paul, and Dave Wagner. "Abraham Polonsky." In *Tender Comrades: A Backstory of the Hollywood Blacklist*, edited by Patrick McGilligan and Paul Buhle. New York: St. Martin's, 1997. 481–94.

Buhle, Paul, and Dave Wagner. *A Very Dangerous Citizen: Abraham Lincoln Polonsky and the Hollywood Left*. Berkeley & Los Angeles: University of California Press, 2001.

Burman, Mark. "Abraham Polonsky: The Most Dangerous Man in America." In *Projections 8: Film-makers on Film-making*, edited by John Boorman and Walter Donohue. London: Faber and Faber, 1998. 230–72.

Ceplair, Larry, and Steven Englund. *The Inquisition in Hollywood: Politics in the Film Community, 1930–1960*. New York: Doubleday/Anchor, 1980.

Ciment, Michel, and Bertrand Tavernier. "Entretien avec Abraham Polonsky." *Positif* 114 (mars 1970): 14–23.

Cook, Jim, and Kingsley Canham. "Abraham Polonsky." *Screen II* (Summer 1970): 57–73.

Delahaye, Michel. "Entretien avec Abraham Polonsky." *Cahiers du cinéma*, no. 215 (septembre 1969): 30–39.

Dickos, Andrew. "Abraham Polonsky." In *Street with No Name: A History of the Classic American Film Noir*. Lexington: University Press of Kentucky, 2002. 70–75, 194–97.

Eisenschitz, Bernard. "Abraham Polonsky par lui-même." *Positif* 84 (mai 1967): 7–17.

Gelman. Howard. *The Films of John Garfield*. Introd. Abraham Polonsky. Secaucus, N.J.: Citadel, 1975. 7–9.

Hamilton, Ian. *Writers in Hollywood, 1915–1951*. New York: Harper & Row, 1990.

Navasky, Victor S. *Naming Names*. New York: Viking, 1980.

Pasternak, James D., and F. William Howton. "Abraham Polonsky." In *The Image-Maker*, edited by Ron Henderson. Richmond, Va.: John Knox Press, 1971. 17–27. Introd. "On Abraham Polonsky," by Gordon Hitchens. 16.

Polonsky, Abraham. *"The Best Years of Our Lives." Hollywood Quarterly* 2.3 (April 1947): 257–60.

Polonsky, Abraham. *"Odd Man Out* and *Monsieur Verdoux." Hollywood Quarterly* 2.4 (July 1947): 401–7.

Polonsky, Abraham. "Hemingway and Chaplin." *The Contemporary Reader* 1.1 (March 1953): 23–31.

Polonsky, Abraham L. "Une Expérience utopique." *Présence du Cinéma* 14 (juin 1962): 5–7.

Polonsky, Abraham. "How the Blacklist Worked in Hollywood." *Film Culture*, nos. 50–51 (Fall–Winter 1970): 41–48.

Polonsky, Abraham. "Making Movies." *Sight and Sound* 40 (Spring 1971): 101.

Polonsky, Abraham. "The Effects of the Blacklist on a Writer." *New York Times* Oral History Program, part 1, no. 16.

Polonsky, Abraham. *Body and Soul: The Critical Edition*. Edited by John Schultheiss. Los Angeles: Sadanlaur, 2002.

Polonsky, Abraham. *Force of Evil: The Critical Edition*. Edited by John Schultheiss and Mark Schaubert. The Center for Telecommunication Studies. Northridge, Calif.: California State University, 1996.

Polonsky, Abraham. *Odds Against Tomorrow: The Critical Edition*. Edited by John Schultheiss. Los Angeles: Sadanlaur, 1999.

Schultheiss, John, and Mark Schaubert, eds. *To Illuminate Our Time: The Blacklisted Teleplays of Abraham Polonsky*. Los Angeles: Sadanlaur, 1993.

Schwartz, Nancy Lynn. *The Hollywood Writers' Wars*. New York: Knopf, 1982. Completed by Sheila Schwartz upon the death of her daughter, Nancy (1952–78).

Sherman, Eric, and Martin Rubin. "Abraham Polonsky." In *The Director's Event: Interviews with Five American Film-Makers*. New York: Atheneum, 1969. 3–37.

Siegel, Robert. "Abraham Polonsky." In *The NPR Interviews*. Boston: Houghton Mifflin, 1994. 62–67.

Zheutlin, Barbara, and David Talbot. "Abraham Polonsky." In *Creative Differences: Profiles of Hollywood Dissidents*. Boston: South End Press, 1978. 55–99.

Index

Printed in the United States
by Baker & Taylor Publisher Services